WEDGWOOD & SONS

Very rare mark used for a short period in 1790.

These marks are rarely found on pieces of a very high character. Adopted about 1840 but used for only a short period.

WEDGWOOD
ETRURIA
WEDGWOOD
ETRURIA
Wedgwood
Etruria

JOSIAH
WEDGWOOD
Feb. 2nd 1805

Mark of Josiah Wedgwood II. Supposedly a new partnership or change in the firm. Found only on some basalt tripod incense burners. It may be the date when the design was first registered, 1805. Sometimes '2nd Feby' appears instead of 'Feb. 2'.

This mark, now in use on bone china, was adopted in 1878 when the manufacture of bone china was revived. It is printed in various colours.

WEDGWOOD

WEDGWOOD

The mark upon the bone china or porcelain, made 1812–1822, always printed either in red, blue or in gold.

England was added to the mark Wedgwood in 1891 to comply with the American Customs Regulation known as the McKinley Tariff Act.

ENGLAND

WEDGWOOD

From 1769 to the present day this mark has been impressed in the clay on Queen's Ware, or printed in colour. In recent times the words Etruria and Barlaston and the name of the pattern have in many cases been printed in addition to the trade mark. From 1780, ornamental Jasper, Black Basalt, cane, terra cotta and Queen's Ware are always marked with this stamp. The name 'England' was added in 1891.

Mark used today on bone china, developed from mark of 1878.

WEDGWOOD
Bone China
MADE IN ENGLAND

WEDGWOOD

This mark, printed in colour, is being used today on Queen's Ware, starting in 1940.

OF ETRURIA
WEDGWOOD
& BARLASTON
MADE IN ENGLAND

Collecting Small
Antiques
and
Bygones

Fig. 1 Hull Coach with horses and miniature luggage (*Victoria and Albert Museum. Crown copyright*).

Collecting Small Antiques and Bygones

Richard van de Gohm

JOHN GIFFORD
London
1975

TO

SUZANNE

© 1975 R. van de Gohm

First published 1975 by
John Gifford Ltd.,
125 Charing Cross Road,
London WC2H 0EB

ISBN 0 7071 10345 2

Printed in Great Britain by
Clarke, Doble & Brendon Ltd.,
Plymouth

Contents

List of Plates (Black & White)

49, 50, 51. Set of three silhouettes
52. Miniature of a Georgian gentleman
53. Pewter Measure with brass rim
54. Fine Coalport Dessert Service
55. Doulton salt-glazed stoneware
56. Doulton salt-glazed jugs
57. Vase in salt-glazed stoneware. $17\frac{1}{2}$ inches high
58. Vase in salt-glazed stoneware. $15\frac{1}{2}$ inches high
59. Jug made for the Staffordshire Volunteer Regt.
60. Tureen, stand and cover
61. Teapots and covers
62. Teapot in Black basalt
63. Early bone china pieces
64. The Portland Vase
65. Vases with covers
66. Early morning teaset
67. Worcester Jug
68. Worcester Vase and cover
69. Worcester Plate
70. Pot Lid
71. Egg cruet
72. A Victorian baby's rattle in silver
73. Cigarette case in silver
74. A selection of silver spoons
75. Silver locket
76. Silver Candlestick, George II
77. Sugar Caster. George III
78. Snuff Box in the shape of a shoe
79. Snuff Box made in papier mâché
80. Cup and Ball. Victorian child's toy
81. Cup and Ball. An excellent example of quality turning
82. Victorian Miniature Armour for Horse and Man
83. Noah's Ark, made of straw and wood
84. 'Caroline' cottage showing interior furnishings
85. A beautiful doll's house
86. Miniature set of four chairs
87. Mechanical Toy. Made in U.S.A.
88. Doll in costume of 1830
89. Child's Toy Horse and Coal cart
90. 'Happy Family' playing cards

List of Plates (Colour)

Line Drawings

An Appreciation

Man's knowledge is accumulative. Each generation starts by extracting the learning it needs from the great reservoir of knowledge provided by those who came earlier to this world; it then adds its own contribution.

Richard van de Gohm would like to express his humble and sincere thanks to all the scribes, researchers, discoverers, and keepers of records who have preceded him, and provided much of the information that made this book possible.

He hopes sincerely that he has, in some small way, added a little knowledge and pleasure to this generation, and through the media of the written word, made some small repayment for the wealth of knowledge that was made available to him in his generation.

Introduction

The ability to collect and appreciate antiques is no longer confined to the smaller section of the community with above-average incomes.

More and more people are finding that they can own articles in a broad sense antique, especially if they content themselves with the lesser pieces. The so-called 'lesser pieces' need not be lacking in either quality or antiquity. It is simply the rarity and demand that pushes the auction room prices to astronomical heights, not necessarily any special quality the article may possess. Why do we find old things appealing? Ask ten different collectors and get ten different answers. Some collect because they have an interest in a modern counterpart and like to have exhibits of its history. Some collect antiques for what they are—examples of everyday life of yesteryear; others find pleasure in the aura that surrounds old things, and of course, many have an eye on the investment potential. The author, a collector himself, is aware of the modern collector's needs in terms of interest and information. He has in consequence been guided by this knowledge and the many helpful letters he has received from all over the world, in connection with his earlier successful books on the subject, to provide this useful and informative volume for your bookshelf.

BOOKS

1. Books

Whatever the subject, it is a certainty that at sometime, someone has written about it. Books are truly universal, every country has its wealth of antiquarian books published over the years, which cover every conceivable subject, and are broadly divided into fiction and non-fiction.

Books undoubtedly outstrip all other forms of collecting; even people who do not profess to be collectors own the odd interesting volume.

The appeal of old books may lie in the visual attractiveness of fine bindings; the content of engraved works; the text matter; or of course, in a combination of all of these things.

Many collectors are excited more by the sheer beauty of the binding than by the book itself, and in consequence, rarely read the contents. But whatever your personal interest, it is certain that a worthwhile collection can be built up even with relatively modest means.

It is as well to begin by learning a little about the sizes of books. Abbreviations used in catalogues will then be more meaningful to you.

THE FOLIOS

When a printed sheet is folded only once, making in fact four pages, it is known as folio, but as single sheets are difficult to sew into sections, numbers of sheets are inserted, one within the other, until a suitable pack is formed. Folio sizes usually provide large books, such as atlases, books on architecture, art, and topographical subjects.

THE QUARTO

When a printed sheet is folded twice, it forms four leaves, or eight pages, and it is known as quarto or 4to. Quarto sized books are rather square-shaped and they are often used for subjects involving travel.

Modern books are often printed on double size paper, or two sheets inserted, which gives a sixteen page section.

THE OCTAVOS

The printed sheet for this size is folded three times, resulting in a total of sixteen pages, or eight leaves. It is the most commonly used size.

THE TWELVEMO

The folding now becomes a little more complicated. The sheet is folded twice in one direction, then twice the other way, giving twenty-four pages or twelve leaves.

THE SIXTEENMO

Similar folding to the twelvemo provides sixteen leaves or thirty-two pages.

Once the sheets are folded into sections they are gathered and sewn together, after which the end papers are added.

To ensure that the various sections are collated in the correct order, they are given a signature, which comprises a small capital letter or numbers, at the foot of the first page of each section.

The pages in a book are made by printing a large sheet of paper and then by folding as described above. Therefore the ultimate size of the book depends on the size of the sheet *and* the way it is folded. Detailed below are most of the sizes that were in common use; these, of course, were sub-divided into large and small.

Foolscap	$13\frac{1}{2} \times 17$	inches
Post	15×19	inches
Crown	15×20	inches
Demy	$17\frac{1}{2} \times 22\frac{1}{2}$	inches
Medium	18×23	inches
Royal	20×25	inches
Imperial	22×30	inches

From the foregoing it will be obvious that a Crown Octavo is $7\frac{1}{2}$ inches by 5 inches, and a Royal Octavo is 10 inches by $6\frac{1}{4}$ inches. There are other formulae that decide the format of a book, which depends upon how the sheets are folded, and then how these sheets are gathered into quires, but it is enough to know the major, and most commonly-used sizes.

Printing as a craft goes back only some 500 years. Recorded history in other graphic forms goes back several thousand years. It has been written on stone tablets, parchments, scrolls, and even painted on the walls of caves.

The first real books made their appearance sometime during the

5th century A.D. after the fall of the Roman Empire. Much of the old writing in the form of scrolls and tablets had been destroyed, but many were saved by monks who hid them in their monasteries, and other safe hiding places. The monks, always scholarly, continued with the writings on parchment, and often added drawings or paintings to decorate the sheets. As the sheets grew in numbers, they were sewn together in sections so that the sequence of writing was maintained. It also kept the sheets tidy, and made them easier to handle and to read. Later several sections were gathered together and bound between wooden boards, the outer surface of which were often beautifully carved. Sometimes leather was used to form the outer covers. The subject matter contained in these early books was invariably of a religious nature, and any surviving books of this type will most likely only be found in the archives of monasteries or in the museums of the world. It is possible, of course, that a few exist in libraries of millionaire collectors.

The discovery of the process for papermaking has been attributed to the Chinese, who first made paper some 2,000 years ago. It is interesting to know that modern paper manufacturers still use the same basic principle, although many refinements in paper quality have taken place since those early days.

The Chinese used plant fibres from wood, grass, mulberry and other similar fibrous plants. The 'raw' material was pounded into a pulp and then boiled in water. When the water cooled the fibrous material was left virtually in solution. A fine mesh, in the form of a sieve, was plunged into the water, and then gently lifted out again. The mesh let the water drain through, leaving the fibres more or less randomly disposed as a pulp. This pulp was then pressed between felt to remove as much water as possible and the final operation was simply to dry the soggy paper sheet in the sun. This early paper was naturally coarse in texture, but nevertheless, quite usable.

Not only did the Chinese invent paper, they also invented printing. However this came much later, around A.D. 600.

Early printing used woodcuts for 'type'. A block of wood was carved with letters or designs in such a way that the printing face was proud of the block. Ink was applied to the proud surfaces and either paper, papyrus, or parchment pressed onto these surfaces which transferred the image. In this way, any number of copies could be made.

Obviously every page of a book would need a separately carved block to produce it, but once the blocks were available, any number of books could be produced.

The real production of books in any quantities, backed by publishing houses and professional authors can be said to have really started about the middle of the 15th century, but even so, books were still expensive to produce, and were not available to the masses until later. After all, a book is not much use unless you can read, and it was not until education spread to the masses during the 17th century that there was a real demand for books in quantity.

Johann Gutenberg, a German, who resided in Mainz sometime between 1440 and 1450, revolutionised the whole concept of printing by inventing movable type. This meant, of course, that once a page, or book, had been printed, the type could be broken up into individual letters, and re-composed for further use.

Now browsing around old bookshops is almost a national pastime, and every English town of any size has its antiquarian bookseller who will have many interesting old books for the collector, and quite likely, he will also issue a catalogue periodically. Antique dealers, market stalls, jumble sales, and even junk shops can occasionally prove rewarding to a persistent collector, but a book dated earlier than 1650 is rare, it is likely that most of the books currently available will be of slightly later vintage.

Really fine English antique bindings are generally expensive, and these are usually out of the reach of modest collectors, thus we must restrict our early collecting days to something less elaborate, such as early 19th century signed bindings, or the plainer trade bindings.

Whatever type or field of collecting interests you, do give some consideration to the condition of the book. It is not usually wise to invest in heavily restored books, or those in a bad state. It is much better to have a few good quality volumes, than a bookcase full of soiled and ragged specimen. It must be remembered, however, that the leathers used in England, with the exception of the best morocco, did not last too well.

Books with good interiors, but with broken bindings or torn boards, can be re-bound by hand relatively cheaply, and this is a practice that can only enhance the value of the book.

The binding leathers will give some indication of the age of a book. Mediaeval manuscripts commonly used deer skin, or sheep skin, which initially was either white or pinkish. During the 16th century, the majority of books with decorative bindings were covered in calf, either blocked in blind, or tooled. From about 1525 onwards, the use of a soft vellum became very popular for the smaller undecorated books. The first half of the 17th century saw the advent of morocco, usually in brown, or an olive green. (Morocco is tanned goat skin.) From about 1650 blue and red moroccos first appeared, and these were used for the finest bindings of the Restoration period. Gold tooled vellum bindings were also fashionable during the early 17th century, but the material gradually fell into disuse on the plainer bindings in favour of sheep or calf skin.

During the 18th century, sheep skin was used for the more common or less expensive works. From about 1770, early forms of book cloth were used to speed up the process of binding and to provide a satisfactory binding in a cheaper material. This early forerunner of the many beautiful cloths available on modern books was in fact a type of canvas.

It is interesting to find old books bound in paper-covered boards; this type of binding was never intended to be final, but simply a temporary protection until the book could be bound properly, perhaps to suit a particular owner's personal taste which may have included some personal device or motif.

Fore-edge painting provides an unusual aspect for book collectors. It was a technique originated in the 17th century by the English and revised about 1785 by Edwards of Halifax.

Fore-edge painting was literally painting the fore edge of every page in the book so that, when the leaves were held trapped between fingers and thumb, and then bent backwards so that the fore edge of each page spread out, a painting appeared. These pictures were often views or conversation pieces. When the book was in its normal closed position, the edges of the paper were gilded in the normal way, which not only afforded protection for the book, but effectively concealed the painted picture.

Quite often, the picture will be unrelated to the contents of the book, but this does not matter providing the book has merit in terms of binding. It will be difficult to find books of this nature at a reasonably inexpensive price. There are many fine 18th and 19th century books on travel and topography, usually illustrated with fine engravings. Unfortunately, the demand for these prints is such that many books find their way into the hands of print dealers who unhesitatingly break them up, even if they are in excellent condition, to supply their market. The prints are removed, coloured, and sold individually.

Modern reference books, especially those designed for the medical profession, are often produced with transparent film pages that can be lifted to show successive sections through the various organs in the body. The older books achieved similar results by using cut out printed paper patterns. These unusual books make fascinating additions to an otherwise specific collection. For instance, 'Nouvelle Encyclopedie Practique de Mecanique et d'Electricite Atlas' by Henri Desarces, is a typical example of such books. The individual 'pages' are stiff boards with a basic picture printed on them, and the successive layers or sections through the illustration are separate leaves of paper, cut out to the required shape, and printed *on both sides.* The electric train illustrated in the book has no less than twenty different little sections of paper that can be lifted to reveal the mechanisms underneath. This book is not antique, it was printed in 1924, but such books are real collectors items since it would be much too costly to attempt to produce such a book today. Victorian and earlier books published specifically for children can provide an excellent adult collection, for example *Der Strammelpeter* by Dr. Heinrich Hoffman, published in Germany about 1876. Although the text is in German, it is profusedly illustrated with intriguing etchings, all of which are hand coloured.

General Care

Having taken the trouble to start a book collection, it is as well to know how to look after it. Store them by all means in a bookcase in any living room of the house, but remember excessive dry heat will make both the paper and the leather bindings brittle. Put them in a location where the direct rays of sun or the heat from a fire cannot reach them. Centrally heated rooms are ideal providing the atmosphere is not too dry.

Excessive dampness is also injurious, as this leads to the growth of moulds, and staining of the pages. Damp, unventilated box rooms or attics where condensation collects, will soon ruin a nice old book. A sulphuric atmosphere can cause decay of the leathers.

The leather bindings can be treated with a special dressing to preserve them, and to enhance their appearance. Some of the preparations made for shoes provide an excellent media for use on real leathers, but do not use commercial saddle soap, or any of the furniture polishes or creams.

Insect pests can be a problem, but they should not occur if the books are stored correctly. Some small insects like to feed on the paste, or chew the paper. If it is necessary to make the odd repair to a torn page, do use a non-staining paste such as photographic paste. If, however, a book needs complete rebinding leave it to the experts, it will not be a very expensive job, and it is likely that the book will increase in value by more than the cost of the re-binding anyway.

GLOSSARY

Azured: A term derived from the method of indicating the colour azure in heraldic engraving, shown by a series of slanting, horizontal lines.

Beau livre: Books with original illustrations. In this sense, wood or copper engravings, lino cuts, and lithographs would be considered 'original' works, as the artist would have executed the plate. Illustrations produced by these techniques automatically set a limit to the numbers of illustrations that could be produced due to plate wear.

Bevelled Edges: Descriptive of the edges of the boards, or covers, which have been angled along the three outer edges, before being covered with a binding cloth or leather.

Blind: A term used to describe decorations or lettering on the binding that has been impressed only, and is devoid of any colour, such as gold, silver, black, white, etc.

Block: A block made of wood or metal, without any handle or protuberances, carrying a design for decorating the cover of a book, intended for use in conjunction with a blocking press.

Boards: The board cover of a case bound book.

Calf: Leather made from the hide of a calf, commonly used in book bindings for old books, and books of very high quality.

Cartouche: A type of decorative label sometimes very ornate with scroll outer framing, but the word is also used loosely to describe any round, oval, or decorative label.

Colour Plate Books: A broad description for books with colour plates, irrespective of the process used to produce the colour, i.e. printed in full colour, or aquatints, engravings, or lithographs that have been printed in black and subsequently coloured by hand.

Deckle Edge: The uncut edge of hand-made paper, usually slightly wavy around the edges.

Endpapers: Double leaves added at the front and back of a book, the outer leaf being stuck to the inner face of the cover. 16th and 17th century leather and vellum bound books were sometimes without end papers.

Etruscan Style: From about 1780 to 1825 calf bindings were decorated with classical designs by the use of staining acids. This type of finish is termed Etruscan style.

Foxing: Brown coloured spots disfiguring the pages of a book, caused by damp, and impurities in the paper.

Halfbound: This usually describes books that have the spine and the outer corners of the boards only covered in leather. The remainder of the covers are finished either in paper or cloth.

Lexant: A type of morocco, loose grained, and held in high esteem for the past 100 years.

Limited Edition: An edition which is restricted to a definite number of copies.

Morocco: Originally used to describe leather made from the skin of North African goats, but used now to describe any goat skin leather.

Panel: Rectangular outlines, or panels, either in between the bands of the spine, or on the sides of a book. The outline can consist of a single line, or a number of lines, blind, or in gilt.

Re-backed: Renewal of the spine, or back strip.

Re-cased: Fixing a book that has become loosely formed, more firmly between the covers.

Roll: A tool used to obtain a continuous or repetitive design. The design is on the outer periphery of the roller and imprints the design as it is rolled over the material.

Sheep: A soft, almost grain-free leather, obtained from sheep.

Wrappers: Paper covers, either plain, marbled or printed. Equivalent to a modern paperback.

BOTTLES AND DECANTERS

2. Sealed Bottles and Decanters

During the 17th century, wine shops did not display a colourful array of attractively labelled bottles. The merchants received their wine from the continent in casks, and sold the wines to their customers in the same containers.

Glass bottles for storing wine seem to have been used first around 1623. Such bottles may well have served the dual purpose of storage and for the table. This would explain the ridge around the neck, just below the mouth, that is found on most early wine bottles, which could only have been used as a means to secure the cork with string.

Early decanters were nothing more than a bottle with a stopper of cork or pewter. Well-to-do folk had bottles made with their own seal moulded on the surface for identification purposes. It is possible that such bottles were sent to the importers for refilling. These early 'sealed bottles' have now become popular collectors items, and are becoming increasingly difficult to acquire. The type of bottle described as 'onion' is English, and has a large round bulbous body, with a short thick neck. 'Shaft and globe' describes a more elegant 'onion' which has a larger and thinner neck, and the body is less squat. The 'shaft and globe' developed in four main stages from the early 17th century to about 1740. In stage one, from 1620–1660, they had bulbous bodies, long necks, flat lips, a string ring about $\frac{1}{2}$ inch below the lip, and a low kick (a kick is the domed indentation seen in the base of the bottles, necessary for early bottle-making). In stage two, from about 1650 to 1685, the angle of the shoulder became more acute, and the body more tapering towards the base. During stage three, from 1680 to 1715, the body widened and became more dumpy, the neck more tapering and shorter, and the kick was quite high. In stage four, from about 1710 to 1740, the body was more square to the base, or with a tendency to an outward slant, with a well defined shoulder at the base of the neck.

From about 1730, the 'shaft and globe' bottles were superseded by the more conventional cylindrical type.

George Ravenscroft (1618–1681) is a famous name in glass, in 1674 he took out a patent for making flint glass. The Glass-Sellers Company were so impressed with this new product, they agreed to

23

take his total output, with the provision that he adopted their standard designs.

From sealed bottles to decanters is an almost indefinable step. Decanters are still basically bottles, but they have a better sense of design and purpose. The 'shaft and globe' shape was always popular for clear glass decanters, and is still being used in modern designs.

From about 1750 we find decanters engraved, gilded or enamelled, with the name of the intended contents, such as Gin, Sherry, Rum, Brandy, Whiskey and of course Wine.

Bristol blue decanters, as their name suggests, were supposedly made at Bristol, from dark blue glass. They were decorated in gold, with the pattern of a wine label suspended from the neck; this type of decanter is rare. If however you are fortunate, and procure such a piece, you may find it signed by the maker—Isaac Jacobs. If no signature is found, it will be almost impossible to define its origin, as other makers copied the design and need not necessarily have come from Bristol.

From about 1765 to 1800, the decanter became more tapered with a less pronounced connection between body and neck. One of these varieties was shaped like an Indian Club and had vertical lines and horizontal hoops cut into its surface.

Closely following this period we find the Prussian type, with fluting halfway up the body. This may have been added to give an additional surface area to facilitate cooling of the contents.

A considerable contribution was made by Irish and Scandinavian manufacturers; Waterford manufacturers produced many popular Prussian types. At the end of the 18th century we find rings appearing on the necks to prevent the vessel slipping out of the hands. Belfast manufacturers appear to have preferred only two rings, instead of the more conventional three rings.

Decanter stoppers were rarely finished by grinding until after 1745, but from this date onwards, it was commonplace.

Stoppers were made to suit individual decanters, therefore it will be difficult to replace one that has become lost or broken.

When buying a decanter, check the stopper, make certain it fits properly, and that it is the correct type. You will find many specimens offered by sale with ill-fitting or replacement stoppers.

Stoppers can be an interesting subject in their own right, and they are often offered for sale without decanters.

BRASS

3. Brass

Man started using metal many centuries ago, well before any historical records existed. Old civilisations were familiar with tin, copper, bronze and iron, and of course, gold and silver.

Copper and tin were often found deposited quite near each other, and it is probable that this proximity originally combined them accidentally to provide the alloy bronze. Bronze has been in use from approximately 1000 B.C! About this time, iron also was being smelted in Central Europe, and had certainly reached Britain well before the arrival of Julius Caesar sometime during 55 B.C.

During the middle ages, Germany was developing the mining of copper and the subsequent manufacture of brass. Flanders was also one of the early users of brass, which was employed to embellish churches with effigy brasses. At this time, Britain was using the alloys of copper to provide armour and implements of war.

Before we start collecting brass it is as well to understand the difference between brass and bronze, and so avoid any possible confusion. Antique bronze is generally accepted to be an alloy of copper and tin, and has a decided red hue. It is a very malleable material that lends itself to forming by hammering. Brass is an alloy of copper and zinc, or copper and calamine (zinc carbonate) and has a yellow hue. Its main advantage over bronze is that it can be cast

Fig. 2   Sovereign case in brass (*Mabel Gohm*).

25

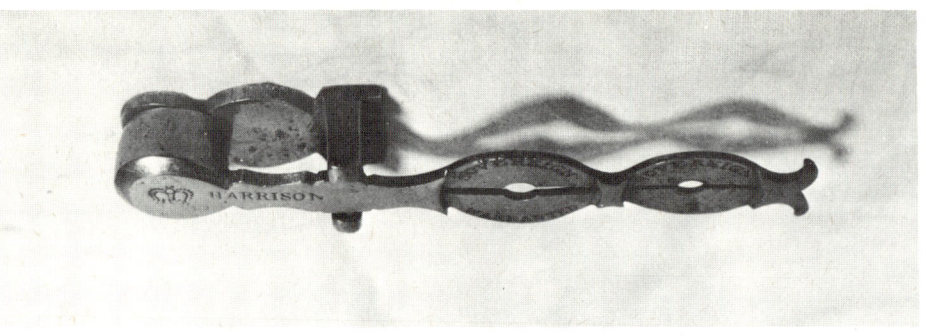

Fig. 3 Scales for weighing sovereigns and half sovereigns. Marked with a crown to prove accuracy. Made in brass by Harrison. *c.* 1870 (*Mabel Gohm*).

satisfactorily, even in thin sections, for the manufacture of furniture brasses, i.e. hinges, hinge plates, and so on.

The first brass manufactured in this country dates back to approximately the 16th century. Brass, however, was used in this country centuries before it was manufactured here. Early brass work was executed from material that had been imported from Germany and the Netherlands in flat sheets. This early imported material was mainly used by the church for church brasses, which are now eagerly sought by collectors interested in brass rubbings.

The first brass made in this country during the Elizabethan period was made of copper and calamine, but it was, in fact, more like a bronze than the brass we know today.

Latten is an old word for brass, and refers specifically to brass sheets that have been made from ingots, and flattened by beating with a horse- or water-powered hammer; consequently latten can be recognised as a flat brass sheet which shows the marks of hammering.

It was during the reign of Queen Elizabeth I that the first patent was granted to William Humfrey and Christopher Schutz. This gave them the monopoly of working in the new material brass. It was not until sometime during the 18th century that the method of producing flat sheets by hammering was superseded by the more modern methods using the rolling mill, a method that is still used.

Brass is an excellent craftsman's material, it has a good colour, and it is ductile and malleable. It can be joined easily, polishes very readily, and has a relatively high resistance to the oxidising action of the atmosphere.

Many articles can be made from brass sheet, by cutting, hammering and forming. But such is the versatility of the material that

Fig. 4 Lucerne Lamp with two wick holders. Made from separate brass castings and assembled with brazing spelter (*Mabel Gohm*).

it can be both cast and spun. The method of spinning is to secure a disc of brass between the tailstock and the headstock of a lathe. The headstock will carry a pattern shaped to the desired form. This pattern can be made of any hard wood, or if a large quantity of spinning is required, it can be made of metal. The disc is now rotated in the lathe and a tool pressed against the rotating surface, forcing the disc to conform to the shape of the pattern. Articles that have been produced by spinning show concentric circles made by the pressure from the tool.

Castings are produced from a master pattern and the use of a special sand. The pattern is put into a box that is split in the middle, and the sand rammed tightly around it. The box is then opened to allow the pattern to be removed without disturbing the sand. When the two halves of the box have been put together again a cavity in the sand equal to the pattern will be left in the centre of the box. Metal is then poured into this cavity. When cooled, the metal will be a solid replica of the master pattern.

27

The Great Exhibition of 1851 was undoubtedly the shop window that introduced the Victorians to the brass bedstead. These beds were constructed from drawn brass tube, a technique that was relatively new at that time, and ornamented with cast brass terminals. The advent of drawn brass tube gave designers the opportunity to work with a new form of the material, and it was soon being used for curtain rails, chandeliers, candelabra, children's cots, stair rods, and a host of other uses, not forgetting the four poster bed.

Collectors of brass are unlikely to make a collection of Victorian beds, or curtain rails, but they can be used most effectively in conjunction with modern decor.

You could, of course, start your brass collection with horse brasses. These decorative pieces of horse furniture have been known in England for over 2,000 years, but it was not until the 1840's that more than a single brass face piece was used.

Pieces earlier than 1850 are rare but from the 1860's they were

Fig. 5 Miniature kettle, brass, with bone handle (*Adrian Bowyer, Beaconsfield*).

Fig. 6 Condiment Coaster made from sheet brass with pierced design.
Date unknown (*Mabel Gohm*).

available in a wide variety of designs. They were used hanging from
the martingale, and on each side of the runners and shoulders.
There were forehead pieces, ear brasses for hanging behind the ears,
and up to 20 pendant pieces.

Briefly, the evolution of horse brasses based on manufacturing
techniques is as follows.

1750 to 1800. Horse brasses from this period are very rare, they
were chiefly made in the form of Georgian sun flashes, and made by
hand from hard latten.

1800 to approx. 1850. These are not so rare, but will be
difficult to find. Usually made from rolled calamine brass, they
were fairly soft and dull in appearance.

Between 1830 to 1860. These were cast in fine brass alloy using
copper and zinc (much the same as present day brass). Also cast in a
high quality brass alloy of the Pinchbeck variety, and often coloured
a reddish gold, with burnished highlights. These are now extremely
rare.

A type of metal known as Emersons brass was also used during
this period. This was a copper spelter metal which produced a
smooth surfaced, brilliant gold coloured brass. Whilst these are not
so rare as the Pinchbeck variety, they are still very uncommon.

29

1860's to 1900. During the earliest part of this period more commercial alloys were used. Castings were finished by file and pierced by drilling, then carefully finished and polished.

Later in this period the brasses were produced by relatively modern methods of stamping from sheet, and these were made almost exclusively in Birmingham and Walsall. Early examples, lead filled, are now very rare.

Stamped brasses, made from sheet by machine, were much cheaper to produce, as they were made in fairly long runs and used less material.

The original purpose of horse brasses is believed to have originated to protect horses from evil spirits. Our ancestors certainly believed in witchcraft, sorcery, and the power of the evil eye, and it is true that the majority of the designs used to incorporate a symbol, which was intended to bring good luck, secure a favourable glance from some ancient and benevolent god, or to offer protection to both the horse and driver from the evil eye. During the middle ages, sorcery and witchcraft were prevalent, and the effects of such beliefs can be observed today by the number of people who are still superstitious.

Horse brasses as such are a comparatively modern piece of horse furniture. They certainly did not exist much before Victorian times, although lucky charms and amulets in one form or another may well have been used in the past. There is no real evidence to show that horse brasses were intended for any purpose other than to decorate a horse.

Since the horse brass became popular for interior decoration and as a collectors item, modern fakes have been made in great numbers. Fakes are usually cast, and treated with acids to give them an older appearance that is not easily copied. It can, however, be very difficult to distinguish between fake and genuine examples until you have gained experience of the subject.

Whilst making no attempt to provide a fully comprehensive history of horse brass design, the following explanations may prove of interest.

THE ACORN

This is a lucky symbol associated with agriculture.

ANCHOR

The motif or symbol of Saint Nicholas, an anchor superimposed upon a sun disc was used as a trade mark of the Bull Brewery Company.

BELL

Bells have a special significance by implication they are noisy instruments, which will frighten off evil spirits. Bells also have religious connections.

BEAR

A popular Lincolnshire design.

CHRYSANTHEMUM

A flower like brass, probably based upon the early lucky world design.

CHURN

Usually associated with dairy man's horses.

CLASPED HANDS

A classic piece of Victorian design that originated about the time of Victoria's jubilee, and her many associations with friendly societies, etc.

INTERLACING KNOTS

The endless knot was originally a Buddhist emblem of security.

CRESCENT

This symbol is probably used more than any other, and was used either in its pure form or incorporated in many designs. The crescent shaped moon was a symbol of the moon goddess, and was believed to have special powers of protection against evil spirits.

RAILWAY ENGINE

These are interesting brasses sometimes showing a railway engine on rails, and sometimes without. These were made originally for Railway Company horses.

PAIR OF FISH

Probably a religious symbol but it is also an old Buddhist emblem of good luck.

FLEUR-DE-LIS

A very old symbol of good luck depicting a stylised version of The Lotus of Iris. This emblem has become identified with the Royal House of France.

SAINT GEORGE AND THE DRAGON

The patron saint of England, it was no doubt used on horse brasses because Saint George was one of the patron saints of the horse.

HEART AND SUN RAYS

Reputed to have originated in Warwickshire.

HORSE SHOE

A well known lucky motif. Often shown in a cluster of three.

ROSE

The association of the Tudor Rose with England makes this an obvious decorative piece.

SHAMROCK

This is of course the emblem of Ireland and has its associations with good luck.

STARS

Stars with eight points and five points or rays have been used for horse brasses, and have associations with old mystic cults.

THREE TUNS

The Ancient Company of Vintners used the three tuns as their coat of arms; brewery horses often were decorated with brasses showing a tun or a barrel.

The brief descriptions of horse brass designs given above cover only a few of the possibilities. Should you wish to know more of the origin and meaning of the various designs that have been used for horse furniture, these have been well covered in a useful little book by R. A. Brown, Secretary to the Hackney Horse Society, and titled

Fig. 7 An unusual Potato Ring in brass with, presumably, original wooden bowl. *c.* 1780 *(Adrian Bowyer, Beaconsfield).*

Horse Brasses, Their History and Origin. This book has been published by R. A. Brown.

Brass candlesticks have been in existence from as early as the 12th century, but they are now, of course, very rare and they are unlikely to be found, other than in museums or as part of church regalias. Therefore we must content ourselves with pieces from the 18th century onwards.

During the period 1700 to 1725, they were made octagonal and ballister in shape. From about 1725 to 1760 the ballister became vase shaped, with a shell base. During the latter part of the century the base became square and the general design more classical.

Old brass is difficult to date. There were no hall marks to guide us and neither were many pieces marked in any way. However, it is possible to get a rough idea of the date of a candlestick by examination of the method of construction. Up to about the late 17th century, the stem and socket were cast in one piece and the base was either attached by means of a screwed thread, or by a burred-over projection. The projecting tongue was passed through a hole in the

33

centre of the base, and then hammered or burred-over to form a head which held it securely in place, in much the same way as rivets hold plates together today.

A new method of casting was introduced about 1670. Instead of the very solid, heavy castings used up to that date, the new method allowed both the socket and stem to be cast as separate pieces, which were subsequently brazed together. The main advantage of this method was of course the obvious saving in material.

Nineteenth century candlesticks were more or less solid, one-piece castings.

As previously stated, it is often very difficult to distinguish between genuine old brass and fairly modern examples, but we can get a reasonable indication if we look under the base of our candlesticks, or any other hollow cast object and look at the surface. Most old brass will have concentric rings made by a turning tool; if the base has a rough impression formed by the sand during the casting process, it can be taken that the article is a modern production.

Brass foundries have existed in Britain since about the middle of the 18th century. There were certainly foundries in Birmingham at this time, producing a great variety of articles, some of which were very elegant and well worth collecting, others not so elegant and somewhat crudely made. However, the collector need not be dismayed, as there is certain to be something he likes, such as old brass oil lamps, fenders, footwarmers, coalhods, braziers, funnels, furniture mounts, locks, skillets, not forgetting the wide range of nautical equipment and scientific instruments.

MINERS' LAMPS

Miners' lamps are not found often in brass collections, but they are always sought after by collectors of old industrial equipment, or by general collectors who wish to convert them to electricity and use them to light a porch, or as a decorative piece of brass in a furnishing scheme. Because of the similarity between the various makes they do not in themselves make a very suitable subject on which to base a specific collection.

The miners' or Davy lamp was first produced about 1815 to provide safe illumination for miners working thousands of feet underground in a possibly highly dangerous atmosphere, requiring only a naked flame to cause an explosion and another pit disaster. The Davy lamp was basically an oil lamp with an oil reservoir and wick, but it was enclosed by a wire gauze cage. The wire gauze permitted air to flow but had the advantage of dissipating heat, so that should the flickering flame attempt to pass through the protective gauze, it was cooled. Therefore, a Davy lamp is simply an ordinary oil lamp surmounted by a gauze collar and a metal cap to which a large hook is attached for carrying or suspending it.

The majority of glass chimneys are clear; a yellow or violet glass is a rarity. The violet glass indicates that the lamp had a special purpose—the detection of gas. Because of its colour it filtered out all the light rays except of the same colour as the glass, therefore, when gas was present, the tip of the flame showed mauve, or violet.

Dr. Clanny introduced a variation in about 1840, this being simply a glass chimney to increase the illumination. A further improvement was added later—this consisted of a metal shroud to enclose the gauze which protected the flame from strong currents of air. This lamp became known as the Clanny.

There were of course many other designs of miners' lamps produced during the 19th century, both in England and on the Continent. Such names as Eloin, Boty, Gray and Museley are just a few of the better-known designers. Obtaining the odd lamp in good condition should not be difficult or expensive; there is a plentiful supply and what is more surprising they are *still being made* for use by some collieries.

CLEANING AND CARE

There are many excellent proprietary polishes available providing they are used with reasonable care. Badly discoloured brass should be washed first in an ammonia solution to remove any surface dirt or grime. Then if you wish you can make up a solution with vinegar and common salt which will brighten the brass. Thoroughly wash and polish with a soft cloth afterwards. Furniture mounts, and handles on drawers, are best removed before cleaning, otherwise there is risk of spoiling the surrounding woodwork, and of filling the interstices with polish residue or bits of cloth. If, however, they are not readily removable, the proprietary product Duraglit can be used with care.

BYGONES AND TREEN

4. Bygones and Treen

BYGONES

A bygone is a special kind of antique. All antiques are, to some extent, bygones, but a general description would define a bygone as a functional item that had been replaced by a more advanced and improved article for doing the same job.

Bygones are interesting in themselves, but the true collector will not be satisfied in just possessing the article. He will want to know about its past history, its function, how it worked, and if possible, from whence it came.

The 20th century is the age that introduced automation, and very sophisticated methods for making things. Old crafts have been superseded by elegant modern machines that produce more accurately, and in greater numbers; consequently the old craftsman's tools have fallen into disuse, and are slowly but surely disappearing. Old methods of farming have been superseded by mechanical aids; tractors now carry the milk churns from the cow shed to the pick-up point, the milkman no longer delivers milk in cans, and many of the old farming implements lie rotting in barns or fields. Although there are still wheel-wrights, saddlers, thatchers and coach builders, they are, no doubt, availing themselves of the benefits of progress, their old tools dusty and rusty in some forgotten corner.

The following suggestions for collectors are not categoric, but reflect the author's own ideas of what should constitute a bygone.

TOOLS

There are a great number of tools that have become obsolete, and very soon will become expensive and difficult to find. Old craftsmen's tools of the carpenter, saddler, thatcher, cobbler and old farm implements are required by museums and collector alike. Not only are these articles required for their interest, but they are being used extensively as interior decorative pieces for hotels, steak houses, and the like.

There is one disadvantage of collecting these items; one can hardly display an old plough in the dining room, but the variety is sufficiently large to permit items to be selected that can be contained within the normal house.

Fig. 8 Glass Fly Trap. Base of the interior was filled with honey and the top stoppered. Flies entered through hole in base. Victorian (*Adrian Bowyer, Beaconsfield*).

HOUSEHOLD

These are usually small items and can be, and are, used as decorative pieces in old cottages, public houses, and even in new hotels, or simply collected for their own sake.

Hand made door hinges, locks, footscrapers, cauldrons, spits, grid-irons and scullery pieces, not forgetting old mouse traps, could be assembled under this heading.

SPINNING WHEELS

Spinning wheels have almost become a modern furnishing piece, especially if you are fortunate enough to own a period house or a

Fig. 9 Veterinary's Knife, appropriately engraved with the owner's name, 'J. Gelding'. Steel blades in brass sheath. *c.* 1880 (*Mabel Gohm*).

very old cottage. But do not be fooled by modern reproductions; the old ones were made to do a job of work, not for ornamental purposes. Utility spinning wheels designed for cottages and crofters were practical machines and were made of hard wood and without much ornamentation, but those made for use in the drawing rooms of the elite were more elegant affairs in walnut, ebony, or oak and inlaid with mother-of-pearl.

TINDER BOXES

A tinder box is a container for holding tinder (a material that ignites easily) a steel striker, and a piece of flint. The steel and flint are struck together to give a spark which causes the tinder to smoulder and with much huffing and puffing to burst into flames—that is if you are lucky.

Tinder boxes were made in wood, sometimes beautifully carved; in tin, with the means of holding a candle, and in various designs from brass, copper and plate.

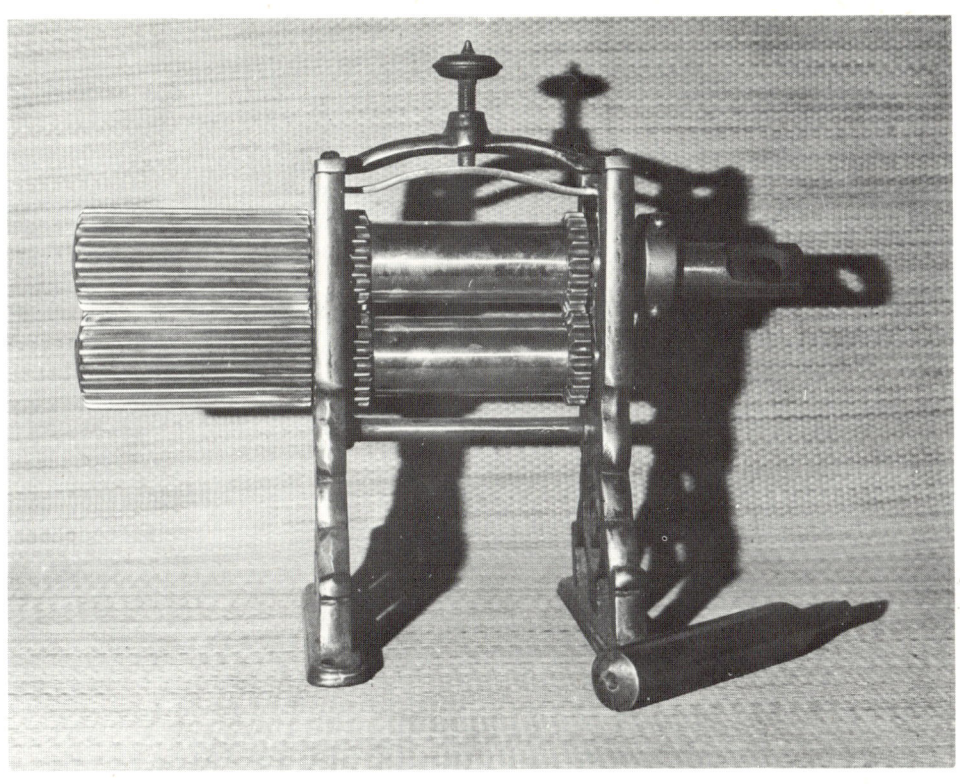

Fig. 10 Ruffle mangle. Two cylindrical irons were heated in a fire and inserted into the hollow ruff or crimping rolls (*Adrian Bowyer, Beaconsfield*).

A development of the tinder box evolved later and became known as the 'strike a light' or tinder pistol. This resembled a pistol in shape, complete with stock. When triggered, the hammer fell, the flint struck the steel, and the resultant spark ignited the tinder situated in a receptacle below the striker. The 'strike a light' sometimes had a candle holder just to the fore of the tinder receptacle.

MAGIC LANTERN

The earliest magic lantern dates from about the late 17th century. It played an important part in the home entertainment of the wealthier families. In principal they have changed very little with the passage of time, but they have, of course, become more elegant in design. The lantern slide is often more interesting than the lantern itself. Up till the end of the 19th century, the vast majority of slides

39

were hand painted. The first moving pictures were obtained by the careful use of two slides; for example, one carrying the sea, and the second one carrying a ship, These would be projected simultaneously, and the slide on which the sea was painted was then agitated to give a realistic motion.

The best period for hand painted slides is undoubtedly between the 1850's and 1860's, a period roughly co-inciding with the best animated slides. Animated slides were produced to give artificial fireworks, fountains with life-like moving water, animated figures, and a host of other ingenious ideas.

PHONOGRAPH

The old phonographs with their cylindrical records are fast becoming collectors items, and the records themselves are of particular interest, especially those with the voices of artists long past, or historical personalities.

Even early gramophones with their large trumpet-like horns, and collections of 78 r.p.m. records, are becoming increasingly scarce.

SMOKING PARAPHERNALIA

Although we have mentioned certain smoking articles in other parts of our book, the general collecting of smoking bygones seems worthy of mention as a basis for a specific collection.

Meerschaum pipes, tobacco jars, cigar cutters, pipe stoppers, snuff rasps, clay pipes, and even match boxes can be included if desired.

MECHANICS

Many old, out-dated pieces of machinery such as early typewriters, cash registers, sewing machines, and such-like are interesting collectors who realise that much of the recent technical advances have quickly put these early Machine Age devices on the scrap-heap, and in no time at all they could become rare and perhaps valuable items.

SHOOTING STICKS

Shooting sticks are by no means a modern invention. They were certainly made during the 19th century. Some had three legs made of bent wood with a cane seat which folded for carrying, but these

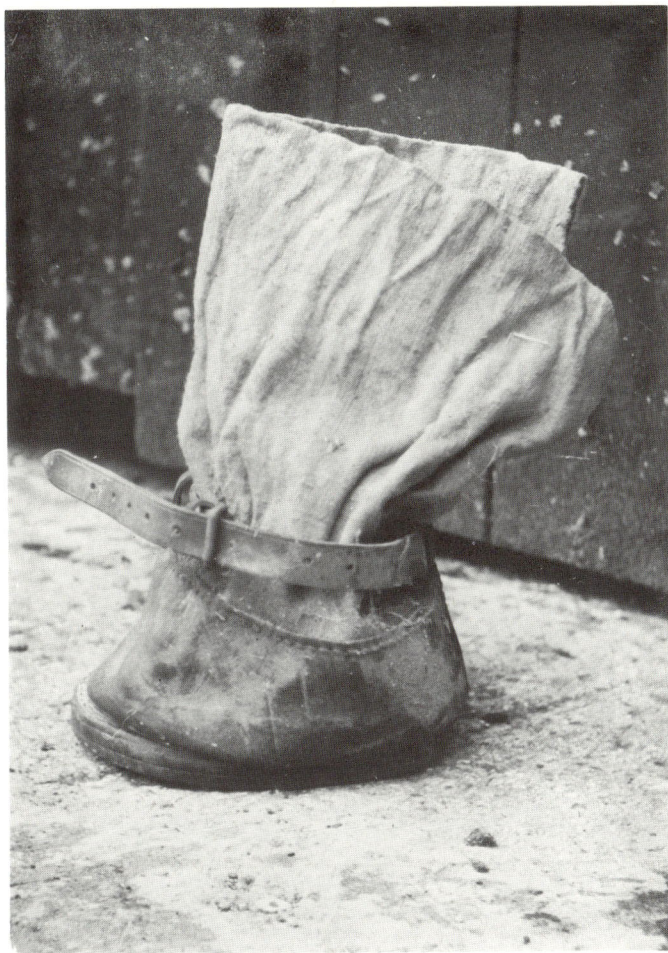

Fig. 11 Horse Boot used to protect the injured foot of a work horse. Not rare, but uncommon. (*R. van de Gohm*).

were bulky. Another type consisted of a single stick on which the handle was unscrewed and then repositioned by another socket to form a tee-shaped seat. There was also a completely wooden shooting stick that in design resembles its modern counterpart, but it was of course much heavier.

BREWING IMPLEMENTS

The practise of brewing one's own beer was once quite common, and implements used include hard wood shovels and forks, mash-stirrers, and coopered oak sinks.

41

FARMING OBJECTS

The 'boot' illustrated was constructed with a thick leather sole and side pieces, and a canvas sleeve. Its purpose was to protect the foot of an injured plough horse. The foot, after being treated, was bandaged, the boot fitted over the bandages, and the sleeve laced or strapped to the horse's fetlock.

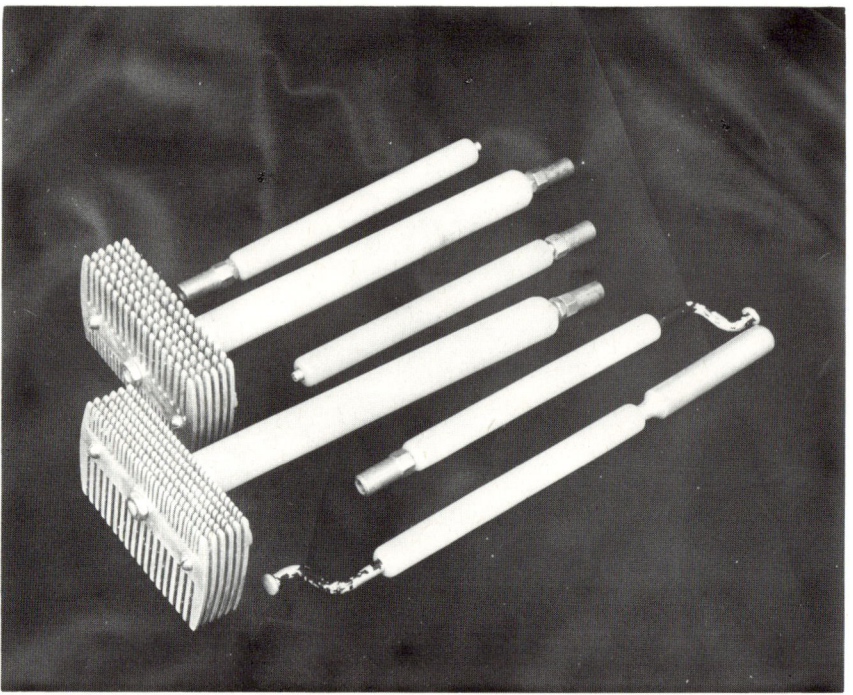

Fig. 12 Set of curry combs, steel with composition handles. The cranked arms were used to curl the mane of the horse. Mid Victorian *(Pamela Watkins)*.

SHAVING TOOLS

Articles connected with shaving include old razors, often encased in wooden boxes of quite elegant design, but they are also found in boxes more crudely shaped. Boxes used by barbers often contained more than one razor. Apart from the main instrument used in shaving there are many accoutrements including hones, soap boxes, wig and cravat holders, toilet cases including razor, scissors, shaving brush, tooth pick, etc., and of course old shaving mugs.

There are shaving utensils in silver, such as silver soap boxes, and shaving dishes, but the prices of these are likely to be prohibitive.

42

Fig. 13   An unusual bygone. The harness, found in a New Forest barn, was used to train horses to hold their heads up. The spike had an adjustable fixing to which two fixed reins could be attached to the bridle and gradually tightened (*R. van de Gohm*).

HARNESS

The rather unusual piece of harness illustrated was used to gradually increase the tension on a pair of reins and so train the horse to hold its head high.

TREEN

Treen is a term that at present has no precise definition. In some instances it is substituted for the term 'bygones in wood', but what kinds of 'bygones'? Furniture, chests, benches and stools were mainly constructed from wood, but by definition, they have not been superseded by a more functional piece of furniture and therefore furniture can be excluded. Because the term 'treen' lacks a precise meaning, it is more often than not omitted from works of reverence on antiques

Fig. 14 Treen Pot painted in imitation tortoiseshell (*Adrian Bowyer, Beaconsfield*).

and is loosely used to describe any wooden objects that are not readily classifiable by existing nomenclature.

The word treen appears to be the old plural for trees, and the Oxford dictionary defines it as (i) made of tree, (ii) of belonging to trees, and the word appears in many old poems such as the following:

> The Wrathful winter, hastening on apace
> With blustering blasts had all y'bar'd the Treene.
> Sackv. Induct. Mirr. Mag.

Fig. 15 In the back row are traditional cheese moulds with weep holes in the base. Front row (from left to right) coopered piggin; three dimensional butter mould in the form of a crown, used formerly at St. James' Palace, and a selection of various other butter prints, three of which have ejectors. All are English *(Pinto Collection of Wooden Bygones. Birmingham Museum and Art Gallery)*.

Yet another old definition describes a vat to be 'a treene vessel,' so we come to a possible compromise, and one that has been generally accepted, that treen classifies the objects produced on a lathe by the turner, completely or in part; for example oatmeal rollers, chalices, cups, bowls, pastry markers, and caramel ribbers.

Treenware was commonly made of sycamore, and the platters, bowls, etc., were used as tableware before pewter superseded it. It is interesting to know that in the first 50 years of the American colonisation, it was customary to eat food from wooden platters, trenchers, and bowls.

CLOCKS

5. Clocks

Man has been influenced by time even before he understood the meaning of the word. He divided the year into seasons; divided day and night; and divided the day by the positions of the sun. Later his assessment of time became more accurate by the use of astrological means, and subsequently, by the use of hour-glasses, sundials and candles, the latter marked to measure the hour as the candle burned down. The innovation of the clock provided the first really scientific instrument for measuring time as we know it. The intricate design of gear trains and escapement devices of antique clocks, produced without the aid of modern precision machines for gear cutting and turning, must surely represent a milestone in man's technical development in fine engineering.

It is not possible to date the first of the clocks as we know them today with any real accuracy, but there is evidence to support the fact that a water clock existed in China as early as the 11th century. This type of clock was powered by a consistent and constant flow of water that operated a step by step mechanism related to time.

Jacopo Dondi of Padua, Italy, made a clock in 1344 and for this achievement he was rewarded by being given the title of Del Orologio, a title that is still born by his present-day descendants. Unfortunately, the details of this clock have been lost, but at least it does establish the fact that clocks existed in Europe during the early 14th century, or probably earlier, and it can be assumed that the simplest early mechanical clock with foliot and weights dates from about 1300.

Early mechanical clocks derived their power from suspended weights; consequently, it was necessary to site them in a static position such as a wall of a room. They naturally lacked portability, but the introduction of the coil spring and the elimination of the weights solved that problem.

Peter Henlein of Nurnberg has been credited with the invention of the coil spring for clocks, but this is a little doubtful. Spring-driven clocks were first introduced about the middle of the 15th century, and to compensate for the varying torque, obtained by the spring slowly unwinding, the fusee was invented, probably in Flanders or Italy. The fusee consisted of a very small and flexible chain that fitted snugly into a spirally grooved pulley which was connected to the barrel of the main spring, so that when the spring was fully wound

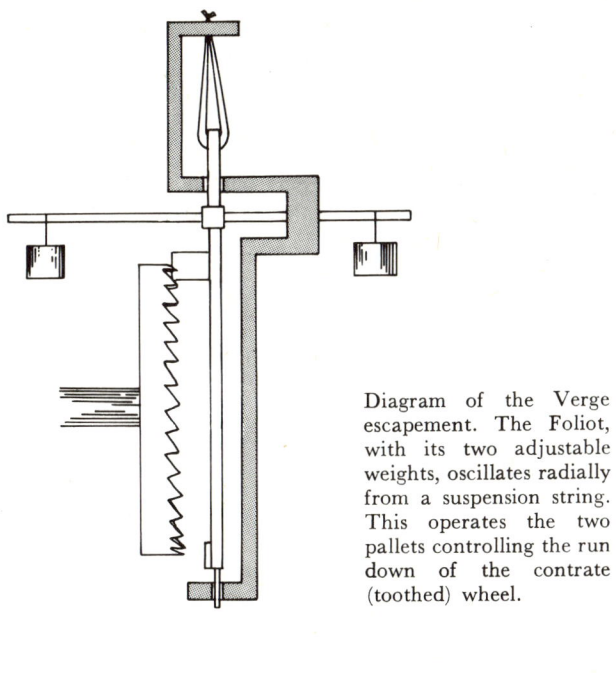

Diagram of the Verge escapement. The Foliot, with its two adjustable weights, oscillates radially from a suspension string. This operates the two pallets controlling the run down of the contrate (toothed) wheel.

Anchor Escapement

and exerting its strongest torque, the chain was wound around the smallest diameter of the spiral pulley. As the spring unwound and the torque progressively became weaker, so the diameter of the groove in the pulley effectively increased as the chain uncoiled down the ever-increasing diameter of the spiral groove. The fusee employed the well-known principle governing levers and was designed to ensure that the same 'pull' was transmitted to the gear train irrespective of the varying amount of tension in the main spring. Prior to the end of the 17th century, it was usual to employ catgut in lieu of the chain.

A device known as the stackfreed originated in Southern Germany about the same period as the fusee. This device, found in early watches, consisted of a spring-loaded roller bearing on a shaped cam attached to a gear wheel that only had teeth around a portion of its circumference. This special cam-wheel was driven by a pinion on the main spring shaft. The roller pressing on the cam acted as a brake applying diminishing pressure as the main spring uncoiled. The incomplete gear limited the unwinding spring to a range whereby the force was considered to be relatively constant.

Although Galileo had observed the principle of the swinging pendulum, it was Cristiaan Huygens who first applied the principle to control clocks in 1657. Basically a given pendulum will take the same time to swing from one side to the other, irrespective of the length of the arc subscribed, i.e. if the pendulum swung only one inch, it would take the *same time* to travel this distance as it would if it was made to swing freely over say four inches. Thus the pendulum could be used to control the driving force and when used in conjunction with the anchor escapement invented *c.* 1670 by William Clement, it led to better and more accurate timekeeping.

British clocks and watches can be said to have been made from the late 17th century. Between the 14th century and late 16th century, some clocks were made in London, but these were mainly the work of foreign refugees residing in this country, such as Nicholas Vallin.

English clock movements were noted for their quality, but the cases, although excellent, were somewhat simple in design and often used marquetry and veneering for decoration. The French, on the other hand, were noted for their beautiful cases rather than their movements, but this does not mean that they did not produce excellent clockwork; on the contrary, they contributed much to the development of the clock movements.

American clockmakers date from about 1715, and although it is possible that a few clocks were made before that date, there are few surviving examples. The majority of 18th century clocks were long case, or grandfather type, made individually by hand and fitted to a case made in the same workshop.

American clocks during the 17th and 18th centuries were mostly owned by the wealthy. This is understandable, because most of the clocks in America at this time had to be made from parts imported from Europe. Early colonists of some financial standing obviously took their clocks with them, together with their other goods and chattels.

In the early 18th century most of the American clocks came from England, and so did most of the early clockmakers, such as Abell Cottley, who settled in Philadelphia in 1702.

Fig. 16 Lantern clock of all brass construction, weight driven with verge escapement. It is rarely that original verge escapements survive because they were not considered to have sufficient accuracy, and many were converted to the anchor escapement. Height 15 inches. Maker: Thomas Stones, London. 1690. (*J. Klein, Twickenham*).

Fig. 17 Longcase clock with an 8-day movement. The case is walnut veneered on oak. It is almost certain that the maker originally intended the dial to be square, but added the arch to keep abreast of the changing fashions. Height 7 feet. Maker: Thomas Perkins. (*J. Klein, Twickenham*).

Fig. 18 Skeleton clock, probably Victorian, and almost certainly made by an apprentice prior to being admitted into the Clockmakers' Company. The moon phase action is rare on a clock of this type. Height 9 inches. (*J. Klein, Twickenham*).

Sometime between 1750 and 1800, wooden movements were used for many of the clocks. This was because brass was both expensive and difficult to obtain. The brothers Timothy and Benjamin Cheney of Connecticut were among the earliest American clockmakers to use wood for the purpose of makng the 'works'.

Fig. 19 Small 18th century bracket clock typical of the type made in London during this period. The case is ebony veneered on oak and the top decorated with a brass basket surmounted with a carrying handle. Probably intended for the bed chamber because it lacks a full striking action. Height 14 inches. Maker: Thomas Wise, London. 1687. (*J. Klein, Twickenham*).

Eli Terry, another American clockmaker who flourished between 1790 and 1826, produced a considerable number of clocks with brass movements. Later, sometime during 1809, he formed a company with Seth Thomas and Silas Headley to produce clocks, but with wooden movements.

Clocks were, of course, made throughout Europe, but it is generally agreed among experts that from the end of the 17th century to about the middle of the 19th century, English clocks led the world. Collectors are likely to find good examples of this period expensive' but a good investment, especially as antique clocks are now tending to rise in price.

Naturally, clocks, like all antiques, need attention from time to time (no pun intended) and a certain amount of cannibalism does take place, attractive late 18th century dials often being added to early 19th century eight-day movements.

Skeleton clocks are both interesting and decorative. As the name implies, they consist of 'the works' most attractively displayed under a glass dome. These clocks were apprentices' pieces, usually unsigned, and made to demonstrate the craftsmanship of the apprentice. The amount of handwork required to file the parts was extensive; consequently they were not made in quantity by qualified craftsmen required to earn a living from their craft. Bracket clocks of the 17th and 18th centuries were clocks that were made for mounting on a wall, the bracket being designed usually as an integral part of the case, but very few of the original brackets have survived. It is not unusual to find a drawer in the bracket for holding the winding key. The back plates of many antique clocks were intricately engraved, but after about 1725 their decoration gradually became simpler until, by the end of the 18th century, only a cartouche was added.

Before the days of luminous hands and numerals, clockmakers attempted to provide means of telling the time in the dark by illuminating the clock faces with oil lamps. This practice could not have been very successful because so few of these night clocks have survived, presumably because they caught fire. Night clocks were provided with a reservoir for the oil on the back, and from one to three wicks to illuminate the clock face.

Clocks with chimes or striking action will command a higher price than non-chiming clocks. In fact, the more intricate the mechanism and the more functions the clock can perform, the higher the price.

Long case clocks not in working condition can be obtained relatively cheaply and will offer hours of pleasure to collectors with a mechanical turn of mind and an enthusiasm for do-it-yourself. Cases in walnut and mahogany are usually the most desirable, and,

Fig. 20   Bracket clock with verge escapement. Mahogany
case shows Chinese influence on the top. Height 20 inches.
Maker: William Bull of Stratford, Essex. *c.* 1770. (J.
Klein, Twickenham).

consequently, the most expensive, but oak was used by a large number of cabinet makers, and these offer the collector with an eye for antique clocks and a limited purse an opportunity to acquire a good example. Naturally, good quality working examples of long case clocks will be expensive. The long case clock was very much part of the furniture, and their design followed the current furniture trends. The Dutch phase of William and Mary will be found to favour marquetry, whilst during the reign of Queen Anne plain veneered walnut was popular, and this was followed by a fashion in japanned cases. From about the middle of the 18th century we find mahogany prominent.

Dainty carriage clocks are ideal acquisitions, as they have a particularly versatile quality that permits them to be included in almost any decorative scheme—antique or modern. They are generally a little expensive but offer excellent investment potential.

Not content with the achievement of the clock itself, clockmakers further exhibited their ability by making various types of mystery clocks. These clocks were invariably very attractively designed, but were intended to mystify an observer by some means or other; for example, the clock made by John Schmidt about 1810 which he named 'The Mysterious Circulation' or 'Chronological Equilibrium'. This clock, mounted on a heavy rectangular base, consisted of a ring on which the figures were engraved, and a single pendulous hand which could swing freely, but always settled at the correct time. The secret was in the bob end of the hand, which contained a watch movement which drove the hand round the face. This was the only functional part of the clock, the base being simply decoration.

Another very impressive mystery clock was made using a column of glass rising from an ornate base, surmounted with a clock face of glass and a single hand. It was possible to look right through the face and column without seeing any mechanism for turning the hand. In fact, this extremely clever illusion was created by having the movement in the base and transmitting the drive by a second glass column within the outer, which rotated and turned a second glass dial to which the hand was fixed.

If you should wish to see the oldest surviving mechanical clock in the world, take a trip to Salisbury Cathedral, where you will see it in its restored state. It dates about 1386. The second oldest clock can be seen in the Science Museum in London; it was made originally for Wells Cathedral in 1392 and by the maker's marks it is believed that both clocks were the work of the same clock-maker. The following is a list of British Clockmakers, and the dates cover the period between which signed pieces are most likely to be found.

Fig. 21 Fine French ormolu clock with exquisite details in the elaborate case. *c.* 1810.

1707–1723	Antram, George
1757–1799	Arnold, John
1697–1738	Bradley, Langley
1682–1709	Colston, Richard
1818–1880	Cole, Ferguson
1740–1788	Cox, James
1702–1733	Delander, Daniel
1693–1730	Duchesne, Claude
1774–1829	Earnshaw, Thomas
1627–1697	East, Edward
1731–1772	Elliott, John
1750–1797	Emery, Josiah
1625–1725	Fromanteel, (various)
1695–1730	Garon, Peter
1686–1730	Goode, Charles
1682–1718	Gould, Christopher
1713–1751	Graham, George
1681–1764	Gray, Benjamin
1715–1776	Harrison, John
1726–1771	Hindley, Henry
1787–1815	Holmes, John
1664–1695	Jones, Henry
1650–1710	Knubb, John
1650–1711	Knubb, Joseph
1640–1662	Knifton, Thomas
1770–1814	Lister, Thomas
1781–1811	McBabe, James
1779–1810	Margetts, George
1704–1720	Moore, William
1740–1794	Mudge, Thomas
1750–1795	Norton, Eardley
1695–1732	Pinchbeck, Christopher
1735–1783	Pinchbeck, Christopher Jnr.
1765–1810	Prior, George (elder)
1815–1830	Prior, George (son)
1674–1724	Quave, Daniel
1590–1655	Ramsay, David
1778–1824	Recordon, Louis
1771–1831	Reid, Thomas
1696–1750	Robinson, Francis
1798–1830	Roskell, Robert
1633–1652	Selwood, William
1666–1710	Stanton, Edward
1699–1745	Tomlinson, William
1671–1713	Tompion, Thomas
1580–1630	Vallin, Nicholas
1775–1820	Vulliamy, Benjamin
1809–1854	Vulliamy, Benjamin Lewis

1730–1790	Vulliamy, Justin	
1675–1715	Watson, Samuel	
1697–1725	Webster, William	
1738–1788	Whitehurst, John	
1697–1725	Williamson, Joseph	
1671–1725	Windmills, Joseph	

AMERICAN CLOCKMAKERS

The first and last dates given represent the earliest and latest records of the clockmaker. When known, actual birth dates (b.) and date of demise (d.) have been used instead.

Benjamin Bagnell	1712–1740	Charleston
Garven Brown	1750–1776	Boston
Benjamin Chandlee	1763	Pennsylvania
Timothy Cheney	b. 1730–d. 1795	Manchester
Benjamin Cheney	2nd half 18th cent.	Manchester
William Claggett	b. 1696–d.1749	Newport
Abel Cottey	1690–1710	Philadelphia
John Farmer	2nd half 18th cent.	Philadelphia
Thomas Gordon	1758–1771	New York
Daniel Graham	1805	New York
Thomas Howard	1775–1783	Philadelphia
Samuel Martin	1805	New York
Philip Price	1817–1825	Philadelphia
David Rittenhouse	1751–1770	Norristown
Robert Scott	1779	Virginia
Peter Stretch	1717	Philadelphia
Samuel Taylor	1799	Philadelphia
Eli Terry	b. 1772–d. 1853	Plymouth
Joseph White	1811–1817	Philadelphia
Benjamin Willard	b. 1743–d. 1803	Grafton, Lexington and Roxbury
Ephraim Willard	b. 1755–d. 1805	Medford, Roxbury and New York
Simon Willard	b. 1753–d. 1848	Grafton and Roxbury

Further details will be found in *Watchmakers' and Clockmakers of the World* by G. H. Baillie, published by the N.A.G. Press Ltd. This book is very comprehensive and contains thousands of names.

GLOSSARY

Acorn Clock: A type of clock shaped similarly to an acorn, and made to rest on a shelf. Usually American.

Arbor: A spindle or axle to which gears and wheels are fixed.

Astrological Dials: Dials which show the relationship of the planets to each other at any time.

Balance or Balance Wheel: The oscillating wheel in a clock or watch usually operated by a spiral spring, to control the 'rate' of the mechanism, running down.

Balance Staff: The spindle on which the balance wheel is mounted.

Balloon Clock: A design of clock in which the case is waisted, giving a balloon shape effect. Popular during the late 18th and early 19th centuries.

Banjo Clock: Clocks shaped like a banjo. Produced in America *c.* 1800.

Banking Pins: Two pins fixed so that they limit the motion of the lever in a lever escapement.

Barrel: The cylindrical, usually brass, box in which the mainspring is housed.

Bezel: The metallic ring, usually angled, forming the frame of the glass.

Bob: The weight on the end of a pendulum.

Bolt and Shutter: A shutter covers the winding squares and must be pushed aside before the winding key can be inserted. The action of pushing the shutter aside brings in an auxiliary drive which maintains the power drive during the act of winding.

Bracket Clock: A clock, usually of the 17th and 18th centuries, designed with its own bracket, often with a drawer to house the winding key.

Buhl: Inlay of brass or silver, usually on a base of tortoise-shell.

Bushing: A means of repairing worn pivot holes by inserting a small tube-like insert.

Calendar Clock: Any clock that indicates date or month and year. Earliest known clock of this type was made in 1364 by Govanni Dondi of Italy, which showed the length of daylight for every day throughout the year.

Cam: Component part so shaped that a rotary motion can be transmitted into a linear motion, e.g. a disc with a spindle off centre would cause an arm resting on the top of the disc to move up and down when the disc was rotated.

Cannon Pinion: The pinion on which the minute hand is usually attached.

Case: The container for the clock or watch movement. The design of the case in a variety of materials has considerable influence and lends much to the appeal and fascination of antique clocks.

Case Pair: One case within another. From the latter part of the 17th century it was usual to provide watches with a secondary or outer case, usually highly decorative.

Centre Seconds: A clock or watch on which the second hand is mounted on the same centre as the hour and minute hands.

Chapter Ring: The circle, found in early clocks, on which the hour numerals are engraved.

Chromograph: A stop watch in which the hands can be started and stopped without actually stopping the mechanism.

Chronometer: A very accurate time piece.

Circular Error: A swinging pendulum does not describe a true arc, but describes a cycloidal path. Therefore, for a short distance either side of the vertical, the true arc and the cycloidal path coincide. Any irregularities in time due to the swing of the pendulum outside this coincidental path is said to be due to circular error.

Clepsydra: A timekeeper using water as a motive force. A water clock.

Click: The pawl that retains the ratchet wheel of the winding drum. It is the sound of this pawl running over the teeth of the ratchet wheel that is heard when a clock is wound.

Collet: A special washer used to fix the hands firmly to their respective shafts.

Compensating Balance: A balance so designed from bi-metal that the effect of heat and cold are neutralised and the time-keeping is unaffected.

Contrate Wheel: A gear wheel in which the teeth point at right angles to the body of the wheel. Used to transmit circular motion at right angles.

Crown Wheel: The escape wheel of the verge escapement.

Crutch: Forked lever with prongs at right angles used to transmit power to the independently supported pendulum.

Curl Pins: The two pins trapping the outer end of the balance spring, adjusted by the regulator to alter the effective length of the spring.

Detent: A device that 'holds back' or detains a pawl or click.

Epicycloid: The curve traced by a point on the circumference of a circle as it rolls around another circle. It is the shape used to flank the gear teeth so that a smooth mesh is obtained.

Equation Kidney: A cam shaped like a kidney used to provide both forward and backward motion. Used to indicate the difference between Solar and Mean Time.

Equation of Time: The difference between Solar Time (shown on a sundial and varying each day), and Mean Time—the conventional 24 hours.

Escape Wheel: The wheel that provides the driving impulses to the balance or pendulums.

Escapement: The device by which the driving force is checked and controlled. The verge escapement was the earliest and although it was not a particularly good device by modern standards, it revolutionised early clocks. The anchor escapement was a later development which refined the accuracy. The cylinder, detent, duplex, pin-pallet, tic-tac, and the deadbeat are all forms of escapement devices.

Fan: A rapidly turning vane on the final shaft of the strike train; operates as an air brake.

Foliot: The earliest form of controller always found with a verge escapement consisting of a horizontal rod fixed to a pivoted bar which carries the verge pallets.

Fusee: A cone shaped pulley, spirally grooved, and connected to the main spring barrel by a length of catgut or later by a fine chain. It was used to compensate for the varying force exerted by the spring from fully wound to fully unwound.

Gong: A piece of hardened wire, coiled and struck to produce a sound similar to a bell.

Grandfather Clock: A long case clock in which the pendulum and weights are housed.

Grandmother Clock: A smaller version of the Grandfather clock.

Hairspring: A fine volute spring used to swing the balance wheel.

Jewels: Bearings made from jewels to reduce both wear and friction.

Lantern Pinion: An early type of pinion produced from two circular discs with wires fixed between them, something like a miniature treadmill used to exercise mice.

Locking Plate: A circular disc with notches set at increasing intervals around the perimeter. It controls the correct number of blows for each hour or quarter-hour.

Lunar Dial: A dial showing the lunar periods.

Mainspring: A length of tempered steel coiled to provide the power in portable clocks.

Main Wheel: The first and usually the largest wheel in the train. Meshes with gear connected to the mainspring.

Micrometer Adjuster: A graduated wheel fixed to the pendulum for finely adjusting the weight to regulate the clock.

Movement: The mechanism of a clock.

Mural Clock: One that is designed to hang on a wall.

Pallet: Part of the escapement mechanism. It provides the link between the escape wheel and the pendulum or balance.

Pendulum: There are various types of pendulums, but in principle they all consist of a swinging rod with a weight on the lower extremity.

Pinion: A small gear with an axial length longer than its diametrical width.

Pivot: The reduced end of an arbor or shaft on which the shaft rotates.

61

Positional Error: Errors in time caused by the position of a watch, e.g. face down, on its back, etc.

Potance: The bracket supporting the lower pivot of the crown wheel arbor in a verge escapement.

Rate: The regular length of time that a clock gains or loses over a stated period of time.

Rating Nut: The nut below the bob weight on a pendulum used to raise or lower the bob and so regulate the clock.

Sedan Clock: A watch with a large dial made to hang in a conveyance.

Skeleton Dial: A chapter ring in which the metal is pierced and cut-away leaving only the numerals and minutes.

Stackfreed: An early German device designed to control the power output of the mainspring so that an even torque resulted (see text for full description).

Strike-Silent: A mechanical device that permits the chimes of a striking clock to be stopped or started at will.

Sunray Clock: A late 17th century clock designed to emulate the sun rays. The clock had a circular dial with carved wooden rays radiating from the outer circumference.

Suspension: Describes the method of suspending a pendulum, knife edge, spring etc.

Time, Mean: An average time based on a 24 hour day, and a year of $365\frac{1}{4}$ days.

Time, Sidereal: Star Time. Calculated by the successive passage of a known star across the meridian. A sidereal day equals 23 hours, 56 minutes, 4 seconds.

Torsion Pendulum: A pendulum consisting of a long torsion spring with bobs suspended at the lower extremity. The bobs rotate in one direction and in doing so wind the spring. The spring then unwinds causing the bobs to move in the opposite direction. This device is used mainly for clocks only required to be wound once a year.

Tower or Turret Clocks: Clocks made for installing in towers or spires of churches.

Train: A succession of gear and pinion wheels.

Weights: Usually made of lead, weights were used to provide the motive power of stationary clocks. From the late 17th century good quality clocks had their weights encased in a brass sleeve.

COINS

6. Coins

There are probably more people interested in coins than in any other field of collecting. Early coins are small antiques, and their fascination stems from the fact that they have been handled by men of the past and provide an unbroken historical record depicting past events and personages. Unlike many other antiques, they are not unique, but usually exist in sufficient quantities to provide for both large and small collections.

Early man had little need for coins or money. He obtained his food by hunting, made his home in a cave or built it from the natural materials that surrounded him, and made the other necessities for himself. The things he could not provide for himself for one reason or another, he obtained by barter, the oldest form of trade.

During the course of barter, certain values or standards were established. Obviously in early times we can easily imagine, say, two earthenware pots equalling one arrowhead, assuming the arrowhead took twice as long to make as the earthenware pot, or was in greater demand. Cattle have been a form of currency for centuries, and even today some African tribes pay dowries in cows. The cow, however, can be a variable standard depending on whether it is large and fat, or small and bony. Also it is a rather large 'denomination' and causes problems when 'purchasing' articles of much smaller values.

Ancient Egypt, for all its wealth and trading involvement, did not have any currency in the form of coins, but had, however, made some attempt to produce standard weights and scales.

Personal seals were used at least 2250 B.C. by persons of authority. The seals were used mainly for endorsing contracts, proclamations, and similar documents. The seal, either in the form of a signet ring, or as a separate stamp, had its owner's motif or design carved or engraved into it, so that when it was pressed into hot wax or clay, the 'mark' of the owner was impressed.

The universal acceptance of metal objects marked to show their standard weight, combined with the representative motif to indicate authority or ownership, give a basis for the next evolutionary stage—coinage.

When the first coin as such was struck is anybody's guess. There are no records to tell us, but it can be assumed that the first coins were the result of evolution and the usual driving force—necessity,

Fig. 22 Model One penny piece. This interesting coin is toy money, or money used as a plaything (*Richmond Stamp Co.*).

Fig. 23 George III Halfpenny. 1806 (*Richmond Stamp Co.*).

Fig. 24 Crown size Hungarian 5 pengo piece 1939 (*Richmond Stamp Co.*).

Fig. 25 Victoria Crown 1887. Jubilee issue. First year with this particular head. (*Richmond Stamp Co.*).

Fig. 26 Gold Sovereign 1871. (Note young head of the Queen.) (*K. Stone Collection*).

Fig. 28 George III Half Sovereign 1820 (*K. Stone Collection*).

Fig. 30 Victoria Florin. 1891 (*Richmond Stamp Collection*).

Fig. 31 Victoria Sovereign, 1900 (*K. Stone Collection*).

Fig. 27 Reverse side of the above. End of the shield design (*K. Stone Collection*).

Fig. 29 Reverse side of the above (*K. Stone Collection*).

Fig. 32 Reverse side of the above. (*K. Stone Collection*).

THE WATER JUMP.

Left. The Water Jump. A Stevengraph pure silk woven picture. This picture is found occasionally titled 'Rennen mit Hindernissen', suggesting it was either made for the German market in Britain, or actually made in Germany. (Studio Suzanna).

Below. Antique Print 'A Ferncutter's Child' by Bartoloti after R. Westall. $12\frac{3}{8}'' \times 9\frac{3}{8}''$. A beautiful example of a stipple engraving printed in colour. (Parker Galleries, London)

A FERN-CUTTER'S CHILD.

Four items from a 'desert' service in the 'Nautilus' shape. Complete service consisted of a centre and stand, two sauce tureens and stands and nine compositers. Decorated with design No. 384 from Josiah Wedgwood's pattern book of 1770. Marked 'Wedgwood.' made Etruria 1798. (Josiah Wegdwood & Sons Ltd)

Wedgwood Black basalt vase No. 1 in Wedgwood shape book of 1770, marked 'Wedgwood & Bentley' Height 12ins. Etruria 1775 (Front). Wine Vase also in Black basalt 'Sacred to Bacchus' with pressed figure of Bacchus holding spout. Marked 'Wedgwood & Bentley' Height 16ins. Etruria 1778 (Rear). (Josiah Wedgwood & Sons

18th century printed Queen's ware teapot decorated with scene depicting the 'Death of Wolfe'. c. 1780 (Front).

rather than the outcome of a single inventive mind. Archaeologists generally agree that the first coins were made about 640 B.C. during the reign of King Ardys. The oldest known coin to carry an inscription is a stator, made from electrum, issued under King Alyattes of Lydia (650–560 B.C.).

The study of coin development from these early beginnings to the sophisticated coinage of the present day is a long voyage, richly enhanced with history, but it is not necessary to make this voyage before starting a collection. Ancient Greek and Roman coins are generally expensive and need a little study, but coins of the British world, and general world coinage, can be far less expensive for the beginner if he concentrates on coins within his personal price range.

Oriental coins can be rewarding for collectors with some knowledge of Oriental scripts and history, but if collecting with investment in mind, these are best left with the expert.

The subject of coin collecting has been well covered by specialist books, and a wealth of catalogues, detailing current prices, are available for the price of a stamp.

The value of coins are dependent upon their exact design, legend, mintmark, date, current demand and condition. Condition is of major importance, and for reference purposes the following grading is generally accepted in England.

FDC=Fleur-de-coin. Unused coins in a mint state, without any scratches, marks, or signs of wear.

Unc =Uncirculated. Coins as issued by the Royal Mint, but due to modern methods of production may not necessarily be perfect examples.

EF =Extremely Fine. Coins that appear never to have been in circulation, but on close examination may show very slight surface scratches or marks.

VF =Very Fine. Coins that have been little used, and only show slight traces of wear on the raised surfaces.

F =Fine. Weak impression due to faulty striking, coins exhibiting considerable wear on their raised surfaces.

F =Fair. Coins on which the inscriptions and main features are still recognisable, but exhibit signs of wear.
Poor, badly-worn coins are not worth adding to a collection unless, of course, they are extremely rare.

The earliest coins found in Britain were circulated some few hundred years B.C. by the migratory Belgic people from the Continent. These early coins were gold staters, designed in imitation of the stater of Philip II of Macedonia. Early in the 1st century A.D. some silver coins were produced in imitation of Roman examples.

First coins of the Anglo-Saxon periods (A.D. 575 to 775) were silver sceats, with designs influenced by late Roman coins, but during the 8th century, silver pennies were struck; these were made the same size and weight as the denier. A little later the weight of the silver penny was increased to 24 grains or one pennyweight. This coin was used until the 13th century, with variations in design, and the addition of a royal portrait.

From about 1279, the groat, or fourpenny piece, half-penny and farthing were included, together with coinage in gold.

During the Renaissance period, coins were made in larger denominations, in both gold and silver, with designs more elegant and intricate.

Up to 1662 coins had been made by hand hammering, but this method was then abandoned and the mechanical mill and screw presses took over. Coins now became more precise and symmetrical in shape, much as they are today.

Maundy money owes its existence to a religious service which is held to commemorate the act of the washing of the disciples' feet by Christ. This service is one of the oldest, maybe it is *the* oldest, of the Christian religious services.

The Maundy service always takes place on the Thursday before Good Friday, in a cathedral of note such as Westminster, St. Albans or Chelmsford. The service is always attended by the reigning Monarch or by the Monarch's representative, and during the service the money is distributed to a number of senior citizens. The money is distributed to an equal number of men and women, and the total number of each is determined by the number of years the Monarch has lived. The amount of money received by each individual also corresponds to the number of years lived by the Monarch. For example, let us assume the Monarch has reached a 42nd birthday, then 42 men and 42 women would each receive 42 pence.

Maundy money struck during the reign of George VI is now becoming quite valuable as a collectors' item.

It is interesting to know that in 1932, George V personally distributed the Maundy coins, and it was the first time that a reigning Monarch had done so for the past two hundred and fifty years or so.

A word about cleaning coins. Providing the example is reasonable, make no attempt whatsoever to clean it; more damage is done to coins by cleaning than by any other cause. Copper coins should never be washed in water or cleaned with metal polish; any dirt in the crevices should be removed by brushing. Gold and silver coins can be carefully washed in soapy water if they are really grimy.

Do not forget that a badly cleaned coin will lose most of its value.

Would-be collectors should avail themselves of a copy of Seaby's 'Standard Catalogue of British Coins'. It is a reasonably priced book which covers the period from the Belgic Migration to the present day in a very competent manner.

GLOSSARY

Aes: The term used for coins made of copper and bronze.

Argentum: The term used for silver coins.

Aureus: The term used for gold coins.

Billion: Silver coins with a high copper content.

Blank: The blank disc of metal before it is formed between dies.

Die: Block of metal in which the design for a coin is cut, used to impress the coin blank with the actual design.

Edge: The milled edge of modern coins; the edge may be smooth and inscribed, or left plain.

Electrum: Natural amalgam of gold and silver found in Asia Minor. The metal used for the earliest coins.

Exergue: The part of the coin below the main design, usually occupied by the date, and separated by a line.

Fabric: The metal from which a coin is manufactured, including the finish obtained by production.

Field: The flat areas on the coin surface not occupied by the design.

Flan: The complete piece of metal after striking.

Graining: The milling around the edge of a coin.

Hammered: Old method of making coins, by placing the blank between dies and hammering by hand.

Incuse: Design sunken into the surface, opposite to relief.

Inscription: Words usually shown around the inside perimeter of a coin, but can also occupy other positions.

Legend: Another term for inscription.

Milled. Coins struck by dies operated in a coining press.

Mint Mark: Symbol or letters on a coin indicating place where it was struck.

Mule: Non-standard coin, one that has been struck from two dies not normally used together. Sometimes a mule will have the current type on one face, and the previous type on the other face.

Obverse: The side of a coin showing the monarch's head. The principal side of the coin.

Pattern: This is a coin bearing a design never adopted by the Mint for circulation, a trial piece.

Patina: This is the result of the natural oxidation of the metal surface; it is a kind of bloom acquired with age and handling.

Proof: A coin specially struck from new dies, 'prooving' the dies.

Reverse: The less important side of a coin, opposite to obverse.

Stater: A piece of a given weight, usually a coin made of gold or electrum.

Struck: The term used to describe coins made from dies. The surface of such coins have a hard smooth finish.

Type: Refers to the main central design.

cuir:	cuirassed	
diad:	diademed	
dr:	draped	
laur:	laureate	Common
m.m.:	mint-mark	abbreviations
quat:	quatrefoil	
pl:	plume	
rad:	radiate	
var:	variety	

FANS

7. Fans

Fans in one form or another have probably been in use since the middle ages, at least in European society. In hot Eastern countries, their history will go back to Biblical times and the palm leaf.

Very few examples of European fans have been traced earlier than about 1700, and it is improbable that such examples will find their way into the hands of a new collector. Therefore, let us take a practical view of the subject and start looking at fans of the 18th and 19th centuries onwards.

Very early folding fans were decorated with geometric designs and simple, straightforward patterns, but the later examples became more ornamental, and depicted landscapes, scenes, and more elaboration in general design.

The functional part of a fan is called the leaf, which can be made of parchment, silk, crepe, paper, net, or gauze. The radiating arms are called 'sticks' and these are usually in wood, ivory, tortoise-shell, or mother-of-pearl. The outer frame into which the fan was folded was called the guard, and this was usually made in the same materials as the sticks.

A variation from the conventional type is known as a brise fan, which has sticks with broad-bladed ends, often decorated by slots and pierced designs. A coloured ribbon was threaded through a series of slots to position each blade in a slightly overlapping position with its neighbour when opened.

The brise fan came into use as early as 1680, but it did not become fashionable until about 1715. The brise fan was also produced with plain, unperforated blades; this provided a plain area for decoration in oil colours, the design appearing on both sides, and it was finished finally with a coat of lacquer.

During the Georgian period, the brise fan was used to provide a novelty—the puzzle fan. It had more blades than the normal brise fan, and depending on the way it was manipulated it could present four different pictures. The trick was in the way it was strung.

Most desirable fans were produced in Italy and France, in Baroque style, until about 1740.

Sticks were usually carved or pierced, and mounted with silver piqué, this combination being a favourite style for bridle fans. During the Regency period, evening fans were small, and often decorated with spangles.

Fan leaves were often hand painted, and prior to about 1840, the painters rarely signed their work, but from 1840 onwards it became a common practice. From about 1850 to 1900, artists, both skilled and mediocre, painted fan leaves, either professionally or just to amuse themselves. Many amateur painters turned it into a hobby.

Sticks and guards were often produced on a large scale by cottage

workers and considerable importations were made from the Orient, which were subsequently fitted with leaves of European design. During the early part of the 18th century, at least in England, printed leaves made their first appearance. These were of poor quality, and painted cheaply, though it is not surprising since these

Fig. 34 *Fan with design painted on* vellum. English. Mid 18th century *(Victoria & Albert Museum. Crown copyright).*

were considered to be expendable items, and consequently are now relatively rare.

The quizzing fan, first introduced about 1735, had a hole cut in every stick covered with a transparent material. When the fan was opened 'peep-holes' appeared adjacent to the outer border, which

permitted its owner to hide behind her fan but still see what was
going on around her. This was a useful little piece of female equipment when one considers the risqué plays of the time, and the need
for a woman to appear modest. There were probably many other
occasions when such a fan could be used to advantage.

The collector may now have to concentrate on fans of the
Victorian era; although these cannot be compared with 18th

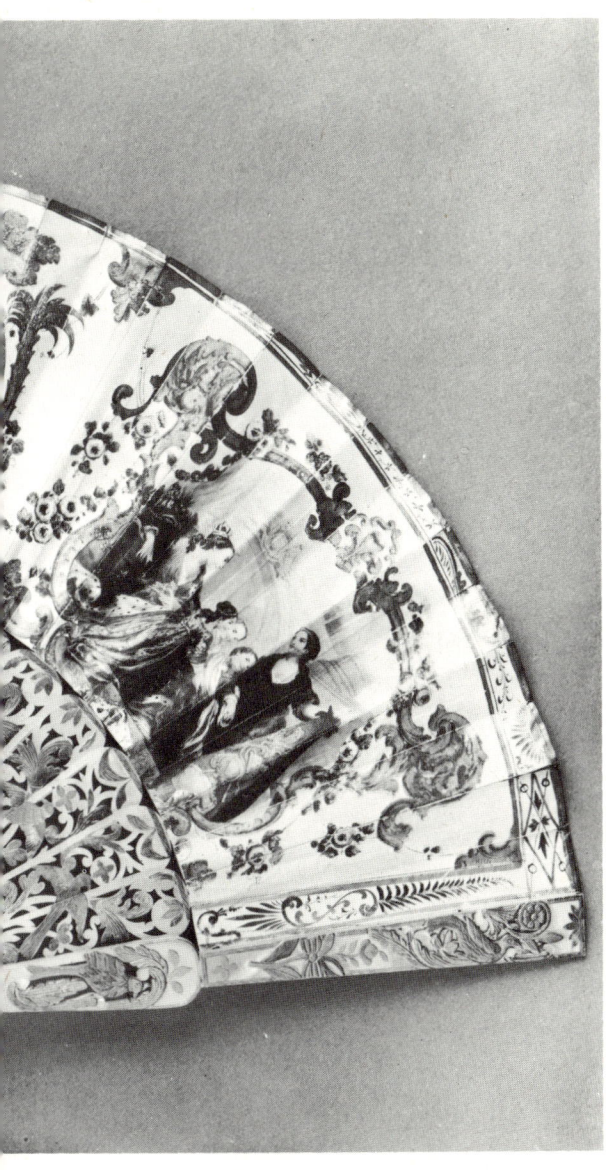

century examples for quality, they are nevertheless very attractive. The fan did not play a very important part in Victorian society; it was used mainly in conjunction with evening wear.

About 1850, fans of coloured feathers became fashionable; these were known as 'Cora' fans. Closely following this fashion we find fans painted in watercolours, most of which were imported from France and decorated by well known artists. Lithography and hand coloured prints were used to produce fans of a cheaper quality.

Large ostrich feather fans made their appearance late in the century, and small fans of lace appliqué were still popular, but the turn of the century virtually saw the end of the fan as an item of fashion.

A rather exotic example of the 1870's was a fan made from peacock feathers. The sticks were made very delicately from ivory, and the feathers arranged so that the 'eyes' of the tail feathers formed the stick terminals. The feathered leaf was finished with a hand-painted scene.

Another bewitching example is the black net fan, with sticks of blackwood painted and gilded. These often were decorated with an anecdotal scene.

Small fans, sometimes shaped like the scallop shell, had sticks of mother-of-pearl and white net leaves decorated with silver and coloured sequins.

Spanish style fans of many kinds were very popular; a typical example would have wooden sticks, painted and decorated, and a leaf of satin painted with some typical scene.

Lace was a popular leaf material, and examples using fine white Nottingham, mounted on mother-of-pearl sticks, with a painted centre panel, would now be considered a very collectable item.

It is surprising that not one British-made fan was exhibited in the Great Exhibition of 1851. This must also have surprised and disappointed Queen Victoria, who in 1870 organised an Exhibition and gave a prize of £400 for the best fans. In 1878, the Worshipful Company of Fanmakers held a competition, and again 11 years later, but by then the popularity of the fan had declined beyond redemption.

FURNITURE

8. Furniture

Sometime in the distant past man decided to make his earthly existence a little more comfortable by making simple 'aids' to help with the necessary tasks and functions encountered in daily living. Just when or how these 'aids' came into being can only be a matter of conjecture. No one can date the first chair or table, and it is unlikely that it will ever be possible to do so. But if we let ourselves travel backwards in time, it will take very little imagination to produce a mind-picture of primitive man evolving such chattels.

It was undoubtedly more comfortable to sit on a fallen tree than to sit on the haunches, or to squat on the ground. Saplings laid side by side and covered with dried bracken must have provided a better bed than the hard earth or floor of a cave. A log upturned, or a large flat rock, would have provided a table that could have been used for many purposes without having to bend the back. This imaginary picture of early man and primitive furniture is, of course, pure conjecture, but it is a fact that man did know and understand how to use timber well before recorded history.

Furniture has been discovered in the tombs of Ancient Egypt dating back to about 2600 B.C., or earlier. These examples, produced by relatively simple tools such as the adze, axe, chisel, saw, mallet and hammer, exhibit not only a high degree of craftsmanship, but also indicate an advanced stage in the evolution of furniture.

Some furniture dating from 15th century England still survives, but very little will be found in its original condition. There are a little more surviving examples from the 16th century. This early furniture was mainly Gothic in style, and often painted.

During the reign of Henry VIII, the Renaissance began to influence design, and Italian carvers and decorators came to work at Hampton Court.

During the early 16th century, the previous Gothic forms had classical ornamentation superimposed, resulting in a mixture of both styles. This compromise lasted, more or less, throughout the 16th century.

The true classical style virtually became established by Inigo Jones (1573–1652) after he had visited Italy, a journey that was to have a great influence on Jones and English furniture.

Inigo Jones, founder of the English school of classical architecture, returned to England in 1614, and a year later he was appointed Surveyor of the Kings Works.

Oak was the predominant timber used during Tudor times, and the furniture was generally heavy in construction. Early examples were austere in design but functional. It was a time when furniture was not considered to have much importance. Even owners of large houses restricted themselves to the barest essentials of beds, tables, stools, bench, and chests for general storage purposes. Chairs were used only by the master and mistress of the household. Such was the poverty of furniture, that chests normally used for storage were often pressed into use for seats, tables, and even beds. Chests, coffers and chairs with high backs were often carved.

Up to the 15th century, furniture was constructed rather crudely from planks and fixed with pegs. The planks were slotted into end frames, and then pegged. This method, however, was superseded early in this period by the innovation of joinery techniques employing the mortise and tenon. These were not the perfect examples later produced by the cabinet-maker, but nevertheless it represented a real step forward in furniture construction.

During the reign of Henry VIII the middle classes had become prosperous and found themselves with money to spend. This resulted in an increase in the building of private houses and a corresponding increase in the demand for the supply of furniture. Henry encouraged immigrant foreign craftsmen into England who brought with them the styles of the classical Renaissance, which also helped to make the Gothic designs and motifs an outmoded style.

During the second half of the 16th century the Netherland influence can be seen in the bulbous legs of tables and chairs. This was the period when chairs, in effect stools with backs, began to supersede the stool.

The Elizabethan period was a more sophisticated period. It was influenced by French and Italian designers; carvings of swages of fruit, eagles, medallions, and strapwork were used in rich ornamentation. Inlaying in coloured woods, and turning, became popular. (Turning is simply the method of making legs, spindles, etc. by rotating a length of wood in a lathe and shaping with sharp cutting tools whilst it is 'turning'). The Elizabethan period is considered by some experts to be one in which a certain amount of ostentatious and vulgar decoration was used, but this is a matter for personal taste. Oak was still the predominant wood.

The gate-leg table was a Jacobean innovation, and table tops, which until this time had been mostly rectangular, became oval or round. It was a period that moved away from the heavy Tudor and Elizabethan styles into lighter and more elegant designs, and Oriental lacquer work made its appearance, but mainly through importations. Metal workers joined forces with the furniture makers, and handles of simple design in both brass and wrought iron were added.

During the reign of James I chairs began to be upholstered; until this time it was customary to use loose cushions. Drawers were fitted to chests and cabinets for the storage of small objects, and a little later, about 1640, mirrors, at first small, were added.

The Commonwealth period is not notable for any major artistic innovations, but it did however introduce chairs with slung leather backs and seats.

Late Stuart furniture was greatly influenced by the immigrant foreign craftsmen who came to England with Charles II and his court when they returned from exile. Much of the best London examples were made by these craftsmen, who introduced techniques that were in use on the Continent, such as gilding, lacquering, marquetry, and veneering.

Lacquer cabinets made from imported panels were mounted on very ornate carved stands, the stands being usually silvered or gilded. European craftsmen were now copying the Chinese panels and had become quite skilful in the use of varnishes or lacquer. Because the panels from Japan were considered to be the best quality, and in consequence probably the most expensive, the art of lacquering became known as japanning.

Oak was now becoming unfashionable, and was superseded by walnut. Walnut continued in popularity for some seventy years, until it was ousted by mahogany.

Joinery now ceased to be a crude and undeveloped method. It blossomed out into a true craft that was practiced by both joiner and cabinet-maker. English artisans also had the opportunity to widen their scope and skills by the study of Oriental workmanship. Inlay work was executed with a precision and delicacy that had not been possible previously. Inlay materials included ivory, bone, ebony and hollywood.

Cabinets, which were a development of early chests, became very sophisticated and artistic, with secret compartments and drawers which are a delight to modern collectors.

Walnut has always been valued for its beautiful grain, or figuring, but it has always been a costly wood, and in consequence it will be difficult to find pieces in solid walnut. The practice of covering a more common wood, like deal, with thin sheets of walnut (veneer) was an obvious method of providing the excellent finish of walnut at a less prohibitive cost.

During the last quarter of the 17th century, chairs, settees, and day beds were made with turned frames, and the seats and backs of woven cane. It was quite common for the legs and rails to have ela-

79

borate spiral turning. The well established cabriole leg was a feature of the following William and Mary period. In general shape, the cabriole leg was styled like a flattened 'S' with a section that tapered from a thick top to a thin foot. It was not of English origin, but came to us from the Netherlands. In fact, much of the furniture of this period was strongly influenced by the Dutch cabinet-makers, who gave us curved tied stretchers for chairs, and dome-topped cabinets.

Marquetry was a fashionable decoration, and much of the original work was executed by immigrant Dutch cabinet-makers. Later of course, the English were also producing marquetry decoration, and it is sometimes difficult to distinguish between the work of the English and the Dutch. Furniture of this period made in the Netherlands for the Dutch is generally larger and heavier than its English counterpart.

During the next period, Queen Anne, the English craftsmen, having by then learnt quite a lot from their foreign counterparts, made full use of their skill and ingenuity to produce excellent quality furniture, but in the English style. The cabriole leg, still much in vogue, was ornamented at the outward curve, or knee, by shell carvings or carved heads. Chair legs, which until now had been strengthened by stretchers, became unsupported, and the splat, that is the panel situated in the centre of the back, became highly decorated with carvings. This period also saw the introduction of the Windsor chair, with its plain wooden seat and lath back.

Mahogany from San Domingo in the West Indies (known as Spanish mahogany), was dark in colour with slight colouring and was more often than not used in the solid form.

The lighter mahogany later imported from Cuba and Honduras, was introduced to England during the reign of George I. It was not until the Georgian period that the timber was established as a successor to the then prevailing walnut. Oak, beech, and chestnut were also still in use, but to a lesser extent.

This was a time when new types of furniture made their appearance; the bureau, for example, which had drawers, and a writing compartment, and shelves covered by doors above. The bureau doors were either panelled or glazed with clear glass or mirrored glass. Mirrored doors were expensive due to the problems of making the glass flat enough to give an undistorted reflection.

Dining tables were quite small, but they were usually designed with a loose leaf, which when inserted, provided a larger table. Although side tables were used for serving food, the sideboard as such did not evolve until later in the century.

A typical settee of the Queen Anne period appeared to be more like a combination of chairs. The main, long, common seat frame, was

Below. Staffordshire Spaniel, front legs integral with body. More desirable examples have these legs separated from the body.

Above. Martinware Vase. (Southall Public Library)

Above. Flask in Nailsea glass. (Loco Antiques)

Above. Martinware Vase. (Southall Public Library)

Martinware Pierced Vase (Southall Public Library)

Jade Necklace. Chain & mounts in gold. Fashioned in England from Burmese jade. 1900.

Pot Lid 'The Game Bag'.
(Loco Antiques)

Two Fairing Pieces. (Loco Antiques)

Millefiori paperweight.

mounted on multiple legs, and the back consisted of two or three separate chair backs.

The Georgian period, which covers most of the 18th century, was a period when form became more important than ornamentation. The cabriole leg was developed to perfection by such masters as Chippendale.

Thomas Chippendale published his well-known book of designs, *The Gentleman and Cabinet-makers' Directory*, in 1754. He was very much influenced by the rococo style, which at that time was enjoying high favour in France, but he also made use of Gothic, and Oriental designs. He was, and is, best remembered for his beautiful chair designs, with skilfully carved openwork slats, and broad seats in the contemporary French style.

The term 'Chippendale' is used to describe the style of furniture from this period, but it does not mean that all Chippendale furniture came from his workshops. During the 19th century his design book was used extensively by makers of reproduction furniture who produced articles in similar styles. Original Chippendale, produced in his own workshops, have carvings that are clean, crisp, and deep, and it is worth a visit to a museum or country house to see this original work so that it can be really appreciated.

Chippendale did not lack competition; there were other designers of high reputation whose work is valued by collectors of today, such as Ince and Mayhew, Edwards and Darley, William Vile, William Hamelt, and Mannering and Johnson. The stand for the bedroom in which the wash-basin and other articles of the toilet could be featured, was one of Chippendale's innovations.

The Regency period is best noted for its 'Neo-Classic Style' of furniture which, in fact, was inspired by the designs of Pompeii in Italy, where archaeologists were excavating examples of historic interest, and from Greco-Roman designs. The Regency period was an artistically unsettled period, with new forms of expression being sought continually. Designers used Egyptian, Chinese, and Gothic styles in addition to the Greco-Roman.

Egyptian motifs commonly found on Regency furniture include serpents, lion supports, lotus leaves, and sphinx heads.

The victories of Nelson were also responsible for a leaning towards marine subject motifs such as dolphins, anchors, tridents, and others. Carving was no longer the predominant method of decoration; in fact, it was little used, except perhaps where it was difficult to eliminate entirely, such as on the legs of tables.

Rosewood was the fashionable wood of the period, but kingwood and amboyna were used, to a lesser extent, but mainly for furniture of high quality.

81

High quality furnishing became the accepted standard with the advent of French polishing introduced just prior to 1820, and it is worthy of note that earlier 18th century furniture was often 'brought up to date' with a fine glossy coat of French polish.

Brass inlay was another Regency feature; it had the decorative quality of marquetry, the virtue of being longer lasting, and gave a real aura of elegance to furniture. Mounts, also made of brass, were commonly used at this time for toe-caps for table supports.

Chinese furniture was largely japanned and decorated with mandarins and other Oriental motifs.

(The Empire style of furniture is virtually indistinguishable from Regency. The term is more applicable to the French period between 1799 and 1814, but out of regard for the French development during this time and its effect on our own development, this period of English furniture is sometimes called 'Empire').

And now to the last of the antique periods—the Victorian, with its flamboyant ornamentation, abundance of flowing curves and rounded corners.

The favourite woods were rosewood and mahogany, and to a lesser extent oak. It was a period of great expansion, both in population and industry, and in consequence there was an increased demand for goods. Mass production in a modern sense did not really get underway until later in the 19th century, although some machines were employed to produce carved pieces, and for limited other operations. The extra demands on the furniture industry were met by simply employing more workers.

Early Victorian furniture still reflected the Grecian style with its sabre leg dining chairs, but from about 1835 revived Gothic began to gain favour and in a few years, certainly by the time of the Great Exhibition of 1851, most furniture exhibited the influence of revived Gothic with its pointed arches, so typical of Gothic architecture, as opposed to the semi-circular arch of the classic styles.

The Victorian era was one of exploration in design; styles were often mixed and this did not always result in pleasing furniture; however, for collectors interested in furniture it can be a very fascinating study.

American furniture followed the general European trends in design. In Europe the capital cities of each country became the fashion centres for the whole country, but along the American Atlantic coast there were many large towns or cities that became regional centres for the manufacture of furniture. These regional centres naturally provided the furniture fashion to the surrounding towns and villages and, because each centre developed locally from individualistic ideas, the American furniture developed regional characteristics.

Early American furniture, based on contemporary English designs, became quite 'localised'. Furniture made in Philadelphia before the Revolution shows a strong English influence, either generated from design books, or executed by London trained craftsmen. Philadelphia chairs in the Chippendale style were beautifully carved with equal quality to those produced in England. Massachussetts furniture was fairly simple in detail, but it had an elegant form and good proportions, unlike the furniture of New York which was strong and heavy in proportion and detail, reflecting an early Dutch influence.

After the Revolution, the newly formed States still had regional differences in furniture within their boundaries, but as better communications and travel developed, the styles tended to merge. The influence of England still prevailed until about 1800, when the French began to creep in. After the French Revolution, immigrant French craftsmen settled in large numbers in New York, and developed the style of the French Directoire and Empire furniture.

Some confusion can arise between the descriptive terminology of the Americans and English when discussing furniture; the same name for a piece of furniture can actually have a totally different meaning to an American and Englishman. For example, to an Englishman a bureau is a desk with a sloping top, but to an American it can mean a four-drawer chest.

Students of early American furniture would find John Jay's Homestead in Katonah, New York, of particular interest. The original farmhouse dates back to 1787, but since then it has been enlarged as successive generations felt the need for more space.

In 1958, Westchester County purchased and deeded the homestead to the State of New York, which restored the historic site and opened it to the public in 1964.

Whilst the homestead is in itself of undoubted interest, it is the fine collection of colonial furniture and bygones that it contains that makes the homestead so exciting. Each room is furnished more or less as it would have been in John Jay's time, and much of the furniture, kitchen utensils, and books were originally owned by this famous New York Governor.

The history of furniture, like any other antique category, is a complicated and diverse subject requiring considerable study if knowledge in depth is required by the collector. For new collectors it is suggested that a start can be made by studying the furniture of a particular period, or by tracing the history of a particular article of furniture, such as chairs, or similar smallish collectable items.

A general but by no means precise guide to the three divisions into which furniture can be classified is as follows:

Age of oak	Up to about 1650
Age of walnut	From 1650 to 1750
Age of mahogany	From 1750

Furniture is hardly a convenient subject for a general collection it is much better suited to museums with space to accommodate and display the articles to advantage, and, by no means a small consideration, the means to buy them anyway.

If, however, one is so inclined, it is possible to use antique furniture in the home, and at the same time consider them as part of a collection. This provides the best of two worlds. An obvious

84

Fig. 36   John Jay's Homestead,
Katonah, New York State. (*Photo:
Courtesy, New York State Board for
Historic Preservation*).

advantage of such an arrangement is the fact that, unlike modern
furniture, its re-sale value will almost certainly be in excess of the
original purchase price, assuming the original purchase was a pru-
dent one.

VICTORIAN CHAIRS

Balloon-back Chairs

Balloon-back chairs were used for the drawing room, bedroom,
and dining room. They were a very popular shape until about the
middle of the period, and they were still being made up to about
1890, although not in such large quantities.

The back of the chair had a curved top that 'waisted in' as it approached the seat, the outline somewhat resembling the shape of a balloon in flight. Seats were usually upholstered and the legs were the usual cabriole style, but after about 1850 drawing room chairs had French style cabriole legs. Early balloon-backs did not have such pronounced waisting, or cabriole legs. The rear legs were often part of the back, and the front legs formed by turned balusters.

Bentwood Rocker
Bentwood furniture was produced by bending strips of beech, made pliable under steam, to form the frame. The particular rocking chair, made by Thonet of Vienna, had a light bentwood framework to support the back and seat. Strips of wood were carried down and under to form the curved rocking members. The bentwood rocker was the product of mass production techniques.

Children's Chairs
Many chairs were designed specifically for small children—solid little rocking chairs with turned rocker supports and arm rests; sturdy little balloon-backs with curved arms and upholstered seats, tall, slim chairs in bamboo, and many other attractive miniature examples of adult furniture.

Easy Chair
The early easy chair was made with a mahogany frame. Seat, back and filled-in padded arm rests were upholstered. Back and arm rest sides were deeply buttoned. Original upholstery material was usually leather, but other materials were used.

Later in the period, easy chairs were made to appear lighter by removing the upholstery from between the arm rest and seat, and replacing it with turned wooden spindles. Leather was still the popular covering, and horse-hair the common padding material.

Fan-back Windsor
The back of this chair was designed with two turned supports on the outside with rails in between, which were set into a circular seat, and tapered outwards until they met the straight top rail. This gave the fan shape.

Legs were turned and supported by turned stretchers.

The Fan-back Windsor chair was in vogue during the late 18th century, and was made throughout the Victorian period, with minor modifications in turning and top rail.

Fig. 37 Armchair. Satinwood with painted decoration. English. Second half 19th century (*Victoria and Albert Museum. Crown copyright*).

Lady's Easy Chair

The back and seat of this chair was virtually made in one piece, supported by a curved continuous frame not unlike a modern slatted garden chair.

Legs were curved, and each pair connected with a single turned stretcher. The chair, because it was without any arm rests, was low and comfortable; it also had the advantage of permitting the voluminous skirts worn by women to drape naturally, unrestricted by arm rest supports.

This chair was made during the first half of the Victorian period, but the shape originated in Regency times.

Lath and Baluster Windsor

This was a heavy solid wooden armchair with turned baluster legs, and double cross-stretchers. The seat was solid wood, with a back made from curved laths, and a decorative splat. Splat decoration was usually made by cutting the wide piece of wood into an attractive shape, but it was not carved. Arms were supported on turned baluster pillars. Beech was commonly used and often stained to imitate rosewood, or painted.

Morris, Adjustable-back Chair

Designed as an easy chair for the drawing room, it had an adjustable bar at the back to alter the angle of recline. The back consisted of a wooden frame which supported a separate squab; the seat had its own separate cushion and the arms were upholstered. Castors were often fitted to all legs. This design became so popular in America that chairs of similar design are still known as 'Morris chairs'.

Papier-Mâché Chair

Papier mâché was not quite so suitable structurally for furniture as the furniture makers had hoped. Victorian papier mâché chairs are invariably made with wooden legs and frame to overcome this deficiency.

These chairs were beautifully japanned and decorated with gilding and mother-of-pearl inlay, and the backs were sometimes painted with beautiful views. (For description of techniques employed in producing papier mâché see appropriate heading).

Smokers Bow

So named because it was a favourite of the smoking room, and had a bow back. This was formed by a thick semi-circular piece of wood supported from the solid wooden seat by either seven or eight

turned spindles. The legs were beautifully turned and strengthened by turned double stretchers. As the period developed, the legs and spindles became less ornamental.

The shape of this chair also made it suitable for barbers' shops and public houses.

Spoon-back Chair

Spoon backs were invariably small upholstered chairs without arm rests. The name spoon back refers to the spoon-like shape of the back, which to some extent follows the shape of the human back. It was usual to upholster these chairs with Berlin woolwork.

REGENCY CHAIRS

Carver's Chair

The 'carver' is an armchair and, as its name suggests, it was probably used at table by the person carving the meat. It is also thought to have derived its name from a chair in the possession of Governor Carver.

Early period carvers had sabre legs but not so bold as Hope's. The arm rests swept down from the back stiles to end in a semi-circle, similar to the end of a scroll. The lower part of the scroll was fixed directly to the seat frame.

The top rail was often fitted with a brass handle to facilitate the handling of the chair, and it was often decorated, most attractively, with brass inlay.

A weakness in the design was caused by the cross grain of the wood used in making the curved arms, as these were cut from a single plank.

George Smith Armchair

This style of armchair was fashionable for a few years early in the 19th century when anything Egyptian was in vogue. The most distinctive feature of this style was the front legs which were designed and carved to resemble the legs of animals, including terminations with a complete hoof. The front legs were extended and carried up to form the front supports to the padded arm rests, which were most elaborately carved. Other decorations often incorporated were griffins and sphinxes in brass.

George Smith was a cabinet maker, who published a design book in 1808 entitled *A Collection of Designs for Household Furniture and Interior Decorating*. In this book he showed examples based on studies of ancient Egyptian, Greek and Roman styles.

Fig. 39   An example of a superb Regency style armchair. Beech, carved in relief and painted black with gilt details. The lion design is typical of the period. *c.* 1810 (*Victoria and Albert Museum. Crown copyright*).

Hope's Chairs

Early period pieces illustrated in Hope's *Household Furniture* were strongly classical, usually with boldly curved sabre legs. One of his styles shows a carved sphinx supporting one end of a straight arm rest, the other end joining the curved back stiles about half way up. The top rail was wide, but of a simple design and extended beyond the stiles. Another typical design, again sabre legged, has a slightly curved back which, radiused at the bottom and curved into the seat, made the back and seat a one piece construction. Front side, and back top of the frame terminates in scroll-work.

Hope's X-back Chair

This is another chair that was based on ancient Grecian designs. Both front and rear legs were curved strikingly outwards, forming a shape known as the 'Sabre leg'. The back stiles were ornamented with a concave top rail that extended beyond the stiles, and a further support joined the two stiles just above the upholstered seat, forming a rectangular space. Into this space two curved pieces of wood were mounted, back to back, to create the 'X' shape. Thomas Hope, who was responsible for the design of this chair, was a wealthy banker and antiquary. His work *Household Furniture and Interior Decoration* was published in 1807, and undoubtedly his designs greatly influenced the taste of the period.

Library Chair

The Library Chair was an interesting example with a dual purpose. It could be sat on or quickly converted into steps for reaching the higher shelves in the library.

This chair had one end of the curved arm rests fixed directly to the seat frame, the other joining the back supports about half way up. The top rail was slightly curved, otherwise quite plain. The squab-type seat, arms and back were made in one piece and hinged along the front edge, so that by standing in front of the chair and pulling the back towards you, the seat and back described an arc until the top rail rested on the floor, which exposed four steps.

Rope Back, or Trafalgar Chair

The Rope Back was a Grecian style dining chair, so named because the back centre bar was often made to represent a twisted rope. The rope, having marine connections, is obviously responsible for its other name, Trafalgar. The general design was clean with plain curved legs, and back stiles very slightly curved terminating in a scroll.

The slat forming the top rail was often embellished with brass inlay.

93

GEORGIAN CHAIRS

Adam Shield-back

As the name suggests, the back of this very elegant chair was shield-shape. The seat was upholstered, and the back padded to leave an outer frame of wood, which emphasised the outline. Rear legs were relatively plain, but the front legs were fluted and carved in a distinctly French classical style. Robert Adam (1728–92), the designer, was trained originally as an architect by his father. He spent some years travelling and studying on the continent, and although, no doubt, an excellent architect, it is with his work in connection with classical style interior decoration that his name will be generally associated.

Comb-back Windsor

The Comb-back Windsor is an attractive country armchair. Like most Windsors the seat was solid and slightly hollowed to fit the buttocks. The simple tapering legs were inserted into holes under the seat and stretcherless.

The tall back was made with thin rods, topped by a simple rail. Both arm rests were formed from a single, curved, wooden member, supported by short double tapered rods on the sides. The back rods passed through holes in the rear of the arm-rest and terminated in sockets in the seat.

A later version of the Comb-back had turned legs, strengthened by stretchers. The back rods tapered from a shaped top rail into the seat, giving a fan shape. The arm rests, although still made from a single curved member, were not filled in with rods. They were supported by two simple lath-like struts.

Hoop-back Windsor

The Hoop-back of the chair was made from a single piece of wood, bent to form a rough inverted horse-shoe. The two ends of the horse-shoe fitted into two holes in the seat, forming a framework that was later filled with wooden rods. Arm rests were made from separate pieces of wood, fixed to the back frame, and supported at the tips by curved members connected to the seat.

The seat of solid wood had a rectangular projection at the rear from which two diagonally positioned struts supported the back near the top.

Ladder-back

The Ladder-back comes mainly from the northern part of England. The back framework was made by an extension of the rear legs,

Fig. 40 Armchair. Ash Ladder back with rush seat, designed and made by Ernest Simpson. *c.* 1888 (*Victoria and Albert Museum. Crown copyright*).

forming stiles that were connected by horizontal slats, either plain or shaped. Front legs also were extended above the seat to support one end of the arm rest. The seat proper consisted of a frame, more often than not rush filled.

Spindle-back

The Spindle-back has much in common with the Ladder-back. The extensions of the front legs forming the arm rest supports were turned baluster shape. The back main frame was made from extensions of the rear legs supported by members or rails. In between these cross members, rows of turned spindles were inserted. The spindles were either equally spaced in rows, or bunched towards the centre, and sometimes a combination of both methods was used.

Wheel-back Windsor

Generally followed the design of Windsor Comb-back chairs except that the legs were turned and supported by stretchers. It had a back formed from a bentwood frame, instead of a top rail and stiles. The most distinctive feature of this chair was the removal of the central rods from the back, and the introduction of a shaped and fretted splat, the motif of which was a spoked wheel, hence the name, 'Wheel-back'.

VICTORIAN SMALL TABLES

Occasional Tables

An occasional table is a light, easily portable, small table that can be moved to suit any occasion. There were a great number and variety of such tables produced during the Victorian period.

Pembroke Table

These tables were supposedly named after the lady who first ordered one, namely the Countess of Pembroke. They were first used about 1760, and they were known also as breakfast tables.

The table was either rectangular or rounded and had two small hinged flaps which were held in position by two swinging wooden brackets. It often had drawers fitted, and legs without stretchers.

Sofa Table

This was a small, invariably narrow, table, with two drawers in the apron. Each end of the table had a small flap. The legs were either fitted one at each corner, or the table was supported on trestle-like brackets, connected by stretchers half way up, or low down near the floor.

Sutherland Table

The Sutherland table was virtually a small gate-leg table. Any advantage this design may have had over the Pembroke is the fact that it folded quite small, but when folded, it tended to be unstable.

Fig. 41 Sofa-table. Mahogany enriched with ebony. *c.* 1820 (*Victoria and Albert Museum. Crown copyright*).

It had four turned main legs terminating in two blocked shaped feet. Hinged flaps were held in position by two legs which swung out from the main frieze, or apron.

Work Tables

There were, of course, many styles and types of work table. One particular style in vogue about 1840 had an inlaid chequered board on the top obviously for chess and draughts. The octagonal table top was hinged to permit access to the interior compartments which held sewing materials. The compartment in the middle had no bottom, but it had suspended below it a bag made of Berlin Wool-cloth.

The top was supported by four curved pieces of wood which met under the table and joined a central ornate pillar; this pillar was mounted on a cross-shaped piece of wood, the four points of which carried castors and was heavily ornamented with scroll carvings.

97

Wood used for this very elegant table was invariably walnut.

Later Victorian work tables were of a similar basic design, but were often simpler, with a tripod base, and an inverted tripod supporting the top. The woolwork bag was replaced by a pierced work 'basket' but bags were still used made with pleated silk and soft leather.

REGENCY SMALL TABLES

Dumbwaiters

Dumbwaiters were a firm favourite of Regency households which used them mainly for dessert. There were many designs, but the majority were two or three tiered structures, mounted on a centred column terminating in a base from which three or four legs curved downwards to brass lion foot castors. The circular tiers rotated to simplify selection of the various sweetmeats placed on them.

Library Tables

During the early part of the 19th century, the circular library table became fashionable. Until this date the earlier examples were usually rectangular.

The circular table permitted several persons to work at the table simultaneously. The centre of the table was fitted with drum-like, circular shelves, tiered one above the other, virtually forming a circular bookcase. Such tables often had drawers fitted for the storage of writing accessories.

The Regency period tables were very elegant, and many fine examples have survived.

Loo Tables

Loo tables were used in the drawing room as games tables; in fact their name was derived from a card game popular during the period.

They were circular tables supported on a single ornate pedestal from which three or four curved ornate legs were mounted.

Side Tables

Side or pier tables were generally used in the dining room. There were many designs, and it was common to support the table by lion monopodia or by Egyptian figures and mythical creatures. Some styles had a platform near the base fitted with silvered glass to reflect objects placed on it.

The tops of some side tables were made from solid marble, and elegantly ornamented with brass inlay and applied brass motifs.

Sofa Tables

Sofa Tables of the Regency period were very elegant. The Pedestal Sofa Table had four legs meeting at a pedestal support, with feet of brass claws and castors. The single pedestal sat on the pedestal support and the table on the pedestal. The overall design was classical, and decorated with brass.

The Sheraton Sofa Table, somewhat simpler in design, had the usual two flaps, and two shallow drawers. Legs were formed by two inverted 'Y' shaped trestles, strengthened by an ornately turned stretcher.

Average sizes of sofa tables were approximately five to six feet long, and two feet wide. These tables were generally used in the library, drawing room, and ladies' apartments.

GEORGIAN SMALL TABLES

Concertina Card Table

This table was a most interesting development about the middle of the period. It could be used as a side table, or opened out for card playing.

A typical example of this table would have a hinged flap top that folded back on itself when used as a side table. The cabriole legs were beautifully carved, and terminated with a ball and claw foot. The frieze supporting the top had two hinged sections either side that folded like a section of a concertina bellows. To increase the table size it was only necessary to pull the two front legs forward, and fold over the hinged top, like opening a book.

Dressing Table

The dressing table made its debut early in the 18th century. It was literally a table, usually equipped with one long drawer and two smaller drawers each side. The dressing mirror which stood on the table, was a separate piece of furniture comprising a mirror which could swivel between two upright supports mounted on a base which also contained small drawers.

Originally dressing tables intended for ladies and gentlemen were almost identical, but as the gentleman needed the facility to shave, the designs became more specifically male or female.

Chippendale obviously made exquisite examples. By about 1788 they had become very elaborate, especially those designed by Thomas Shearer, the reputed inventor of the side board.

These tables, although originally intended for the bedroom or dressing room, are ideal furnishing pieces for any modern room. Some examples are absolutely exquisite in design, but very expensive.

Eagle Tables

Eagle tables will not be found easily, and even if one should turn up it will be much too expensive for the average collector. However, these tables are much too interesting to be omitted on that account.

Basically, the table consists of a large carved eagle with outstretched wings, its clawed feet gripping a rectangular plinth. The top, often made of marble, was supported on the eagle's head and wings. The eagle was invariably gilded. When complemented with a black marble top and imitation black marble plinth, the overall effect was most extravagant and lavish.

Georgian houses would often use this type of table in conjunction with a mirror, but it is almost certain that you will have to visit a stately home to see such a table today.

Gaming Tables

The gaming table was a popular piece of furniture during the Georgian period, both in England and on the continent. The majority of these tables were designed for playing cards, but many were also made for chess and backgammon, and of course, a combination of all three, plus others.

Tables with flaps, which were supported on gate-leg type supports, with green baize covering the exposed top, were usually made for the gentry and were used mainly in large houses. These tables, made in mahogany, were of outstanding quality. From about 1730, the 'concertina' support was used in a relatively small number (see Concertina Table).

Another device, used a little later, was to swivel the top so that the flaps were supported by the table frame in their open position.

It is interesting to note that early examples with dished receptacles on the top surface of the table were not designed that way for the benefit of containing the gamblers' money, but they were intended to hold candlesticks.

Money-wells will be found on gaming tables, but they are usually relatively deep, and positioned more conveniently nearer to the centre of the table.

Library Tables

Library tables of the Georgian period were usually large flat-topped desks, with the working surface covered in leather. They contained either two pedestals of drawers, or cupboards for holding folios. There was a knee-hole space between the pedestals similar to a modern typist desk.

These tables were sometimes fitted with pull-up reading lecterns, and pull-out writing slides.

100

Fig. 42 Victorian Canterbury, or receptacle for sheet music.

Neo-Classic Tripod

These were useful little tables, especially those that made provision for hingeing the top into a vertical position. This feature made it easy to store, and to display the inlaid or painted top to advantage.

The tripod legs were surmounted with a single pedestal which supported the top.

Tea Table

It was customary, about the middle of the 18th century, to provide a table for each person taking tea. These tables were generally little tripod affairs with a circular top that tilted for storage. Around the edge of the top was either a pie crust moulding or a delicate little brass rail, known as a gallery, to prevent the china from slipping off.

101

MISCELLANEOUS ITEMS

Canterbury

The Canterbury is a rack for holding sheet music. It is suggested that the name originated as a result of an Archbishop of Canterbury ordering the first one.

It consisted of an openwork, rectangular box structure with divisions for music books, and usually had a drawer underneath for sheet music. It was supported on each corner by a turned and castored leg, which made it an easy matter to push it under the piano keyboard when not in use.

Commodes

The meaning of the word 'commode' seems to have changed with time. During the 18th century it referred to a low piece of furniture, provided with drawers, and occasionally with cupboards as well. They were usually very decorative and were intended for use in the drawing room, not the bedroom.

Originally they were, more often than not, supplied in pairs. They were generally quite large and they were intended to fit into the area between windows, with a tall mirror suspended above. Small examples are rare, and matching pairs more so.

Court Cupboard

In appearance, the court cupboard could easily be mistaken for an early sideboard. The court cupboard technically is a two tiered open-shelved stand, the shelves being supported (usually) by turned supports. Some examples may have a small closed cupboard in the centre of the upper shelf.

During the early 17th century it was used for the display of the family silver and pewter. Real antique Court cupboards are rare.

Dwarf Bookcase

This small type of portable bookcase was a new fashion that first appeared in Regency times. It consisted of a case, usually in rosewood, supported by a beautifully turned pedestal at each end. The pedestals sat on a pair of 'Y' feet, strengthened with a single turned stretcher. The front doors were either glazed or fitted with a brass wire trellis, and a shelf provided for two rows of books.

Dwarf bookcases were low pieces of furniture designed to leave ample wall space above them for hanging pictures.

Another innovation of the period was the revolving bookcase—legs supported a central shaft on which the bookcases were fixed in such a way that they could be rotated at will. Shapes were either round, rectangular or any other compatible shape.

An interesting development of the 'bookcase' evolved a most attractive little Regency piece—the set of portable open shelves, the sides of which were often made of brass wire. These shelves were designed so that 'my lady' could carry it easily about the house, when moving from one room to another.

Fire Screens

Fire Screens were first known in England during the 18th century, but it was the Victorians who popularised this decorative piece of furniture by featuring it in almost every room containing a fire place.

One type, popular early in the period, consisted of a single pole supported either by tripod legs or a round base. The actual screen was usually made of a needlework panel or a decorated wooden panel, which could be adjusted up and down to protect the face from the heat of the fire. The tripod legs and base of the upright pole were often decorated with carvings. The most commonly used embroidery was Berlin wool work; those with Soho tapestry are rare, and practically unobtainable. Papier mâché pole screens were a great favourite. These were most artistically made, and decorated with landscapes and figures, or with Chinoiserie designs and gilding.

Tea Containers (Regency)

The teapoy was a Regency invention developed originally from a simple three legged table used about 1750 as an individual table for persons taking tea. Later in the century this custom slowly disappeared, and the tables were then used to stand the tea caddies on. The final stage of development was the incorporation of both caddies and table to make the teapoy.

A typical late Regency teapoy would be made in rosewood, perhaps with four strongly curved legs, terminated with brass lions claws and castors. The pedestal, often rectangular in section, would have an ornamented profile and would support a rectangular chest. Brass inlay was often used as a decorative design feature, but mother-of-pearl was also used.

A late Regency teapoy to be seen in the Victoria and Albert Museum is made in rosewood; it has four relatively plain legs, supporting a plain pedestal base. The turned pedestal supports a chest, under which is hung a tasselled semi-circular half barrel.

Tea Containers (Victorian)

Tea, the British national drink, was an expensive luxury when it was first introduced over 300 years ago, so it is not surprising that it was treated with some reverence, and stored in silver canisters which were kept in a box, later known as a tea chest.

Fig. 43 Pole-screen. Carved mahogany with a panel of embroidery in silks, wool and silver gilt thread. Style of Chippendale first half of 18th century (*Victoria and Albert Museum. Crown copyright*).

Fig. 44 Tea Caddy. Mahogany and rosewood, brass inlay and mounts. *c.* 1750 (*Victoria and Albert Museum. Crown copyright*).

A typical Victorian teapoy is virtually a tea caddy on legs. Generally made in mahogany, with an ornate pedestal legged base. The top consisted of a thick circular box with a lid, which, when opened, exposed one or two fitted tea canisters.

Early Victorian teapoys were usually rectangular, and often inlaid with mother-of-pearl. Later examples were made in a variety of shapes.

Teapoys made in papier mâché were made throughout most of the Victorian period, usually beautifully japanned and decorated. Collectors usually seek examples with finely painted landscapes on the inside of the lid, but these are now quite rare.

Tea caddies of various shapes, and tea-chests of various woods decorated with marquetry, make useful, collectable items.

Other items

Victorian trays were made in a tremendous variety; small circular 'waiters' for presenting a glass of wine; rectangular, oval and curved fronted examples were made in wood and papier mâché and used for a number of special purposes.

Other collectable items include music stools, knife boxes, wine cisterns, stands for vases, basins, kettles, and small display cabinets.

A FEW INTERESTING AMERICAN EXAMPLES

Boston Rocker

As its name suggests, the Boston Rocker was an American rocking-chair. In appearance it was very similar to the English Windsor rocking chair, except for the seat. Windsor chair seats were hollowed to fit the buttocks, but the American version often had a flat or scroll shaped seat.

This chair dates from about 1825, and originated in New England. It became the most popular chair ever made in America. The wood used for early examples was maple and pine.

Butterfly Table

This table is exclusively an American piece of early furniture. Usually they are small, with turned legs with stretchers supporting all four legs. The two halves of the table top fold down leaving a narrow top similar to the modern gate-leg table. Two butterfly brackets swing out to support the leaves in the open position.

Tops are rarely found in the circular form; the usual shapes are oval, rectangular, or square.

Earliest examples date from about 1670.

Carver Chair

The American Carver chair was made from turned legs, spindles, etc., that fitted together by inserting the ends of each piece into a corresponding hole in an adjacent piece. The name is presumed to have originated from the fact that Governor Carver had such a chair. The more elaborate examples are sometimes known as 'Brewster' chairs. The 'Carver' was made in America during the latter quarter of the 16th century.

Chair-table

The chair-tables are now seen rarely. They consist of a fairly robust chair with arm rests. The table top, which was usually circular, was hinged to the back of the arm rests, so that it could be lowered, and supported by the arm rests. This type of chair is sometimes termed a 'monk's seat' but why this should be so is unknown. These chairs were also made in America during the 17th century.

Martha Washington Chair

The Martha Washington chair is obviously American in origin. It was a chair with a high back, upholstered, and provided with open arms in wood typical of the 18th century English style. The name also refers to a worktable containing the implements for dressmaking or sewing, dating from 1780 onwards.

Sofa Table

The sofa table, introduced in England towards the end of the 18th century, was similarly produced in America until about 1840. These tables were designed to stand either along the back or just in front of a sofa. They were drawing room pieces and invariably of good quality.

The best examples are generally agreed to be those in the Federal style, a period commencing soon after the Declaration of Independence in 1776, and continuing until about 1830.

Early Federal style followed the neo-classic style of Europe; later it evolved through the *Directoire* and Empire under the French influence.

The majority of Federal furniture will be found in mahogany, but curly maple was also used in places where Europeans were using satin-wood. Decorative motifs closely followed the European fashions, but the eagle, maybe for obvious reasons, was used more in America than it was in Europe.

ENGLISH FURNITURE MAKERS

1728–1792	Robert Adam	Architect and designer
c. 1760	Philip Bell	Cabinet maker
1718–1779	Thomas Chippendale	Cabinet maker
c. 1740	Francis Croxford	
1833–1886	Edward W. Godwin	Anglo-Japanese style furniture
c. 1766	Giles Grendey	Chairs
d. 1796	George Hepplewhite	Various
1770–1831	Thomas Hope	
1684–1748	William Kent	
c. 1720	John Ody	Chairs
c. 1720	William Old	Chairs
c. 1767–*c.* 1780	Benjamin Parran	Cabinet maker
c. 1689–*c.* 1729	Thomas Roberts	Joiner
1751–1806	Thomas Sheraton	
d. 1769	William Vile	

AMERICAN FURNITURE MAKERS

1612–1683	Nicholas Disbrowe	Hartford	Warnocot Chairs and Chests
1704–1743	John Gaines	Portsmouth	Chairs
f. 1740–1787	William Savery	Philadelphia	Cabinet-making
c. 1745	Thomas Elfe	Charleston	Chippendale style furniture
f. 1732–1766	Thomas Johnson	Boston	Japanning
f. 1730–1799	Robert Crosman	Taunton	Chests
1740–1795	Thomas Affleck	Philadelphia	Various
1717–1785	Gilbert Ash	New York	Chairs and Tables
1746–1829	John Bachman	Pennsylvania	Cabinet-making
f. 1772–1775	Thomas Burling	New York	Various
f. 1769	John Cogswell	Boston	Bombe cane furniture
f. 1747–1775	Thomas Elfe	Charleston	Cane Furniture
1713–1791	John Elliott, Snr.	Philadelphia	Mirror Frames
f. 1756	Benjamin Frothingham	Boston	Desks and Bookcases
1736–1781	James Gillingham	Philadelphia	Chairs
f. 1740	John Goddard	Newport	Various
1745–1795	Jonathan Gostelowe	Philadelphia	Chests and Drawers
f. 1760–1790	Benjamin Randolph	Philadelphia	Various
1758–1831	Aaron Roberts	New Britain	Case Furniture
f. 1740–1787	William Savery	Philadelphia	Cabinets and Chairs
1732–1809	John Townsend	Newport	Cabinet-making
f. 1800–1845	Michael Allison	New York	Various
1770–1826	Henry Connelly	Philadelphia	Various
1775–1811	Ephraim Haines	Philadelphia	Various
1795–1852	Lambert Hitchcock	Hitchcocks-ville	Chairs
1757–1811	Samuel McIntire	Salem	Carving
f. 1783–1847	Duncan Phyfe	New York	Cabinet-making
1745–1848	John Shaw	Annapolis	Case Furniture
1804–1863	John H. Belter	New York	Various
1804–1871	Elijah Galuslia	Troy	Various
f. 1836–1890	John Jelliff	Newark	Various
f. 1812–1853	John Needles	Baltimore	Various
f. 1835–1849	Anthony Quervelle	Philadelphia	Cabinet-making

GLOSSARY

Acanthus: A foliage or leaf design originally adorning Corinthian capitols, but later adapted as a design motif in furniture. The design was used by Chippendale on the knees of cabriole legs.

Art Noveau: This was a style of furniture used at the turn of the 19th century; it was stiff with a tendency towards vertical lines.

Baluster: A pillar usually turned, to support a rail.

Baroque: Refers to the late Renaissance period, when decoration became flamboyant with scrolls and natural motifs.

Beading: A small usually semi-circular moulding, used to form a ridge or decoration on furniture.

Bail: A drawer fitting comprising a half loop of metal, usually brass, fitted to drawers by metal bolts.

Barley Sugar or Twist Turning: A form of turning resembling the twist in barley sugar or the effect of twisting two ropes together.

Bell Flower: A decorative motif consisting of a stylised flower with three or five petals hanging downwards. It was often used as a carving or inlaid in a series, one below the other; also known as Husk motif.

Bracket: A bracket fixed to the wall usually for displaying ornaments or busts.

Cabinet: A piece of furniture, glass fronted, intended for displaying porcelain or other artistic pieces.

Cabinet Making: Craft of furniture-making requiring skill of a high order employing joinery and engineering techniques.

Cabriole Leg: The shape of a leg used almost universally in the 18th century. It has a slow curve like a flattened 'S', representational of the animal form. The foot of the leg terminated in various designs including the claw and ball foot, slipper foot, the pad, and the scroll in the Chippendale style.

Canted: Tipped at an angle.

Carpentry: The making of wooden structures not requiring the skill of the cabinet maker, and uniting timbers with the use of nails.

Caryatid: An upright carved in the human form.

Cheval-Glass: A large rectangular mirror which pivoted in a frame, or moved up and down within the frame. Usually supported on four legs.

Chiffonier: Originally this meant a tall chest of drawers, but used to describe a low cupboard during the Regency period.

Chip-carving: A method of carving used for surface ornamentation; motifs developed by lightly chipping away the wood.

Claw-and-Ball foot: Used on terminations of legs for chairs and other pieces of furniture. Originally believed to have been adapted from the Chinese dragon's claw holding a pearl.

109

Coffer: Coffers are often confused with chests; in fact, they are a chest but the definition demands that they should be covered with some material such as leather, and banded with metalwork.

Cresting: Ornament on the top or crest of a structure sometimes shaped, carved or perforated, as seen in the cresting of a chair.

Daventry: A small chest of drawers with an angled top used for writing.

Dentils: A decoration used beneath the moulding of a cornice representing a series of small rectangles.

Dowel: A wooden peg used for joining two pieces of wood together or for positioning same.

Ebonise: To imitate ebony. This was accomplished by staining the wood.

Fillet: A small narrow strip of wood, usually flat.

Finial: The top decoration, usually a knob situated on the top of a post. Often seen on chair uprights.

Fluting: A classical style decoration involving narrow vertical grooves reminiscent of classical architecture. Often used on straight legs.

Gadrooning: A style of decoration used for edgings in carving. The pattern is formed of straight or radiating lines with raised lobes between the lines.

Inlay: Decoration formed by letting in separate pieces of different coloured materials, such as woods, ivories, tortoise shell, bone, etc., into a recessed base.

Japanning: A technique which became popular in England during the late 17th century, it is a lacquered finish obtained from the use of gums and spirits.

Joinery: Woodwork that has been made using specialist joints such as the mortise, tenon and dovetail.

Linenfold: A carved ornamentation suggestive of folded linen.

Marquetry: A method of decoration involving the process of inlaying woods and other materials into a veneer.

Melon-bulb: The large, melon-like swelling on legs or posts of furniture. Usually elaborately carved.

Moulding: Ornamental strip of wood used to enclose panels, or to finish the edge of a lid and for many other purposes.

Ogee: A double curved moulding or support. The top is convex in shape and changes to concave below.

Ormolu: An alloy of copper, zinc and tin resembling gold, gilt, bronze. A preparation of gold leaf used for gilding furniture.

Patina: In furniture, this refers to the finish of the woodwork; the beautiful soft gloss on antique, well cared for furniture.

Pier Table: A table designed to stand between two windows, i.e. the pier. Loosely used to describe any table that has been designed to stand against a wall.

Rail: This is the top member of a chair, supported by the stiles. It is also any horizontal piece of framing or panelling.

Reeding: This is a very similar decoration to fluting but in this instance the ornamentation is in relief representing a series of slim reeds.

Rococo: A florid and asymmetrical style of decoration using rocks and shells as the motif. It was developed in France from Chinese forms and came to England between 1730 and 1780.

Rush Seat: A seat made of woven rushes, mostly used on country furniture.

Sabre Leg: Sabre shaped, describes the sharply curving leg of the classical style.

Saddle Seat: Resembling a saddle. Solid wooden seats as used in Windsor chairs, which have been shaped somewhat to suit the buttocks and in doing so roughly resemble the seat of a saddle.

Settle: Usually refers to seats with a boxed base, an earlier stage of the settee.

Splat: The upright member in the middle of the back of a chair, often decorated by carving and fretting.

Stile: The upright side pieces of a piece of furniture, usually the outermost.

Strapwork: A band or ornamentation representative of plaited straps. Strapwork is usually found in a stylised form.

Straw-work: The forming of landscapes and geometrical patterns by the use of tiny strips of bleached pink coloured straws. This method of decoration came to England towards the end of the 17th century from the Continent and was used mainly for small pieces of furniture.

Stretcher: The horizontal members connecting legs of chairs and other vertical members of furniture.

Stump Leg: A short thick rear leg slightly curved.

Tunbridge Ware: A form of inlay developed at Tunbridge Wells about 1650. The process used minute strips of wood of many natural colours to build up patterns. Early examples were mainly of geometrical designs but later landscapes and floral decorations were used to decorate boxes, tea-caddies, trays, etc.

Turning: This is a method of shaping wood with cutting tools whilst the wood is rotating in a lathe.

What-not: A type of rack used from about 1800 onwards for books and ornaments. It is a series of shelves supported by four uprights.

GLASS

9. Glass

How and when man first discovered glass is one of the mysteries yet to be unravelled. The Egyptians had certainly mastered the techniques of glass-making more than 3,500 years ago, and from fragments found in various excavations, some experts conclude that the first glass could have been made about this time. Glass in the form of simple beads and small amulets was made some 2000 years B.C., also by the cultured Egyptians.

To most of us glass is a brittle solid, easily broken or damaged, but technically it is a 'super-cooled liquid' and like most liquids, it will 'flow' under certain conditions. This can be seen in a plate glass window that has been standing for a long time; the bottom edge will be found to be slightly thicker than the top edge due to the extremely slow flow of the material under the continual pull of gravity.

The Egyptians produced hollow vessels by shaping molten glass either around cores of sand, or by dipping the cores repeatedly into the molten glass; they also pressed molten glass into open moulds. Glass blowing, the method of shaping hot glass by blowing down a hollow rod, was discovered some 2,000 years ago and opened the way for producing glass in more elegant forms.

Hollow vessels, such as wine glasses, relied very much on the skill of the glass blower up to the late 17th century, and a brief description of the methods employed may be of interest. Let us take a look and see how a wine glass was made.

Molten glass forms a hot sticky mass, that readily adheres to the hollow iron rod used for blowing, or to itself. The blow rod was dipped into the molten mass until sufficient glass adhered to the tip; it was then withdrawn and rolled to and fro on a flat surface to remove any lumps. The next stage was to blow down the rod to expand the molten glass into a bubble of the desired size; this was ascertained by checking with calipers, or with some other suitable gauge. A blob of glass was then added to the end of the bowl and the stem forged. The foot was then added in the same way and shaped, whilst being rotated, with a pair of wooden boards.

A second rod was then temporarily attached to the foot with a dab of molten glass, to hold the glass whilst the mouth was cut from the blow pipe with a wetted metal tool at a position where the rim was required. Any rough edge on the bowl was trimmed with shears and smoothed by fire polishing, a technique achieved by reheating in a

112

Fig. 45 Goblet with engraved decoration of Nelson and the Victory, late 18th to early 19th century (*Victoria and Albert Museum. Crown copyright*).

furnace. The final operation was to break off the second rod which had only been necessary as a means of holding the wine glass during the latter operation. The rough mark produced by the break is known as the pontil mark.

During the majority of the foregoing operations it was necessary to continually rotate the wine glass on the end of the blow pipe during its manufacture. This was executed by the 'gaffer' who sat

113

in a chair with extended arm rests. The rod was rolled to and fro along the arm rests to keep the glass in constant rotation and to prevent it from sagging under its own weight. It must also be remembered that thin sections of glass cool rapidly, with consequent loss of plasticity; therefore, if the operation was a lengthy one, the glass had to be continually reheated in between operations to retain its workability.

Glass moulding is a very old process. Early glass articles were formed by pressing the molten glass into moulds made from stone or clay, and any patterning required was obtained by cutting the pattern into the mould so that when the glass was pressed into the grooves, the pattern appeared on the finished product in cameo, i.e. raised glass.

So that the moulds could be used more than once, the articles had to be designed so that they were easily withdrawn; no undercutting was permitted that prevented their easy removal.

Roman glass workers added a decoration called Pillar moulding; this was a raised ribbing, executed by means of lifting the still-plastic glass by means of pincers.

With the advent of glass blowing, moulded glass could take another step forward. The moulds were now made in two or three pieces in such a way that they could be broken apart for the removal of the specimen. The glass blower proceeded in much the same way as if he were making our wine glass; that is, he inserted his hollow iron blowing rod into the molten mass of glass so that a gob formed on the end, then with successive immersions into the molten glass, he would increase the gob size until there was sufficient glass to make the required article. The plastic lump of glass was then rolled onto a cast iron plate or a smooth stone until the mass was worked to the end of the tube, and the pear shape gob of glass was then inserted into the mould and blown. The gob expanded like a balloon inside the mould and took up the form of the mould. If the article being manufactured was a bulbous item like a bottle, the two or three parts of the mould could be opened and the bottle withdrawn. Should further work be necessary, the pontil rod would have been added to the bottom of the article with a dab of molten glass for finishing.

As the thickness of the bubble of glass is more or less consistent, the finished article would therefore have the same shape both externally, and internally except that bumps on the outside will be depressions on the inside.

Pressed glass should not be confused with moulded glass. A large proportion of Victorian glass was produced by pressing, a process thought to have originated in the United States of America during the late 1820's.

Fig. 46 Wine glass with engraved decoration. Late 18th to early 19th century. (*Victoria and Albert Museum. Crown copyright*).

The principles of pressing glass involved the use of a mould, which consisted of a block of metal that had been hollowed out to comply with the exterior shape of the article to be produced. If the article was larger in girth than at its apex, the mould would be split into two or four parts so that the finished article could be removed.

Molten glass was dropped into the mould cavity and a top tool,

115

or follower, was pressed into the glass; this forced the glass to take up the shape of the mould interior, thus forming the outside shape of the article. The top tool or follower provided the inside shape. Therefore it will be seen that with pressed glass the interior shape and exterior shape can be quite different—facetted on the outside, smooth on the interior.

Pressed glass gives a much sharper definition than blown moulded specimens due to the higher pressure used, and it can be produced at a much faster rate.

The introduction of pressed glass during Victorian times heralded the first stages of mechanization in the glass industry.

The machines required for bringing the two halves of the mould together were relatively cheap, and because of their relatively high output, articles made of glass were produced much more cheaply than hitherto.

During the process of manufacture, both pressed and moulded glass required finishing and annealing, which was executed by fire polishing at the furnace mouth, simultaneously with the annealing process. Pressed glass made after 1850 rarely shows any trace of a pontil mark, as from that date onwards a spring clip was used to remove the articles from the mould.

Although both pressed and blown moulded glass are formed and patterned by the use of moulds, there is a difference that can be detected by the collector. It has already been said that pressed glass has a stronger and better-defined pattern. If we now look at the mould marks, that is the thin lines reproduced on the articles from the segments of the mould, we will find that those from blown moulding are very faint, due to the relatively small pressures that have been used in blowing. Because the forces exerted in the press were very great by comparison, these mould marks tend to be better defined. As the pressure built up in the mould, there was a tendency to force the sections apart, which tended to increase the size of the mould mark.

Pressed glass was used extensively from about 1840 to 1860 for the production of general goods such as dishes, drinking glasses and the usual household paraphernalia, and these can be bought quite reasonably.

There are two old methods of making flat glass that will interest collectors, since it was used for mirror glass, picture framing, and glazing bookcases and cabinets. One method commonly employed was to rotate a large bubble of glass on the end of an iron rod to flatten it. Glass sheet so produced has a thickened area in the middle of it. The second method required a blown, sausage-like cylinder which was cut down one side and rolled flat whilst the glass was in a

116

plastic state. Glass produced in this way can be recognised by the slightly uneven surface easily seen when looked at from a slightly oblique angle.

Glass cutting is a familiar method of decoration; the angled patterns and facets produced give a prismatic effect when light is reflected on their many surfaces, causing the glass to glow and sparkle with colours of the rainbow. Cut glass has a very satisfying feel; its precise, sharp, clean outer faces are pleasant to handle.

The cuts in glass were made with discs of polished slate, and fine sandstone. Cast iron discs were also used in conjunction with a cutting medium of sand and water. After cutting, the surfaces were polished with discs made of cast tin, copper, and even wood and cork, in conjunction with a very fine abrasive such as jewellers rouge, and special putty made with calcined tin.

Glass cutting was a decoration that was not necessarily undertaken by the glass makers; in fact, in the early 19th century, there were many works specialising in cutting only. Glass merchants would buy the undecorated glass blanks for cutters in their employ to finish.

The quality of glass up to the mid-18th century, in respect of refractiveness, was not particularly good; it possessed a cloudiness that prevented good transmission of light rays and consequently cutting was limited to shallow faceting and scalloping, but from the late 18th century, when crystal-clear flint glass was available, the cutting became more elaborate.

Designs were also added to glass by engraving. This was accomplished by scratching the glass with a diamond or by 'pricking' tiny dots to form a pattern. Etching was a quick and relatively cheap process for decorating glass, using hydrofluoric acid as an etching agent. The articles were treated with an acid-resistant varnish and the design scratched on it to expose the glass. It was subsequently immersed in acid, which bit the pattern into the surface.

Glass was often used to decorate glass. Threads, rods, and tubes of glass could be applied to a vessel by heating them to a plastic state and simply touching the two together. A glass rod, when heated, can be drawn out to a considerable length. This has the effect of reducing the cross-section in size, but has little effect on the shape. Bundles of coloured glass rods were 'stuck' together by this method, drawn out, and used for 19th century paperweights (see Paperweights).

The colour is added to glass by the addition of metallic oxides. For example, the addition of tin oxide will make the glass opaque white. Other opaque colours are obtained by adding a further metallic oxide to the tin oxide.

An interesting effect was obtained by 'flashing' or covering the

117

Fig. 47   A beautiful Regency chandelier. English. *c.* 1815.

clear glass vessel with a thin outer coating of glass of another colour, and then cutting patterns through the outer skin so that the clear glass showed through.

Roman and Syrian glass is not for the collector; these are mainly museum pieces. Neither is medieval European or Islamic glass any easier to find; these periods are far too early for a new collector, even if he had the opportunity to add such fantastically rare pieces to a possible collection.

One could not do better than start with English glass from about 1820 to 1900; this is virtually Victorian glass although it is appreciated that, if we are to be particularly precise, Victoria was born in 1837 and died in 1901. One of the most interesting fields of Victorian glass is Nailsea. Nailsea glass is usually characterised by a greenish bottle glass in which flecks of other colours, including white, has been skilfully amalgamated.

It is interesting to note that taxes influenced the early glass industrialist; green glass, which was normally glass in its natural colour, was taxed, but at a lesser rate than clear glass which had been rendered colourless.

Nailsea, from which this particular glass obtains its name, is a town near Bristol where John Robert Lucas started his glass house in 1788, but Nailsea glass was not the exclusive product of John Robert Lucas; it is known that it was produced at Wrockwardine in Shropshire, Warrington, Sunderland, Newcastle, Stourbridge and Alloa in Scotland and probably elsewhere.

The examples produced by these various glass houses are so similar that it is difficult to ascertain their precise origin; therefore, Nailsea will be considered as a general group.

The earliest Nailsea was a brownish green bottle glass decorated with lines of white enamel, and neither mottled or flecked. It is estimated that this was produced between about 1790 and 1820. Between 1800 and 1820 the bottle glass became a light green in colour and decorated with notched ornamentation. From about 1815 opaque coloured glass was introduced with mottled and looped decoration; flecking was also included with this type of bottle. Up to 1845, crossing and interlacing strips of opaque and clear glass was used to decorate a pale green bottle, and this was followed by the same ornamentation on clear flint glass. From about 1845 coloured flint glass was introduced, decorated with contrasting tints.

From the foregoing it will be obvious that we have five broad groups in which to classify our Nailsea glass, and some rough indication of date. One of the most attractive decorations used on this type of ware is known as Looping or Dragging. It is a familiar decoration on iced cakes; threads of contrasting colour are added to

119

the body and then dragged upwards by a pointed tool to form reasonably precise wavy bands around the vessel. This form of decoration has been used since ancient times.

The flecks which appear in Nailsea are usually white or bluish white in colour and feel slightly rough when touched with the finger. The speckles may be so dense that they cover the bottle completely or in other instances will be sprinkled thinly. Yellow and red speckles occur occasionally and are eagerly sought by the collector.

Gimmels are not a modern invention; quite attractive examples were produced in Nailsea. A gimmel is the two-flask container that is used today for oil and vinegar. The two bottles were blown separately and then fused together, their necks curved so that they were pointing in opposite directions. The Nailsea gimmel was usually produced with pink and white spiral decorations, or with white crossing and interlacing strips of opaque glass.

Nailsea candlesticks were shaped from short lengths of glass tube. One end was formed into a down-spreading foot with a folded rim; the socket was also enlarged with a thick rim and ornamented, the smallest was about 6 inches high and the tallest approximately one foot.

The following items are just a few of the forms of Nailsea glass that the collector can seek.

Flasks made in the form of hand bellows often used for perfumes, Jacob's ladders, glass bells, coaching horns, shepherds' crooks, glass masses, riding crops, tobacco pipes, walking sticks, canes and the yard of ale.

The yard of ale was of course a trick glass; it measured approximately 3 feet in length and usually terminated in a hollow bulb. The theory behind the yard of ale is that once it had been filled it cannot be stood upright because of its rounded end, consequently the drinker had to drain it to the bitter end. When the vessel is raised above the shoulder of the consumer during the act of drinking, the liquid in the hollow bulb suddenly deluges down the inside of the long glass into the face of the user.

The more useful examples include very attractive jugs, flasks, perhaps with a pewter cap, serving bottles, tumblers, rolling pins, jars and mugs.

Before leaving Nailsea, a word about friggers. This was a term used to describe unofficial pieces of work. These were executed by workmen or apprentices for their own amusement, pleasure and perhaps profit. The work of friggers is generally included in Nailsea collections. Articles commonly frigged are rolling pins, which were often painted in oil colours with inscriptions and views.

120

Very elaborate ornaments were also produced by friggers including fully rigged ships, sometimes complete with crew members, and fox hunting scenes with hounds.

It is not thought that the general quantity of glass ware produced by friggers is very great, and it is only mentioned here as a matter of interest to the collector.

Irish glass from Waterford, Cork, Dublin, and Belfast is reputed to have a clarity of its own that is characteristic of Irish glass. Although, no doubt, attempts have been made in the past to produce a steel-blue, super-clear glass, much of the Irish glass is similar in clarity to other good quality glass, and does not contain any special colour to identify it. Knowledge of style, rather than a study of the glass itself, is the best way to distinguish Irish glass, which incidentally is invariably of good quality.

The Victorian era saw the birth of slag glass, which has the appearance of marble. It is opaque, mottled, and complete with marble-like veining. It is also known as purple slag or marble glass and as 'end of day wear'. Two of the many better known makers of the glass were J. G. Sowerby of Gateshead and Thornhill Leas near Wakefield, Yorkshire.

Slag, the waste material which floats on the top of molten steel in blast furnaces, was skimmed off and used by the glass makers for mixing with clear glass. Other materials such as sand and colouring were added, depending upon the ultimate requirement of the glass. It may appear that the manufacture of slag was a slap-happy operation, but the whole operation was skilfully conducted.

The name 'end of day wear' referred to the operators in the blast furnace rather than the glass makers. The slag was drawn off shortly before the steel was tapped at the end of the puddlers day.

J. G. Sowerby in the late 1860's was producing slag glass pieces in beautiful variegated colours, opals, blue and green mixtures, and varieties of turquoise.

The Victorians used a wide variety of coloured glass, and were very experimental in its use. The collector will find many items to interest him made from slag glass. All the usual paraphernalia of useful and not very useful articles can be collected. Some of the minor items will include salt cellars, comports, tumblers, pin trays, spill holders, pilgrim bottle vases, and vases of many designs and shapes, dishes and plates.

The Bristol blue glass of the early Victorian period was almost a royal blue, known as King's Blue. The name King's Blue originated after George IV had expressed his delight and admiration of a spirit set presented to him as a coronation gift in 1821. This costly royal blue glass was produced until 1840, but due to the various refining treatments given to the cobalt oxide, important minerals were removed, and the colouring qualities deteriorated.

Collectors of Bristol blue glass will certainly want to collect earlier pieces than Victorian; collectors usually prefer 18th century tableware. Unfortunately the name Bristol blue has become less specific and is now used to describe any dark blue or translucent glass.

The term Bristol Blue did not necessarily originate to indicate where the glass was made. Bristol was the only place where the smalt, which is used to colour the glass, could be obtained, and what is more surprising, there was only one merchant stocking it!

Smalt is a vitreous form of cobalt oxide and is used for tinting the glass blue.

Opaque—white or enamel glass, which is now generally described as 'South Staffordshire', was made in England from about the mid-18th century. It is a material that closely approximates porcelain, and may well have been invented as a cheaper alternative to that material.

Enamel glass has little resistance to heat, therefore it was not used very extensively for domestic articles normally subjected to relatively high temperatures; when such articles were occasionally made, they were invariably robust in section.

The dense whiteness of the glass was obtained by the addition of tin oxide to flint glass. The addition of this chemical, however, made the material somewhat brittle, and although doubly annealed, this brittle property was never completely eradicated. Articles made in enamel glass have a smooth texture, but it is a relatively soft material that scratches easily, the scratches showing dark as they become ingrained with dirt. If examined against a strong light the material will be found to have a creamy translucence.

Pieces of opaque-white glassware are often decorated with designs and patterns, not necessarily executed by the original manufacturer. Anyone so inclined could buy a plain white specimen and add the decorations to suit themselves.

Early decorated examples using unfired pigments and colours, and gilded motifs, lacked the resistance of fired enamels, and with constant handling and the passage of time, they have either been obliterated, or completely worn away. The decorative work was applied with oil colours. Enamels required heat firing, but oil gilding was a low temperature process, and easier to affect.

Another method employed from about 1760 by Sadler and Green was a black transfer print, which was subsequently overpainted with enamel colours.

Many interesting examples of this glass can be collected including chemists' jars, often labelled in gold, snuff boxes, bodkin cases, wine

122

bottles, scent phials, tea caddies, jugs, mugs, flower bowls, vases, candlesticks, tapersticks, cruet stands, and almost every type of hollow-ware normally found in porcelain.

An interesting development in glass was furthered in England by Apsley Pellatt, who was the proprietor of the Falcon glass works in Southwark. Originally a French invention, the technique involved embedding small models of a ceramic material in clear glass.

The models of portraits, flowers and other subjects were formed from a ceramic paste which had two important properties—it did not form gas when heated and its rates of expansion and contraction were very similar to those of the glass into which it was to be sealed.

This was obviously important if the two materials were not to fracture on cooling.

This type of glassware is known as Sulphides, Cameo Incrustations, and Crystallo-Ceramics.

The first of the Crystallo-Ceramics was produced by Pellatt in England about 1820 and continued in production until about 1850, but he was not the only source; other English manufacturers continued after this date, and of course, the French were producing during the same period.

Paperweights, tankards, candelabra, scent bottles, pendants, small bottles and aromatic vinegar bottles, are just a few of the articles treated by this process.

It is assumed that the first American glass was produced by Casper Wistar. He established his manufactory in Salem, New Jersey, in 1739 to produce the normal wares of everyday use, such as bottles and window panes. Wistar was born in Germany in 1695, and during his early American career, he was assisted by four glassmakers, also from Germany.

In addition to the utility products, Wistar's craftsmen produced excellent free-blown pieces, usually in amber, olive or green glass, following the Continental traditions of the times.

Henry William Stiegel of Manheim, Pennsylvania, was operating a glass manufactory from 1765 to 1774; he then went bankrupt. Using English, Irish, and German workers, the works produced mainly bottles and window glass, but tableware, in English and German peasant styles, was also produced in quantity.

Stiegel glassware was usually made from clear or coloured glass, often decorated with enamelling, engraving, or moulded patterns.

John Frederick Amelung, another German, founded a factory in New Bremen, Maryland, in 1784 with the assistance of glassworkers who came with him from Germany. The name Amelung is important in American glass because he was the only glassmaker of his period to sign and date examples of his work.

The quality of Amelung's work was superior to that of his contemporaries, and unfortunately for collectors, it is now rare, although fine examples of decanters, flip-glasses, and items of tableware can be seen in American museums of note.

Another early glassmaking organisation was founded about 1790 with craftsmen from both Amelung's and Stiegel's old works; it was known as the Baltimore Glass Works.

Two former employees of Casper Wistar also started a glass business for themselves about 1780, known as the Glassboro Glass Works, in New Jersey. In 1840 it was purchased by the Whitney Bros.; bottles and flasks were their main products.

The first glass house to operate in Connecticut was the Pitkin Glass Works, founded by Captain Richard Pitkin in 1783, which produced bottles and flasks in olive-amber, and olive green glass.

Other notable American makers were the Pittsburgh (Pennsylvania) Glass Works, founded in 1797; New Geneva Glass Works, founded also in 1797; the Essex Glass Works, founded about 1787 in Boston; and the White Glass Works, founded in 1815 at Zanesville, Ohio.

Wine glasses provide an excellent medium for the collector, offering as they do a fascinating subject for study, especially if the collector is interested in having pieces to show the development of the wine glass. More modest collections can, of course, be formed by limiting the range to periods, types, or styles. The development of wine glass stems was briefly as follows:

1680 to 1710	Inverted Baluster. Period when glasses were adapted from the Venetians bowls. 'V' shaped with wide mouths, very robust designs. Stem bellied, one side tapering, the other side rounded at top.
1690 to 1710	Drop Knop. Stem with urn-shaped bulge just below the bowl to prevent glass slipping through fingers.
1695 to 1715	Angular Knop. Flattened knop, horizontally positioned. Air bubbles or 'tears' introduced as a stem decoration. Ball Knop. Bulge in stem spherical like a glass marble, often placed immediately above a shoulder.
1695 to 1725	Annulated or Triple-ring Knop. Stem with flattened rings, triple-ringed, usually one ring in between two others in close proximity.
1700 to 1720	Multiple Knops. Knop of similar shape repeated.
1710 to 1730	True Baluster. Knop with bellied, rounded base, tapering into the stem above.
1710 to 1715	Acorn Knop. A tooled design in the form of an acorn, sometimes inverted.

Mushroom Knop. Shaped like a mushroom, curved on top, with an acute return to the stem below.

1715 to 1730   Silesian Stem. Moulded pedestal.

The above are general descriptions of stem types, together with an indication of their periods, but do not be surprised to find a stem that does not specifically fit any of these categories. There was no requirement for the manufacturers to follow any specification. Fashion and the necessity to sell their products, together with the individual ideas of the manufacturers, often influenced the finished article.

Tears were added to stems by a simple process. The glass was indented and covered with more molten glass. The air trapped in the indentation, expanded by the heat, formed a bubble, which was elongated when the stem was drawn up.

The base, or foot, of wine glasses up to 1750 had a folded edge, made by turning the rim back under the base and folding flat. This provided a much strengthened rim that was less prone to damage. Later examples do not have this feature.

Bowl shapes also varied considerably in size and shape, depending upon the liquid they were intended to contain. From the early conical bowl with hardly any stem, they employed other shapes known as bucket, round funnel, flanged, cup or ovid, ogee, trumpet, and bell-shaped.

Decorations include cutting, elongated air bubbles in stems (air twist), twisted stems, coloured glass and coloured twists and engraving.

GLOSSARY

Ale Glass: A long narrow glass for serving ale.

Air Twist: Mostly found in drinking vessels, and shafts of candlesticks. Tube-like veins produced by drawing an entrapped air bubble.

Amberina: An amber glass mixture containing gold. Colour ranges yellow to dark red.

Anglo-Venetian Glass: Glassware made of soda-glass in London from about 1570 until about 1680.

Annealing: Process of relieving stresses in glass by re-heating and permitting the glass to cool slowly.

Arabesques: Scroll works of flowers and leaves engraved on hollow-ware.

Aventurine: A style of glass originally discovered by accident in Murano, Italy, effected by adding copper crystals to the melt, which resulted in a dark brown glass, gold flecked.

Baluster: This refers to the shape seen in a balustrade, the graceful swelling central curve also used to decorate the stems of drinking vessels, and candlesticks.

Blow Moulding: Detailed in text. Forming glass by blowing through a tube.

Broken-Swirl: A double moulding process. The glass is first moulded with vertical ribs, removed from the mould and twisted. It is then returned to the mould and vertical ribs re-impressed over the swirls.

Calcedonia: A type of glass, the colour and veining similar to chalcedony, first produced in the 15th century.

Cane: Rods of coloured glass used as inserts for obtaining coloured streaks and forming patterns in paperweights.

Cased Glass: One layer of glass over another of a different colour.

Compote: Bowl mounted on a foot.

Cresting: A fluted fillet used to join the stem of a glass to the bowl. Can be small or extended half way up the bowl.

Crimping: Dents or flutes formed by a tool used on a foot or handle.

Cristal: A term used to describe fine table and decorative glass of all kinds.

Crown Glass: Early form of glass used for windows.

Crystal: A term used to describe the best quality clear flint glass.

Cullet: Clean broken glass melted into new mixtures of glass.

Cutting: Detailed in text.

Cyst: A circular protuberance usually found in the lower part of a wine glass bowl.

Dram Glasses: Other names include Joeys, Nips, Gin Glasses, and Genettes. Small glasses for spirits.

126

Etched Glass: Detailed in text.

Filigree Glass: A decoration involving interwoven spirals of white and coloured glass threads.

Finials: A knob, usually added to covers.

Firing Glasses: A strong, stumpy glass with thick stem and flat foot. Also known as hammering glasses, because they were used to bang the table to show appreciation, much the same as present day hand clapping.

Flashed Glass: A coating of coloured glass over clear.

Flint Glass: This glass was developed by George Ravenscroft (1618–1681) in England. Silica occurs in nature in most rocks including calcined flints, which was used to produce flint glass. Hollow-ware made from flint glass has a decided ring when flicked with finger nails, and has a better refractive quality than any glass made up to this period.

Flute: A deep, conical-bowled drinking glass, or a vertical cut or cuts, i.e. fluting.

Free Blown: Method of blowing glass without the aid of moulds, relying entirely on the skill of the glass blower (see text).

Green Glass: Glass in its natural colour.

Kick: Cone-shaped indentations found in the base of early bottles and decanters.

Latticinio: Filigree glass made by interlacing strips of clear and opaque glass. Originally a Venetian development.

Lattimo: White glass made with lead, early 16th century; made at Murano, Italy.

Lead Glass: Glass in which lead oxide was used as a fluxing agent (see Flint Glass).

Merese: A connecting piece of glass, used to join a bowl and stem, shaped like a button; or simply a wafer of glass.

Mould Blown: Detailed in text.

Picot: Tooled decoration, an edging.

Pomona Glass: A stippled effect obtained by the use of acid. Unstippled portions of the glass were stained a yellowish-straw colour.

Pressed Glass: Detailed in text.

Prunts: Moulded or tooled pieces of decoration that are applied as a separate part to the body of the article during its manufacture.

Punties: Concave cuts in paperweights.

Quilling: Quill-like, also known as pinched trailing. A strip of glass is added and pinched to form repetitive pleats.

Reticello: Lace glass. A decoration with a network of white opaque threads beneath the surface. First produced in Venice about 15th century.

Reticulated: A pattern similar to netting, diamond-like formations of crazing.

Rigaree Marks: Produced by a small metal wheel, with tiny continuous ribs, producing bands of glass tooled in vertical lines.

Romer: A drinking vessel of pale green glass, similar to a wine glass but with a spherical bowl. The stem and foot are hollow, freely decorated with prunts.

Rummer: Short stemmed drinking glass.

Scalloping: A decorative shape like the end of a scallop shell, usually used on rims or series of semi-circles.

Seeds: Tiny air bubbles trapped in the glass, usually caused by an insufficiently heated furnace, which otherwise would drive the air out completely.

Spangled Glass: Decoration obtained by rolling molten glass over particles of metal or flakes of mica. Subsequently fused by heating.

String Rim: The raised band around the top of the neck of a bottle, for securing string or wire to retain the stopper or cork.

Sulphides: Detailed in text.

Swirl: Radiating spirally, as formed in paperweights by canes of various colours.

Swirled Ribbing: A decoration formed by twisting a stem or similar shape that has been previously ribbed vertically.

Tale Glass: A second quality glass taken from the top of the pot; the glass taken from the bottom of the pot is much finer.

Threading or Thread Circuit: A thin thread of glass continuously wound around the rim of a bowl or neck of a vessel.

Three-piece Glasses: Glasses in which the bowl, stem, and foot have been made separately.

Toddy Lifter: A type of pipette tube for lifting hot toddy from bowl to glass.

Trailed ornament: Looping threads of glass added to a bowl or foot.

Two-piece glasses: Glasses made by drawing the stem from the bowl. The foot is then added as a separate piece.

Venetian Glass: This is a soda glass, blown thinly, and worked at relatively low temperatures which required great speed in working.

Vermicular Collar: A trace of glass surrounding a decanter neck or stem, formed into a wave.

Writhing: Swirling ribbing, surface twisting, on bowl or stem.

Three Ivory Figures.

A typical Imara patterned vase.
(Court Antiques Ltd)

Soup plate. English Delft. Late
Victorian. (Mabel Gohm)

An ivory 'Balls-within-a-ball'. The ball is separate from the stand. Both are exquisitely carved with rose and foliage designs. (Court Antiques Ltd)

A pair of late Capodimonte figures. (Court Antiques Ltd)

Lucerne Lamp with two wick holders. Made from separate brass castings and assembled with brazing speller. (Mabel Gohm)

IVORY AND BONE

10. Ivory and Bone

Ivory has been used as a basic carving material since primitive times. From the days of the Romans it has been used continually for personal adornment, statues, inlays, and for thousands of other purposes. The study of ivory could provide a continuous record of man's tastes and fashions through this extensive period.

The best ivory comes from the tusks of African elephants, and the quality of wild elephant ivory is much superior to that taken from captive animals.

The largest recorded tusks from an African elephant were eleven and a half feet, and the combined weight of both tusks was 293 pounds! The sole source of ivory is the elephant's tusk, but other bones have been used, and these are often difficult for the amateur to distinguish from the real thing. These alternatives include fossilised tusks of mammoths, rhinoceros horn, walrus and narwhal tusks.

The majority of ivory carvings are small, mainly because the raw material is limited in size, but it is an ideal substance for carving, and lends itself readily to details of a delicate nature. It has a warm smooth feel, which mellows with age, and it takes a lightly polished finish very easily.

Oriental ivory is particularly pleasing (see Netsuke) but ivory carving is, by no means, exclusively Oriental. Germany and France used ivory for small sculptures well into the 17th century, and Italy, up to the 15th and 16th centuries when bronze took its place, also used the material extensively. Francois Duquesnoy (1594–1647) the originator of the famous 'manneken-pis' in Brussels, worked occasionally in ivory, and Balthasar Permoser (1651–1732) working in Germany produced his Seasons, which were later copied in porcelain at Fürstenberg. He was probably the best known European carver of his time.

In addition to objects of solid ivory, it has also been used for adorning *objets d'art* of many kinds, such as mounted tankards carved with figures in relief, many of which came from the Netherlands in the 17th century.

The carvers of Augsburg and Nuremberg made a variety of objects such as dagger-hilts, powder flasks, plaques, vases, and so on. During the 19th century, a considerable number of religious figures were produced in Dieppe, France.

Oriental ivories originate mainly from Persia, China, Japan, and India. Persian ivories, although invariably of excellent quality, are not often seen in antique shops. Japanese carvings are more plentiful and these are often most skilfully carved with greater attention to detail than the ivories from other Oriental sources. Chinese figures of good quality are probably the best of all the Oriental small sculptures. Chessmen, a favourite Chinese subject, are often found beautifully carved and mounted on a 'balls within a ball' pedestal. This style of mounting, whilst demonstrating the considerable skill of the carver, is not a significant factor when valuing the article. A considerable amount of very intricate work was executed in Bombay, and in other parts of India, but little of it has any real merit.

How does one start to collect ivory, when the subjects available are so numerous? Personally if the specimen is ivory, attractive, and the price is not above my means, I would need no other incentive— I would buy it, and be happy that I had acquired another piece of ivory.

However, the choice is a personal one, and the collector may wish to specialise in figures, netsuke, bodkin cases and small boxes, cane handles, novelties, or some other subject of his own choice. The following descriptions of various pieces may help in that choice.

BALLS WITHIN A BALL

Everyone must, at some time, have seen examples of this oriental novelty in ivory, consisting of an outer ball with a number of diminishing size balls trapped within. Each ball is separate and can move freely within the confines of the ball encompassing it. All of the balls are usually beautifully carved.

The balls-in-a-ball have a long history in the East, and, no doubt, they are still being produced there.

The method used to achieve this apparent impossibility was first to make the ivory into a sphere or ball, and then to drill holes to a certain depth in positions dictated by the requirements of final design. Then with a sharp carving tool, the interstices between the drilled holes were cut away to release a ball, repeated cutting away through another layer released the second ball, and so on until all the balls were free. The decorative carving was executed during this process.

These novelties are also known as Devils Balls, and are often a feature of chessmen of Eastern origin.

EIGHT IMMORTALS

The eight immortals are a collection of Chinese figures, roughly synonymous with the Catholic saints. They have been represented in many media, including porcelain, but, in my opinion, the ivory examples are the best.

They are representative of masculinity, femininity, wealth, poverty, youth, age, aristocracy and plebeianism, though not necessarily in that order, and they are indicative of the Taoist principles that censure the worship of power and material things.

The little figures are named and recognition features have been added:

Chung-Li-Ch'uan	Usually carries a fan.
Ho Hsien-ku	A figure of a woman, usually with flowers, lotus bloom, or ladle.
Lu Tung-pin	Cap pleated and carries a sword.
Li Ti'eh-kua	A really ugly fellow with crutch.
Chang Kuo-hao	Bearded face, carried a drum.
Ts'ao Kuo-chiu	Bearded, carries tickets.
Lan Ts'ai-ho	Carries flowers either in a basket or as a bouquet.
Han Hsiang-tzu	Carries a broken branch.

SNUFF RASPS

Snuff rasps were made and used during the 17th century for grating tobacco into snuff. They consisted of a section of ivory about 2 inches wide and 6 to 7 inches long. The back was carved with groups of figures, or made in the form of a single figure, and the front carried perforated iron grates.

The majority of snuff grates were produced in Dieppe, but they were also made in the Low countries, Germany and England.

CRUCIFIXES

17th century crucifixes were often carved from a single piece of ivory, including the body of Christ. It was also a practice of this period to produce the body of Christ in ivory, and mount it on a wooden cross. These were of European origin.

There is an important Crucifixion by the outstanding German carver Simon Troger (1693–1769) to be seen in the Victoria and Albert Museum (London).

CARE

Hard ivories are inclined to distort and crack, more so if they are kept in a dry atmosphere. Therefore, always store them away from heat and, if possible, in a humid atmosphere.

The outer surface of ivory is yellow, and tends to become more so with age; it can be bleached with hydrogen peroxide, but this action has no real lasting effect, and it is doubtful if such treatment will improve the appearance of a piece. Grease can be removed, without causing any harm, by gently swabbing the ivory with a little pad of cotton wool soaked in benzine.

If ever the need arises, ivory can be softened by immersion in phosphoric acid, and it will regain its original hardness on drying.

BONE

Bone carvings are closely allied to those of ivory; the raw material for both comes from animal 'bone', and sometimes it may be difficult for the layman to differentiate between the two. There is, however, a considerable difference in the cost and availability of each material. Bone may lack the quality of ivory but objects made in this material are very collectable.

We can thank the French prisoners captured during the Napoleonic wars for some very beautiful work in bone. During these wars, which covered a period from 1793 to 1815, it is estimated that over 60,000 prisoners were housed in this country, either in prisons or in prison ships. Like any army, there were all types and trades represented in their number, including ivory and jet carvers, many of whom came from Dieppe, where the local industry of ivory carving had been established well before Bonaparte.

As a means of obtaining money for a few luxuries, and to pass away the time more enjoyably, these craftsmen manufactured articles which could be sold to prison visitors on open days. Surprisingly, the prisoners were allowed and even encouraged to market their products. Some prisons allowed visitors to call once or twice a week especially to trade and to bring raw materials. The raw materials were probably more necessary for the other trades being carried on than for the bone carvers, who had their own way of obtaining materials. They collected the bones from their own meat rations and buried them for a period to get them clean. Subsequently they were split into convenient pieces for carving or for model making.

When the project got under way it was common practice for the prisoners to form groups, each man specialising in a particular part of a model or carving in current production.

Although the prisoners were allowed to follow a craft in prison, the authorities were not over-keen on letting them have proper tools. This is understandable because they could be used for escape purposes. Even as late as 1806 when a new prisoner-of-war camp was

constructed on Dartmoor, they were still making-do with impro-
vised tools. By 1812 the relationship between prisoners and prison
authorities had become more trusting, with the result that paroled
prisoners were allowed out of camp to buy tools and materials
locally.

MODEL SHIPS

The ship models produced by prisoners of war were very fine
examples indeed. They were produced in exquisite detail and as
accurate as they could be made under the circumstances. Remember
the prisoners had no drawings from which they could work, so they
were compelled to rely on their memory.

Metal fittings were produced from any metal that came to hand,
even the earrings of prisoners. Rigging was made from plaited
human hair.

These quite excellent little works of art were sold by the
prisoners from about one pound to thirty shillings. Today a good
model ship will cost at least a thousand pounds!

GAMES

Bone chess-pieces, playing cards, draughts and dominoes, were all
made by the prisoners, initially no doubt as a pastime and as a
means of providing games for their own amusement.

Later these games were packaged in suitable bone boxes and sold
in considerable numbers. Some of the boxes were quite elaborate
with sliding lids, and decorated with water colour paintings.

Playing cards were often quite tiny rectangles of bone with the
symbols added in oil paint.

The French prisoners of war were not the only source of bone
carving. Many small and interesting pieces originated from other
sources, like the pocket domino set illustrated. This is a Victorian
novelty for carrying in the pocket. The dominoes are quite roughly
finished, but the little brass box, leather covered, is beautifully
made with a hinged lid with an inserted bevelled glass window.

GUILLOTINE MODELS

These gruesome models were made with the same care and attention to detail that is typical of prisoners-of-war work. The models
were made in various sizes, and a few even had a model figure, with
hands tied behind his back, in the process of being executed. To add
to the effect, decapitated heads with bloody necks were placed in the

basket under the blade. 'Blood' was added beneath the blade to complete the realism.

MECHANICAL TOYS

Mechanical toys, with limited motions, were made to operate by a series of ratchets and wheels made from bone. Threads connected to the wheels and the operating handle completed the mechanism. Spindles, etc., required for their production, may have been supplied by a local turner; if not, it would not have been beyond the wit of such talented craftsmen to have devised a simple lathe for themselves.

Toys with mechanical motions include women spinning, nursing babies, and soldiers.

CRIBBAGE BOARDS

Apart from the standard bone cribbage board, these were also made in a box form with a sliding lid, with glass let into the sides, under which were set small water-colour paintings.

OTHER EXAMPLES

These include clock-cases, fans, mirror-frames, seals, miniature toys, watch-cases, lace-bobbins, thimbles, needle-cases, etc.

JADE

11. Jade

Jade is to most of us a pale green stone, often exquisitely carved, and surrounded with an aura of oriental mystery. The mystic quality of jade was undoubtedly felt by the Chinese who were carving the mineral in Neolithic times, some 4,000 years B.C., because they also believed that jade possessed magical properties.

Although jade is an oriental, or at least, a foreign material, the actual word 'jade', strange as it may seem, originated in Europe.

Sometime during the 14th century, Marco Polo (1254?–1324?) the famous Venetian traveller and author, returned to Europe from China and described decorative objects that he had seen in vast numbers at the court of the Great Chan. These objects were fashioned from a very hard stone of delicate and varied colouring into the most elaborate ornaments and trinkets by skilful carving. Undoubtedly, Marco Polo was one of the first Europeans to discover oriental jade, although he could not have known it by that name.

The first importations of jade into Europe from China were made during the 16th century by Portuguese merchants and seamen. The Portuguese, always with an enterprising eye on commercial possibilities, opened direct trade with China early in the 16th century, and by 1557 Macao had become a Portuguese outpost, the first in China, and a centre for the export of Chinese goods, including jade.

However, the export of jade out of China could only be executed with difficulty and great secrecy, due to the strict Chinese opposition to jade being taken out of the country. They regarded it as a very, precious material, more desirable than gold because of its supposedly curative and magical properties. The export of jade in these early days was therefore very much a cloak-and-dagger operation.

Jade has always been given the credit of possessing certain healing qualities, especially in connection with the kidneys. It was thought that by simply placing jade in direct contact with the skin, it would prevent diseases of the kidneys and stimulate regular urinary functions.

Naturally, the legend travelled with the mineral from China to Portugal, where it became known as the urinary stone, or 'pedra de mijada' to the Portuguese. Allowing for a little abbreviation and corruption to the words, it is easy to see how the Yu, that means 'jewel' or treasure in China, became the jade of the Western World.

Jade is not a specific term, but rather a general term loosely used to include various mineral substances of a tough texture, which are usually of a green hue and properly embraces nephite and jadeite, but the green varieties of garnet, pectolite, serpentine, sillimanite, and vesuvianite are sometimes included.

Genuine old jade used by the Chinese since Neolithic times was, without doubt, a calcium-magnesium silicate of some considerable hardness, corresponding to $6\frac{1}{2}$ degrees of the Moh's scale (see appendix) and this can be considered the classic nephite. Other minerals are sometimes mistaken by Europeans for the real thing, serpentine being a common one, especially the Chinese variety with a Moh's scale degree of hardness 6.

The familiar modern importations of jade statuettes often seen in gift shops and sold by purveyors of bric-a-brac, are usually not of Chinese origin and not really made of jade, but they are carved in a soft translucent green fluorite, a material easy to work and, in consequence, they have little real monetary value.

Genuine jade is found in a variety of colours and combinations of colours. The fine emerald green variety is known as Imperial jade; the pale green is more common. Other colours are brown, black, mauve, orange, red, violet, yellow and white. 'Mutton fat' jade is, as its name suggests, either a dirty white or grey colour.

Jade, of course, is found mainly in China, but the finest comes from the Mogaung district of Upper Burma, and certain parts of Turkestan. It has also been found in Alaska.

Jade was certainly known to the Aztecs and other civilizations of Central America, but where it came from is a mystery as no deposits of the mineral have yet been found in Central America.

It is amazing that a mineral as hard and difficult to carve as jade should have been fashioned so beautifully using only the primitive tools and methods available to the Chinese craftsman of the Neolithic age. The cutting and shaping was a hand operation, employing tools of bone or bamboo sticks. The actual cutting media was made with an abrasive powder of crushed garnets, mixed with a greasy paste. To form circular depressions or to drill holes, the ancient craftsman made himself a drill from animal bone or a bamboo stick. These tubular boring tools were sharpened with flint or stones to provide a chamfered cutting edge. The area in which the hole was required was smothered with the garnet-impregnated paste, and the drill applied under pressure and rotated.

The method of rotating the drill was simply to wind a few turns of string around it and attach the two free ends to a curved strip of wood, like a bow, and then reciprocate the bow backwards and forwards like a cello player whilst keeping a downward pressure with the other hand. This method is very old, and was used in a very similar way for fire making. It takes little imagination to realise that the carving and fashioning of any single jade piece must have been a very time-consuming and laborious task.

With the advent of bronze in the 15th century B.C., and later iron, the bamboo drills were obviously replaced by these more durable materials, but the general method remained unaltered.

The Maoris of New Zealand knew and carved jade, and even as late as the first half of the 19th century they were still making their normal requirements for day to day living from stone, whale-bone, and hardwoods, and of these materials, the most valued was nephrite, or jade; or if you are a Maori—pounamu.

'Pounamu' was used for knives, axes, adzes, and for war clubs. It was also used in a non-utilitarian capacity for decorative objects such as the hei-tike—small pendants, in the form of a human, which were suspended by a string, and hung around the neck.

The Maoris carved and shaped the mineral with shells, stone, whalebone and with points of hard wood, in conjunction with an abrasive mixture of possibly sandstone and slate. It is also feasible that they used a drill bow much in the same way as the Chinese.

Archaic Chinese jade is of course a study in itself, and such jade is found usually only in museums or in millionaire collections. But, in general terms, it can be said to fall roughly into three divisions— weapons, ceremonial and quasi-scientific. Among the weapons, the dagger, halberd (combined spear and battle-axe) and spearhead are probably the most common. The pi, apparently, was a most important ceremonial object. It has been made from the earliest times, and threads itself through Chinese history into comparatively modern times. It is basically a simple disc with a hole in the centre. It varies considerably in size, and sometimes it is found in sections, pierced with small holes at each end of each section as if intended to be joined by thongs to complete the ring, or it may well be that the holes were intended for fixing the pi to something else. It can be quite plain, or exquisitely decorated. The pi represented Heaven, and probably originated from the solar disc. The tsung, another ritual object, represented the Earth. It is a cylindrical tube with a square centre surface.

A circular disc with the edges serrated had an astronomical use, but just how it was used is not known.

Ritual jades were used also for burials; the orifices of the body were plugged with jade to prevent the entry of evil spirits after death.

The Ching Dynasty (1644–1912) is a particularly interesting period for jade. The inclusion of another colour area in the jade was used to carve a specific feature, such as an insect or leaf, and so give it emphasis. Hollow wares were carved with paper-thin walls, and

137

vases with free handles were carved from an integral piece of jade. Collectors interested in jade should avail themselves of the opportunity to visit suitable museums and see for themselves some of the priceless and exquisite examples of the jade carvers' art, and to see the wide variety of colours. The British Museum, London, and Metropolitan Museum, New York, both have interesting collections.

Dating jade is always difficult, even for experts. There are two indications, the *apparent* age of the material itself, and the style of the carving. The material changes with the passage of time, particularly if it has been buried for long periods, but the new collector will not find these facts very helpful.

Early jades are interesting to study, but may well be out of reach of the average collector; in fact, any good quality jade will command a reasonably high price. Maori jade is being collected more now with the increased interest in the primitive arts, the tikki being a most favoured object. But the prices, quality, and varieties of jade carving generally are so diverse that it is well beyond the scope of this book and the ability of the author to recommend any specific approach to buying for investment.

NETSUKE

12. Netsuke

The national costumes of Japan, unlike European dress, made no provision for carrying the paraphernalia of everyday life. The kimono is a buttonless gown; those worn by the males were supported by a wide sash. As the costumes were pocketless, personal articles were secured to the person by means of a netsuke. A netsuke is in effect a decorative toggle, attached to a cord; the other end of the cord carries a pouch for personal articles such as a tobacco pouch, sweet meat box, snuff bottles, and a small container for carrying a seal and red pigment, medicines, and herbs. Such a pouch is termed an Inro.

The assembly of netsuke, cord, and inro were attached to the person by passing the cord behind the sash so that the netsuke rested on the top edge, thus preventing the cord from slipping.

Generally a netsuke was designed compactly without any projections which would catch in the costume material, and the backs were flattened so that they would fit comfortably against the body. Cord holes, usually two in number, are often joined by a channel to hold the cord. Older netsuke often had one hole larger than the other to receive the cord knot.

A netsuke is usually modelled in wood or ivory, and is frequently found in the human or animal form, but they were also carved to represent many other forms, including reptiles, birds, fruits, insects, zodiac animals, legendary figures and even household utensils.

The Japanese zodiac animals were the rat, ox, tiger, hare, dragon, serpent, horse, goat, monkey, cock, dog and boar. Each animal represented a two-hour period of the day and night; for example 10 p.m. until midnight was the 'hour' of the boar.

Netsuke is known to have made its appearance sometime during the early part of the 18th century: undoubtedly they were used prior to this date but opinions differ; some experts even go back as early as 1600, but be that as it may, the examples available to modern collectors will be of the late 18th, early 19th century vintage.

The Japanese, although perhaps appreciative of their beauty, did not really value their netsuke; they were simply functional objects that served an everyday purpose, and consequently they were discarded when they were damaged.

From 1780 to about 1870 was the best period; many fine pieces were carved and signed by the artist. It was a period when the demand was at its highest peak due to the fashion of wearing tobacco pouches, as well as the usual objects mentioned earlier. From about 1870 onwards there was a general decline in their use.

Shibayama is a name given to a particular method of inlaying metals and mother-of-pearl into the ivories. This type of netsuke was very skilfully executed and makes a most desirable possession.

Netsuke vary in size from about one inch to about five inches, and until about 1965 they were relatively inexpensive, being collected more for their intrinsic beauty than for any investment value that they may have possessed. In fact, some could, at that time, have been purchased for a few shillings. However those days have gone, and now the art investors have pushed the prices into four figures for first quality examples.

Although ivory and wood are the most common materials used for the netsuke, porcelain, bamboo, horn, various metals, gourds and shells have also been used. Artists particularly associated with netsuke are Tomotada (for the cattle subjects); Ikkan (for rat subjects); Hoshin; Gyokuzan Asahi; Masanao; Kokei; Toen; Kaigyokusai; Okatomo; Tomiharu; Mitsuhiro; Yoshimura; Tomokazu; Shugetsu; and the Deme family.

The collector should be aware that from the 19th century there has been a tourist trade in netsuke and, of course, many skilful fakes produced. It is sometimes very difficult for the inexperienced to determine a late copy or fake from the genuine antique article. Usually they lack the patina, may possess sharpness when handled, and could be falsely aged by staining. A large proportion of examples will be found without any signatures, but even signed copies can be faked. If a skilled operator can fake a netsuke, he should have little trouble faking a signature.

In the early days of collecting, rely on a reputable dealer who has the expertise you have yet to acquire through study and by handling many examples. There are no real techniques or tricks to help determine the real value or quality of any piece, it is a matter of experience.

When buying netsuke again use your judgement, look for detail and the obvious skill of the craftsman. Make certain that no part is damaged or broken.

Ivory netsuke may be cleaned with a very soft brush or hand polished but remember they can suffer from excessive heat and light.

PAINTINGS AND PICTURES

13. Paintings and Pictures

The art of painting, in its many forms, has been practiced by man since he emerged from pre-history, and it is one of the oldest art forms. What other art form could go back 20,000 years to the caves of Altamira, and provide such wonderful examples.

How then, can a subject so vast, and covering such a long period, be adequately covered in a few thousand words? Obviously it cannot, therefore in keeping with the aim of this book, we will make the introduction, guide the reader through the preliminaries to whet his appetite, and then leave him to pursue the path of his choice.

Do not be dismayed by the high prices being paid for old Masters; these prices do not necessarily reflect the true value, which after all, is arbitrary. There are plenty of excellent pictures that can be bought without mortgaging your house, and if you use your judgement, they will certainly increase in value, and give many hours of pleasant contemplation.

The opportunity of discovering an exceptional oil painting is unlikely to say the least, but oil paintings, like every other commodity, are governed by supply and demand and of course, fashion. Step outside the fashion and you will find excellent works, either by minor artists, or by lesser known ones, relatively cheaply. If you are fortunate in anticipating the likely demands for fashion during the next few years, who knows what price your painting would command?

Oil paintings have been executed on wooden panels, copper, tin, stretched canvas, and many other supports. All of these are acceptable, and in general terms do not affect the cost or desirability. Large paintings are invariably on canvas for the convenience of the artist.

Catalogues will often refer to a painting as Italian school, or English school. School in this sense is a term used to state that the painting originated in that country, and that usually the artist is unknown. School is sometimes used in another sense—such as School of Rembrandt—meaning that it has all the characteristics of a Rembrandt painting, but was not executed by him. It may have been the work of assistants, or copyists.

Brushwork is another important consideration to the expert. The bristles of the brush, charged with paint and applied over canvas, are as individual as an artist's hand-writing. Experts familiar with the works of a particular artist can recognise his work simply from the brushwork.

Paintings described as 'conversation pieces' are not, as may be expected, groups of people having a chat, but a special kind of painting showing two or more portraits in surrounding scenery, usually appropriate to the subject.

Icons originally referred to a picture of Christ, (or a Saint) that was painted on a separate panel, to distinguish the work from those executed on walls. These are often turning up in sale rooms, usually in most elaborate frames.

An interesting technique of painting is known as 'Optical mixtures'. The object of this technique is to obtain brighter secondary colours by placing primary colours in close proximity, in tiny blobs, so that the eye mixes these colours when viewed from a distance. For example, blue and yellow blobs of paint would appear green.

The word 'primitive' is often applied to paintings of a particular style or date. It sounds informed if the description is used among uninformed circles, but the word is practically meaningless now, except for giving an undeserved importance to the work of amateur artists whose only claim to fame is their lack of technical skill and vision, which is obvious in their childlike daubings.

Size of pictures will be an important consideration for the collector. Very large pictures will require plenty of space to hang them and with present-day houses, this is not always available; consequently the smaller and more manageable pictures are those usually desired. This has an effect on the cost. Excellent quality, large sized pictures will often be cheaper than the poorer quality smaller examples.

Before buying your first oil painting, get to know your own taste. This is not to suggest that a collector does not know the subjects that excite him most, but oil paintings have a tendency to 'grow on you' and pictures turned down with a cursory examination will often become enchanting with longer association. Conversely the opposite can happen. Some art galleries specialising in 'minor masters' will often be pleased to loan a picture on approval, so that the collector has the opportunity to see it in his own home, and to 'get to know it' before making his final decision.

Do not bother to acquire paintings in very bad condition just because they are cheap, unless of course you suspect you have found an old masterpiece. The cost of restoring will often outweigh any original advantage in price, and extensive restoring is unsatisfactory.

Fig. 48 'A Walk in the Park', by Nicolas Florent Crabbels. Oil on board. Size 14 × 12 inches. A beautiful example of the work of a minor master (*Leon Gilbert, New York*).

Still life paintings, which reached their zenith during the 17th and early 18th century, are not avidly sought-after today. I can only assume the lack of action usually projected by such pictures is not in keeping with the modern mood. This is a great shame; many still life subjects are beautiful compositions of natural objects, re-arranged for the sake of design, colour and lighting.

Flower pieces, often executed with great attention to detail, are much in demand as decorative furnishing pieces, and consequently may cost a little more than still life subjects.

Shipping paintings are in high demand, and if the quality is in any way acceptable, prices will be high.

Water-colour painting is an art that has been particularly exploited by English artists, and has the reputation of being the finest in the world. True water-colours applied in transparent washes give a fresh, delicate luminosity to any subject. Almost perfect examples of the medium are seen in the work of Russell Flint; admittedly the works of this master are not antique, but they are well worth examination in the interest of knowledge.

Water colours were used many centuries before the discovery of oil paint, the pigment applied either in washes, or as tempera. Tempera, which is powder colour mixed with a binder, was used until about the 15th century for easel pictures. The binder was either egg white, or the yolk, or even a combined mixture of both.

Techniques employed in water-colours, in addition to tempera, include colour washes used in conjunction with pencil line drawings, which produced a fine, delicate, compact picture, or a loose, free style, dependent upon the mood of the artist. Opaque water-colours mixed with solid opaque white were used on a tinted paper, which gives a strong, vigorous picture. This technique was a little like oil painting, because the colours could be applied thickly, and pale colours could be applied over darker colours or vice versa.

Some of the finest water-colours have been produced using a combination of both transparent washes and opaque colour.

The most prominent name in 'early' English water-colours is Paul Sandby (1725-1809), who was a topographical draughtsman, employed by the Crown. It is not surprising, therefore, that his landscapes are meticulous. Opaque colour, or gouache, was a medium used extensively, and very expertly, by Sandby.

Sandby was the first artist to produce aquatints in this country (see Prints). He was also responsible for a series of etchings, including Hyde Park and Windsor views.

Samuel Prout (1783–1852) was born in Plymouth, but much of his work was executed on the continent. His style was bold, but very controlled, lending itself admirably to the art of lithography (see

144

A page from 'Nouvelle Encyclopedie Pratique de Mêconique et D'Electricite Allas' showing the many printed overlays (see text).

A fore-edge painting of Salisbury. The book entitled 'Picturesque Memorials of Salisbury' is fully bound and blocked in gold. Dated 1834. (Richard van de Gohm)

Curry combs (also supplied in B & W). (Pamela Watkins)

Right. Martinware Grotesque Birds.
(Southall Public Library)

Below. Wine glass with bowl flashed with ruby glass, then cut. (Court Antiques Ltd)

Left. A beautiful pair of unmarked porcelain figures, possible German. (Court Antiques Ltd)

Right. Martinware Grotesque jug. (Southall Public Library)

Prints), a process used by Prout extensively for illustrative works including *Sketches in France, Switzerland, and Italy* and *Facsimilies of Sketches made in Flanders and Germany.*

Prout's water-colours have been copied extensively, therefore his so-called signature on the picture is no guarantee that it is an original.

Thomas Rowlandson (1756–1827) was a water-colourist with an interest mainly centred on man and his pursuits, rather than his environment. He is often considered to be the first cartoonist of his day. His water-colour sketches, although invariably drawn with a subtle delicacy, have the exaggerated and inelegant quality associated with caricature.

Rowlandson prepared a large number of designs for books, and was also a celebrated etcher. His technique was to first produce the original watercolour, and then etch the main features in outline on a copper plate, which was subsequently finished, and aquatinted, or coloured, by others in imitation of the original.

A typical work by Rowlandson named 'Brook Green Fair' can be seen at the Victoria and Albert Museum.

William Henry Hunt (1790–1864) was a well-known painter of flowers, fruit and vegetables, which he painted in exquisite detail.

Clarkson Stanfield (1793–1867) was a very competent artist mainly concerning himself with sea and landscapes.

Much of the work of David Cox (1783–1859) was executed in North Wales, but he also visited Holland, France, and Belgium. His style was vigorous, broad and full of charm. He liked to work on a kind of wrapping paper which had a slightly rough, tinted texture, ideally suited to his style. A similar type of paper can be obtained today, and is known as 'Cox Paper'.

There are many other very competent water-colour artists worthy of study, and their names are as follows:

Francis Towne	(1740–1816)
William Pars	(1742–1782)
Thomas Hearne	(1744–1817)
Edward Dayes	(1763–1804)
Thomas Girton	(1775–1802)
John Robert Cozens	(1752–1797)
John Sell Cotman	(1782–1842)
Peter De Wint	(1784–1849)

You may not be able to afford many paintings by the above artists, but nevertheless, they should be studied so that a standard of quality can be established, which will greatly assist in the evaluation of works by less exalted artists.

145

GLASS PICTURES

The earliest glass pictures date from about the end of the 17th century. They were produced by a process known as verre eglomisé, which is a term used to describe flat glass decorated with engraved silver and gold leaf; some painting may also be included. It was a popular technique in America during the late 18th century for decorating mirrors, wall and shelf clocks and glass panels generally.

The 17th century method of making glass pictures involved the use of a print; most of these seem to have religious subjects and are not in very great demand, but there were some very attractive decorative prints used if you can find them. The author had a beautiful example of 'Nelson', and a very attractive set of 'The Seasons'.

The process involved soaking the print, as yet uncoloured, in water to remove the body, or size. When the print had been dried it was stuck, face-down, onto a sheet of glass and left to dry. Now came the operation requiring considerable skill—the paper was moistened and carefully rubbed away to leave only the thinnest film of paper carrying the printed impression.

When thoroughly dry the back of the print was then coloured. If you look at the back of such a picture, you will note that the tone value of the colours vary from those viewed from the front, due to the effect of print and glass.

The earlier the picture of this type, the better the painting; later ones tend to be less skilfully executed.

SILHOUETTE

The name 'Silhouette' is derived from Etienne Silhouette, one of Louis XV's Finance Ministers, but the earliest silhouettes go back to the end of the 17th century.

Profile portraits were usually produced by throwing a shadow of the sitter's profile onto a screen made of oiled paper and the outline traced with a pencil. The outline was used to cut the shape from black paper which was subsequently stuck to a white background, or the outline simply filled in with black pigment.

Silhouettes are not restricted to portraiture; half- and full-length figures will often be found with sketched-in backgrounds. Occasionally portraits had the hair painted in a lighter tint and gold was used to pick out hair decorations.

Dickens mentions in the Pickwick Papers, 'a profile machine which could be used to execute a portrait in two and a quarter minutes'; this refers to a device introduced early in the 19th century something like a pantograph that had a pointer which followed the outline of

Fig. 50

Fig. 51

Set of three silhouettes painted on card with details scratched through the paint. Signed S. Hürsch and dated 1849 (*David Morley Antiques*).

the sitter's face at one end, and a pencil attached to the other for tracing the outline.

Silhouettes painted on the reverse side of the glass are usually of French origin. Sometimes the silhouette is backed with coloured pigment similar, in fact, to verre eglomisé; others are painted on the reverse side of convex glass and backed with a white card. These are the most interesting, because the actual painting is proud of the background, and casts a shadow.

It is not unusual to find the silhouette cut from black paper and stuck to a white background. Artists who cut their profiles from black paper did so at quite an amazing speed; in fact, they almost took more pride in their speed than the finished profile.

Francis Torond (1743–1812) was a cut paper artist; his work is rare, and expensive. John Miers (1758–1821) is probably the best known of all the profilists, but collectors interested in the subject could do worse than study the works of August Edouart, Isabella Beetham, Edward Foster, J. Buncombe, A. Forberger, and for American collectors William King, who flourished between 1785 and 1805, and Charles Polk.

There are many other names connected with the art of the silhouette, but we have tried to provide a nucleus of the better known artists as a starting point for further study.

MINIATURES

Miniature portrait paintings have always been in demand, both by collectors and folk with an eye for interior decoration. When used for decoration, they are shown to their best advantage if hung in a compact group, or one above the other, on a suitable wall. They can also be displayed in a glass-fronted cabinet.

Miniatures, or 'limnings', as they are named, really became established as an art form about 1540 when Holbein turned his attention to painting small circular portraits on vellem with opaque water-colours. The 16th century miniatures were also painted on playing cards, which made an excellent support.

During the 17th century, the portrait miniature underwent an evolutionary change from an alliance with medieval illuminators to an alliance with contemporary oil painting. A few miniatures of this period will be found painted in oil and possibly on metal.

It was during the early part of the 18th century that ivory was introduced as a ground and support; the natural colour of ivory was an ideal background when used with transparent water-colour.

Nicholas Hilliar (1547–1619) is one of the best known of our English miniaturists. His fame stems from his wonderful portraits of

Fig. 52 Miniature of a Georgian gentleman. Size of painting $1\frac{1}{2}$ inches diameter. Signed A.G., dated 1797. Circular frame black japanned (*David Morley Antiques*).

Queen Elizabeth, and from 1584 he was granted 'the sole rights' to paint her portraits in miniature. Much of this artist's work has been reproduced countless times.

Other 17th century miniaturists are John Hoskins, Samuel Cooper, Isaac Oliver, Thomas Flatman and Nicholas Dixon.

About the turn of the 18th century we will find miniatures painted by Lawrence Cross, Bernard Lens, and later in the century by Gervase Spence, Samuel Cotes, Nathaniel Hone and Luke Sullivan. Between the late 18th and early 19th centuries the dominant artists were Richard Cosway, George Engleheart and John Smart.

Any miniatures by the above artists will be difficult to find and will certainly be expensive.

Miniature paintings are not restricted to English origin. The American continent followed the English example, and their earliest listed painter was John Watson of East Jersey. Little appears to be known about the subject prior to this artist.

The American artists of note are Charles Willson Peale, Joseph Dunkerley, Nathaniel Hancock, Henry Benbridge and many others.

An interesting series of portraits was painted by Charles Willson

149

Peale during the War of Independence; these were mainly officers, including George Washington.

It is worth seeking American miniatures, but they are rare in England. American collectors often have to be satisfied with miniatures of European origin.

Apart from the 'big named' artists, there are many other very competent artists who have produced excellent examples of the art which can be bought for a relatively few pounds. Use your judgement—if the quality is good, and the picture pleases you—buy it! If, however, you wish to study the work of miniaturists of the late 19th and early 20th centuries, then here are a few suggested artists worthy of attention.

JOHN COX DILLMAN ENGLEHEART (1784–1862)

A popular artist of his period, often painted backgrounds of trees, flowers etc., on his miniature portraits.

SIR WILLIAM JOHN NEWTON (1785–1869)

There was a tendency by this artist to use a brown shading on the face of his portraits. His work is usually signed on the back.

SIR WILLIAM CHARLES ROSS, R.A. (1794–1860)

An outstanding 19th century miniaturist, who is reputed to have painted over 2,200 portraits. He was appointed Miniature Painter to the Queen in 1837, and painted many portraits of the Royal Family.

SIMON JACQUES ROCHARD (1788–1872)

A French artist who came to England in 1815.

REGINALD EASTON (1807–1893)

Although a self-taught artist, he became a notable artist in water-colour and in miniatures. Noted for his child portraits.

JOHN HASLEM (1808–1884)

There are not many miniatures to be found by this artist; probably it was not his main vocation. He is better known for his association with porcelain.

WILLIAM EGLEY (1798–1870)

His miniatures are said to have a slight resemblance to those by Sir William Charles Ross, but they lack the fine quality of his composition.

JOHN LINNELL (1792–1882)

John Linnell is better known for his landscape paintings, a subject he preferred to portraiture, therefore miniatures by him are relatively scarce.

Having acquired a few miniatures, give them the care they deserve. Do not let them dry out by hanging them too near a fire. If you do, the ivory is likely to buckle and distort. Do not hang them where they receive the full rays of the sun, as this will cause them to fade just like any other water-colour.

PAPERWEIGHTS IN GLASS

14. Paperweights in Glass

The glass paperweight known as Millefiore, meaning 'thousand flowers', offers the collector a rare opportunity to acquire items that were made over a very limited period.

Undoubtedly the best period was between 1845 and 1849, but if the collector restricts himself to these dates his collections will remain very small indeed, unless he is a man of considerable means. It is suggested that he extends the period from 1845 to about 1880, and so provide an opportunity of buying cheaper. Fine quality, early paperweights made about the middle of the 19th century can command very high prices. In 1965, at a London saleroom, one such piece was sold for £3,000!

The best early pieces were French, and came from factories in Clichy, Baccarat, and St. Louis, but other countries, including England and America, produced excellent specimens. The American paperweights, similar in style, were made during the 19th century by the Millville factory in New Jersey, who engaged craftsmen from St. Louis and Baccarat. Glass paperweights were shown at The Great Exhibition of 1851, but they did not become very popular until sometime later when it was realised that they were indeed small works of art in their own right.

The weights from Baccarat were probably made between 1846 and 1849; this is assumed because the dates incorporated in the designs invariably fall between these two dates, the commonest being 1848, the rarest 1849.

St. Louis weights are not dated so frequently, but from records available it can be assumed that they were made from 1845 to 1849, the dates 1847 and 1848 being the most often seen. The initials SL occur on some, but not all, weights from St. Louis.

The weights from Clichy on rare examples will bear the name CLICHY in full, others will occasionally have just the letter C.

Another type of paperweight that can usually be bought reasonably is the domed or raised block of glass which acts as a magnifying glass and has a coloured print stuck to the underside, showing views of towns, holiday resorts, places of interest, street scenes, and foreign views. There is a considerable range of subjects from which to choose.

It is known that this type of paperweight existed in about 1851, and probably dates from that period, i.e. latter 19th century. As time progressed, the coloured print was superseded by the photographic print, but these lack the colour and appeal of their predecessors.

Prior to 1870, the weights were usually circular, but following this period, they became more elaborate and were produced in the shape of horseshoes, hearts, and other decorative outlines.

The outlet for this type of paperweight was mainly through stationers, and apart from their practical use, had a souvenir value. Therefore it may be possible to start your collection whilst on holiday, or visiting a town on business. Antique shops in these areas are more likely to show interest in such items than those in the London area.

Apsley Pellatt was an English manufacturer of note, who made paperweights with a small slab or plaque of white china with the design shown in relief. This was then embedded in glass. (See Glass Crystallo Ceramic).

Although the first English paperweight is thought to have been made in Stowbridge about 1845. Pellatt is reputed to be responsible for introducing the millefiori into England about this time; he employed French craftsmen, and describes the technique in his Curiosities of Glassmaking (1849).

The early English examples were crude when compared with the exquisite Continental paperweights, but after about 1848 they improved, the most common design of the time being known as 'Venetian Star Work'.

A millefioire paperweight is a crystal ball (not unlike the crystal used by fortune tellers) with a galaxy of brightly coloured flowers imprisoned in its body. Instead of flowers, one might find reptiles, salamanders, snakes, and butterflies, or even portraits.

The technique employed to produce the millefiori dates back to Roman times. First, coloured glass canes were assembled to form a cylinder about three inches across, and then fused together by heating. The next operation was to heat the chunky slug and draw it out until it was about three feet long. Naturally the cane became reduced in diameter but the coloured glass canes remained in their original position. The long cane, when cooled, was then cut into small sections and embedded into clear glass. This technique was more or less standard practice in England and France for the decoration of paperweights.

The embedding process was executed by placing a decorative cross-section in a heated iron mould which softened the glass. A little liquid glass was then poured into the moulds to set the pattern into the glass. It was then covered with clear glass and the shape formed by successively dipping into molten glass.

Another method was to lay sections of glass, coloured and shaped, onto a small bed of glass and set them with a flame. These were then covered with liquid glass and the process of forming and shaping proceeded as for millefiori.

Latticinio type decorations were also executed in this manner. This technique originated in Venetian glass about 1550. It consisted basically of embedding threads of opaque glass in clear or coloured glass to form a lacy pattern.

Decorations in the form of animals, reptiles, etc., were first formed in a mould, and then subsequently encapsulated as previously described. More elaborate designs also incorporated millefiori decorations, or a background of latticinio.

French paperweights are invariably in the millefiori style, bouquets are rare, whilst single sprays of flowers and fruit are more common. Reptile, butterfly and similar decorations are rare, and nearly always out of the reach of the average collector.

The overlay weight had a bulbous glass body which had been flashed all over with a thin layer of opaque coloured glass. Facets were then ground which removed the opaque covering in certain areas to reveal the clear glass underneath, and to provide a window through which the interior could be viewed. The overlay colouring most encountered is dark blue, pink, turquoise, and less frequently rose, and apple green.

The overlay paperweight is a most delightful piece of artistry, but good quality examples are expensive, and they are likely to become more so; in fact, the majority of overlay weights should be considered rare.

You have probably seen hundreds of modern copies of the famous millefiore in gift and antique shops, but these are not valuable and do not warrant a place in your collection. These modern examples are made today in America, London, Birmingham and Perth in Scotland. It is easy to select the real specimen by the overall quality of workmanship, after only a little practical experience.

Serious collectors seek mostly the antique paperweights from France, overlays and those with a single design subject being the most valuable. Dated weights are obviously more desirable than undated specimens, and the colour of the glass should be clear and without blemishes.

The base of a glass paperweight may have an unfinished spot, called a 'pontil-mark'. This was caused when the glass was broken off the pontil rod by the glass worker at the completion of the manufacturing cycle, and can be taken as an indication that the piece is old.

PAPIER MÂCHÉ

15. Papier Mâché

Papier mâché was invented by the French, and as the name suggests it is literally mashed or pulped paper. The original papier mâché centre was Paris, probably because it was a city where the raw material could be had in abundance, due to the excessive advertising carried out by bill posters which were continually being renewed and changed.

Papier mâché is not the delicate material that the name would imply, and many lasting articles were made from it. However, it does lack the durability of wood and metals, consequently much of it has been destroyed by ill use and bad handling in storage.

There were two basic methods of producing articles from papier mâché. The method known as the French style involved the use of high grade paper pulp, or good quality fibrous paper, the oatmeal-like pulp being poured into a suitably shaped mould which hardened under the influence of a slow heat. The English method of making papier mâché was to paste individual layers of paper together, to form a very strong laminate. The laminate was very suitable for the manufacture of such articles as tables, trays, chairs and other articles requiring some inherent strength.

Although the process of making papier mâché was known in Britain as early as the 1670's, it was not really used for the manufacture of articles in any big way until about 1765. At this time small articles in the French style were being produced for the British market.

Henry Clay of Birmingham, a japanner, probably laid the corner stone for the industry in England in 1772, when he took out a patent for laminated sheets of paper formed by pasting individual sheets together. Being a japanner, Clay's interest in the material was sparked by its suitability for japanning. Japanning, a technique of Eastern origin, is a method of painting wood or metals with grounds of opaque colours in varnish; these ground colours were subsequently covered with several coats of clear japan varnish, requiring stoving to obtain the beautiful surface lustre characteristic of the technique. The problem was to prevent wood, which was one of the common basic materials of the period, from warping or even splitting during the stoving process. The English style of papier mâché overcame this problem, and also presented a hard, smooth surface ideally suited to the application of the pigments.

Clay sold his products under the name of Paper Ware. He used a special sheet of paper which was greenish in colour and resembled blotting paper but was probably a little thicker; the name for this paper was Making paper.

Obviously Clay was very successful with his patented process; so successful, in fact, that he was appointed Japanner-in-Ordinary to the King and the Prince of Wales.

It is surprising to find the number of uses that Henry Clay found for his new material. Apart from the obvious small boxes, tea trays and waiters, he included panels or roofs for coaches, sedan chairs, panels for rooms, and even doors and cabins of ships. By the early part of the 19th century, manufacturing techniques and the materials had improved which made it possible to mould the material without the disadvantages of bubbling, found in the early French techniques of moulding.

C. F. Bielefeld, of London, took out a patent in 1845 that widened the application of papier mâché by using it for internal decoration in conjunction with the architect. The Victorians used the material to produce their period ceilings, in skilful imitation of the conventional plaster of paris mouldings. Specialist manufacturers supplied cornice mouldings, central roses and a great variety of general border designs.

Bronze powders, in several colours, were used for decorating from about 1802. The green bronze with graphited shadowing is a characteristic colour often used for foliage.

Sometime after 1843, stencils were used occasionally for bronze pictorial decoration. Jennens and Betteridge of Birmingham introduced mother-of-pearl into papier mâché wares about 1825, and the best examples of this form of decoration were produced between about 1830 and 1840.

Jennings and Betteridge were also producers of furniture on a large scale, some of which must have been exported to America, because they had, sometimes around 1840, an office in New York.

Some of the names associated with papier mâché decoration are David Sergent, noted for his fern paintings; Edward Haselar and George Neville noted for their flower painting; and Edwin Booth for his high quality Oriental work of the 1830's.

By 1850, papier mâché wares were being produced in America by the Litchfield Manufacturing Co. They produced the usual small boxes, tables, trays and so on, but they were particularly noted for their clock-cases. Although they used a similar process to that employed by Clay, the quality of their finish did not compare favourably with Clay's beautifully smooth japanned finish, despite the fact that they employed artists from England.

155

From a collector's point of view papier mâché is a Victorian product, although it was used in China many centuries ago. It offers the collector of modest means an interesting subject that can satisfy the collecting instinct and at the same time decorate the home. Good pieces will be difficult to find, as many of these have found their way to the United States; they can, however, still be found but may require a diligent search.

PEWTER

16. Pewter

Pewter is a tin based alloy, with minor additions of lead, antimony, copper and bismuth, which are added in small proportions. There have been many varieties of pewter used in the past and it is almost impossible to be certain of the type used for any specific piece.

In general terms, Fine Old pewter had one hundred and twelve parts tin to twenty-six parts copper. Plate pewter had one hundred parts tin, eight parts antimony, four parts copper, and four parts bismuth. Superior pewter had one hundred parts tin and seventeen parts antimony. Ley metal had eighty parts tin and twenty parts lead. It will be seen therefore that the main constituent of pewter is tin, and that very little lead was used.

In 1348, the makers of pewter in Great Britain formed their Guild. One of the objectives of the Guild was to maintain the quality and standard of the metal, since there was a tendency at that time to include lead in the alloy in larger proportions than was necessary or desirable. The use of excessive lead, which could dissolve out of the alloy, provided a risk of lead poisoning to the users.

During the mid-18th century, Britannia metal was introduced, this metal being roughly the same composition of good quality pewter, but less solid and of a thinner section. Articles made from Britannia metal were spun and formed from sheet, unlike the normal process of casting and joining that had previously been the accepted method of producing pewter articles.

English pewter dates back to the 10th century and was used until the 19th century, but it was not until after the Resortation that it came into general use. It was during the middle of the 18th century that the increased wealth of England permitted the houses of the day to replace their wooden utensils with pewter, but from then on, over the best part of a hundred years, pewter became the material for everyday commodities and utensils.

Although pewter was made as early as the 10th century, it is unlikely that a collector will find anything earlier than the 16th century. Such pieces are extremely rare due to many factors, one of which was the practice of trading-in old articles for remelting. It is interesting to note that during the mid-17th century, one could trade-in pewter articles and receive about 15s. per lb, and purchase new articles at only about 15s. 2d. per lb., allowing only 2d. per lb. for remelting, labour and profit (pre-decimalisation, of course).

Fig. 53   Pewter Measure with brass rim marked 'Half Gill', engraved on side 'J. Karfoot' (*Mabel Gohm*).

In 1662 an average pewter plate, 9 inches across, cost about 11d. each, very cheap indeed by present day standards; but as the average wage in those days was only about 7 shillings per week, it must have been quite a luxury item, and explains why the peasants had to be content with their wooden platters.

The majority of available pewter will date from about 1700 to the late 19th century. Most collectors consider English pewter to be the best, with its good proportions and functional designs. Continental pewter is usually more ornate and heavier.

From the second half of the 16th century, pewter was decorated with engraved designs, but in comparison with the engraving on silver, the results were somewhat crude. Because the engraved line was not too effective on the relatively soft pewter, wriggle-work was introduced.

Another method of ornamentation was obtained by the use of steel dies, which were used to impress the metal. For example, the ledges and rims of plates were often decorated, in a repetitive manner, by being struck with either a single punch or by the use of various shaped punches.

Yet another method, employed more by Continental workers than British, was to cast suitable pewter objects like hollow tankards and bowls, and to include the decoration in the mould. The moulding faces were engraved to provide motifs, or decorative design in *intaglio*, which of course, imparted a *relief* impression on the finished product. Articles so decorated, however, are rare.

Pewter was used in churches for alms dishes, alms plates and

158

sacramental vessels. It was used in the dwelling houses to provide basins, bowls, ink-stands, candlesticks, mantle ornaments, snuff boxes, tankards, spoons, plates and flagons. English pewter, as previously stated, derives its appeal mainly from its good proportions and functional design. Decoration played only a minor role in the overall presentation.

TOUCH MARKS

A touch mark in pewter does not carry the same authority as the hall marks used on gold and silver. A true hall mark used on precious metals refers to material quality, and date of manufacture; it does not encompass the design or workmanship. Pewter touchmarks have no special value apart from interest and as a guide to their maker, as they do not refer in any way to the quality of the alloy. In many instances dates will appear in the touches but this will not date the articles; they represent the year of registration with the London Guild and not the year of manufacture. But if we know the approximate date of the death of the manufacturer we can at least obtain the period, i.e. it will be somewhere between the date of registration and the demise of the maker.

Pewterers would sometimes add additional touches resembling hall marks. These were usually four in number which closely resembled those used on silver plate. These bogus hall marks were not supported in law nor by the Pewterers Company.

The 'touch' of pewterers were registered with the Worshipful Company of Pewterers as early as 1550, but unfortunately, the Great Fire of London in 1666 destroyed these records.

Here are a few examples of touch marks:

Thomas King	Two hands supporting an anchor displayed in a large oval with a crown above (1675).
Thomas Deacon	Flaming beacon in a large oval with a moulded rim and palm leaves. (1780).
Adam Tate	Outline of a cross with castle in the middle and the initials A.T. on either side (1747).
Henry Adams	Figures of Adam and Eve.
John Cambridge	Heart surrounding a book with palm leaves (1687).
Robert Nicholson	Eagle on a globe surrounded by palm leaves (1690).
John Barlow	Tulip above a plough. (1698).
Thomas Mathews	Mermaid and six roundels with palm leaves (1711).
Robert Patience	Standing figure of Queen with sceptre (1771).
John Wingod	Square and compass (1748).
Paul Fisher	Fisherman in a boat (1798).

CLEANING

There are many diverse opinions regarding the best method to clean pewter, or even whether it should be cleaned at all. This is a matter for personal taste; if the article is in good condition it will usually be sufficient to wipe it with a soft cloth dipped in paraffin oil, lightly dusted with powdered whiting. The finished sheen can be applied with a chamois leather.

Stains and blotches caused by oxidation can usually be removed by a long soak in domestic paraffin. Badly scaled and pock-marked surfaces may need the actions of an acid, and as most acids are difficult and often dangerous to use, it is better to gain a little experience on the easier methods using modern detergents and chemicals, before resorting to the rather drastic treatment by acids.

However, if the corrosion is heavy and difficult to remove, try using hydrochloric acid diluted two to one with water, and if this does not do the job, try the acid undiluted. After treatment in acid, the surface of the pewter will be dull and will require polishing to bring back the lustre. Badly scaled pewter can first be treated with a fine wire wool. This may cause minor scratches that have to be removed, using a finer abrasive such as rouge or plate powder, or by using the proprietary item, Dura-Glit. Always use plenty of this wool and then polish with a dry cloth before the surface is completely dry.

When starting your collection, the temptation to buy any odd piece of pewter that comes your way will be irresistible, but very soon you will feel the need to specialise.

Here are a few suggestions:

You can choose dishes, chargers, plates or flagons, tankards, beakers or bowls. These articles are known as hollow-ware. If you wish to have a wider choice, collect articles that would normally stand on a table, such as candlesticks, salt-cellars, ink-wells, coasters and so on, or on a broader basis, specialise in household, ecclesiastical or tavern pieces.

There is of course some very fine pewter other than that of English origin. There is Scottish, Flemish, German, French, and American. You could, therefore select the country of origin as a theme for your collection.

GLOSSARY

Akerne: This means acorn-like. Early 15th century spoons were decorated with an acorn-like knob and described in medieval times as 'With an Akerne.'

Alloy: A mixture of metals, usually a base metal, to which has been added a metal of finer quality.

Ampulla: A flask, goblet, or small phial mainly used to hold water or oils for sacred purposes.

Ball and Claw: Describes the shape of a foot displaying a ball held in an eagle's or Lion's talon.

Baluster: This refers to the shape seen in a balustrade; it usually means the graceful swelling central curve, seen in the form of a stem of a candlestick, or the body of a flagon or measure. (Characterised by having a bellied middle.)

Beaker: This is from the old English word 'Biker,' usually a tapered sided, or lipped drinking vessel; describes drinking pots and cups.

Black Metal: Pewter with a greater proportion of lead to tin than is normally found in domestic pewter, generally used for organ pipes.

Booge: The part of a plate or dish between the rim and the base which provides the dished configuration.

Bossed: Dishes with raised centre portions are said to be bossed.

Capstan: In the 17th century and early 18th century, salt-cellars and pewter ink-wells of a late style were made in a conical form with a broad base, resembling that of a ship's capstan. These salt-cellars were known as 'Capstan Salts'.

Cardinal's Hat: One of the earliest forms of a pewter dish usually around 15–16 inches in diameter, resembling an inverted Cardinal's hat.

Cassolette: A perfume burner consisting of a bowl with a pierced lid.

Chargers: Dishes usually larger than 13 inches in diameter.

Chased: Decoration carried out with a lining tool or punch.

Chopin: Derived from the French word 'chopine' meaning a pint. It was used to denote the capacity of Scottish spirit measures.

Coasters: Tray for a decanter or drinking vessel, used to prevent the rough bottom of the bottle scratching the wooden table tops.

Cupping Dish: Dishes used by the surgeons for blood-letting; concentric rings inside the bowl were there to measure the amount of blood released.

Ecuelle: Generally a kitchen or scullery utensil such as a porringer or bowl.

Hammerhead: A low, heavy thumb piece used for balluster measure of the 1690's, not unlike the head of a carpenter's claw hammer.

Haystack or Harvester: A wine and spirit measure made by Irish Pewterers from about 1820. They resemble a circular haystack in shape.

161

Hollow-ware: As the name suggests, articles of capacity such as pots, tankards, and bowls.

Mutchkins: Meaning a little cap. A type of tappit hen, i.e. a Scottish measure smaller than a chopin.

Patina: Patina is the term used to describe the finish of pewter surfaces, either obtained by continual handling, age or by ceaseless rubbing with a soft cloth.

Planish: To flatten and smooth by hammering; the action of hammering also hardened the pewter surface.

Pounce Box: A pewter container, not unlike a modern pepper-pot. This container was used to hold pumice, which was sprinkled onto newly written correspondence to dry the ink.

Pricket: A candlestick terminating in a spike, which fitted into the base of the candle itself.

Quaich: A shallow saucer or bowl with two handles. This vessel was mainly of Scottish origin.

Repousse: Decoration obtained by hammering from the underside of pewter articles, i.e. raised by beating upwards.

Spout Pot: Any pot with a projecting spout.

Tappit-Hen: A type of Scottish measure. Name is derived from the old French word 'Topynett' meaning a quart. Most tappit-hens have bun or domed lids but the Aberdeen type, in common with the Irish Harvester, is lidless.

Touch Plates: Touches, Touch blocks. These were in fact early trade marks, the plates of pewter upon which members of the Guild had to strike their personal touches on admission into their Guild. The touch plates were kept at the Guild Headquarters, and used for tracing makers in the event of their wares being below the Guild Standards.

SILK PICTURES

17. Silk Pictures

Just over 100 years ago the weaving industry in Coventry found itself in the grip of a slump, mainly caused by the importation of foreign goods. Thomas Stevens, who had until this time been a ribbon weaver of world renown, found himself with the possibility of closing down his works. It has been quoted that necessity is the mother of invention, and in this instance it certainly proved to be an apt quotation. Instead of bemoaning his fate, Stevens set about modifying his Jacquard looms for the production of bookmarkers, silk pictures and novelties.

The weaving of bookmarkers was started in 1862, and the silk pictures in 1879. This new venture proved an instant success, and soon Stevens had an overwhelming order book. By virtue of the small size, approximately postcard size or less, the picture could be despatched readily to anywhere in the world by post.

Stevens further promoted his business by attending all the important trade fairs in Britain, Europe, and America. He set up specially converted, transportable looms, and had a few of his weavers producing souvenirs for sale on the spot.

Thomas Stevens died in 1888, but the business continued and was still operating in 1939; unfortunately the outbreak of World War II and the subsequent enemy bombing resulted in the complete destruction of the premises and the plant in 1940.

Stevens bookmarkers were many and varied. A particular series that found great favour in Victorian society were those with birthday and Christmas greetings.

Although the novelties and bookmarks of Thomas Stevens are well worth collecting, it is his pictures that are in the greatest demand. These pictures are known as 'Stevenographs', and they are beautifully woven and brilliantly coloured pictures on silk, mounted on card with a bevelled, rectangular opening to frame them. On the back of the card, Stevens stuck a label which stated that he was the 'Sole Inventor and Manufacturer'. Listed on this label was a range of available subjects, and the price, which was a shilling unframed, and two shillings and sixpence if required in a Gold Oxford frame. This latter price included packing in a box! You will be very lucky today if you find anyone willing to part with a Stevenograph; if you do it will not be cheap, and may not be in an acceptable condition.

163

It is almost impossible to date a Stevenograph with any degree of accuracy. The pictures were produced in the form of a long ribbon, or bolt, and mounted as required by demand. Consequently, the stock of bolts could be stored for many years, causing possible deterioration in the brilliance of colour.

Stevenographs have always interested British collectors, but their appeal now interests American collectors, who have a society devoted to their study. This is not surprising because many of Stevens' pictures contain American subject matter, for example 'W. F. Cody', 'Landing of Columbus', 'Signing of the Declaration of Independence', 'Niagara Falls', 'John L. Sullivan'. The English subjects are more varied, and include bicycle races, horse races, jockeys, railway trains, mail coaches, royalty and a host of sporting subjects.

Approximately one hundred and fifty different subjects have been produced, covering an extremely wide variety, but irrespective of the subject, they are all very worthwhile collectors items.

The safest way of ensuring that you have a Stevenograph is to make certain the trade label is pasted to the back, the name woven into the silk, or printed on the front of the mount.

Thomas Stevens never covered his process with copyright, and like most successful ventures, he had his imitators.

He created his early bookmarks about 1860–1880, a period when ribbons were first mounted for framing. At this time similar ribbon pictures were appearing from the looms of competitors such as Odell and French; Ratcliff and Son; and Willie Grant. The work of these weavers was mainly in black and white, although they did produce occasional colour pictures.

As a general guide to age, the list of advertised subjects on the trade label will give an indication—the fewer subjects listed, the earlier the example.

Like prints, the subject will greatly influence availability and price: early trains, coaching scenes and American subjects will, no doubt, be the most expensive.

PORCELAIN AND POTTERY

18. Porcelain and Pottery

Porcelain is one of the more difficult subjects for new collectors and it is not an easy subject for established collectors. During the 18th century, there were many factories producing a multitude of wares, and separating these into their various manufacturers and periods it is not an easy task unless, of course, the articles are well marked. But even the marks are sometimes unreliable.

The basic composition of a particular porcelain is difficult to establish unless you happen to be a scientist. Even so, the establishment of the porcelain is not in itself sufficient evidence to positively identify a particular factory, for the reason that many manufacturers used identical formulae. So one has to become a porcelain detective and gather evidence of paste, glaze, colour, form and if possible the approximate date of manufacture, and, if *all the evidence points* to a particular maker, then we can be reasonably certain that it is so. It must be remembered that, like today, craftsmen painters responsible for applying the designs were employees of the proprietors, and did not necessarily stay with the same proprietor for all their working life. They changed masters and consequently their work will appear on porcelain articles from more than one factory.

BOW

The Bow factory, situated on the eastern outskirts of London, started production sometime in 1744, or very near that date. It was certainly producing by 1750.

In 1744, Thomas Frye, an Irish painter and engraver, together with his partner E. Heylyn, took out a patent for the manufacture of porcelain using imported clay from America. In 1748 Frye took out a second patent which added bone-ash to the formula. This addition is useful because the resultant phosphoric acid can now be detected by chemical analysis, and the presence of bone ash proved. While this is not conclusive evidence that a particular example came from the Bow factory, it does narrow the field of possibilities to those factories using this material.

Thomas Frye managed the factory until 1759. From 1763 the progress of the factory is a little obscure, but it is known that it was finally acquired by William Duesbury, of Derby, who continued to operate the factory until about 1776, when it was closed finally and the moulds removed to Derby.

The Bow factory specialised in useful wares such as plates and dishes, but not exclusively so; many figures were made also. Not very much is known about the early wares, but an inkwell in the Victoria and Albert Museum decorated with sprays of flowers in the Chinese style is inscribed 'Made at New Canton 1751', which indicates an effort to compete with Eastern importation at that time.

'New Canton' is probably the porcelain produced by a factory started in 1750 by two London merchants, using the Bow patent.

The majority of surviving useful wares are decorated with under-glaze blue.

Transfer painting in russet and a purplish black was employed about 1756 and early colour, up to about 1765, included famille rose and Kakiemon style painting, which was practised extensively. (Kakiemon—named after family of Japanese artists.)

Bow figures have small doll-like heads, receding chins, slight modelling of the cheeks, and upturned noses. They often have floral bocages at the back and they are mounted on a base ornamented by scrolls.

Figures after about 1755 usually have a slightly opaque light blue enamel, with a puce outline on the base scroll work. Although not conclusive, a four footed base indicates the probability that the piece is of Bow origin, but Plymouth also had feet of a similar design.

After about 1760, enamelled examples became more florid, and were marked sometimes with an anchor and dagger, painted in red. Later porcelain became rather chalky, with a less compact texture. Consequently, it was lighter in weight than the earlier examples.

Bow is a soft paste porcelain, cream in colour, with a tendency to stain brown where the glaze had been chipped or worn away, and it occasionally has black specking.

CAUGHLEY

The Caughley pottery near Broseley in Shropshire was, until about 1770, mainly concerned with earthenware products under the management and guidance of Ambrose Gallimore. In the early 1770's, Thomas Turner entered into partnership with Gallimore, with the result that the factory was modified and probably enlarged, for the production of porcelain, or 'Salopian' as it is often termed.

The factory continued in business until 1799, when Thomas

Turner, due to ill health, sold the leases to the owners of the Coalport Porcelain factory. Coalport also acquired the materials, and the engraved plates for transfer printing, and so were able to continue working the pottery. About 1814 the factory was closed, and all the useful paraphernalia of production transferred to the Coalport factory.

The earliest Caughley porcelain was first produced about 1775. The wares were decidedly utilitarian, relatively inexpensive dessert, dinner and tea services, together with a variety of pigs, sauce-boats and so on. They did, however, produce a few ornamental vases, but never aspired to figures.

This early porcelain was, in the main, painted, or printed under the glaze in blue, with designs strongly resembling the Nankin porcelains which, at that time, were in high demand. Other designs in Worcester style floral patterns, also printed with underglaze blue, were included in their catalogue.

There is a decided kinship between some of the designs and shapes of Caughley and Worcester, No doubt this was due to the fact that Thomas Turner, prior to joining Caughley, had been employed by the Worcester factory.

The decoration of Caughley in polychrome is reputed to be the work of Humphrey Chamberlain.

During the productive years of the Caughley porcelain factory, many small individual items were produced for the delight of present day collectors, in addition to the various services. The following are just a few examples of collectable items—eye baths, egg cups, drainers, custard cups, candlesticks, mugs, butter cups and tubs, muffin plates, etc.

When comparing Caughley underglaze blue with the products of Worcester decorated in the same way, it will be found that the colour of Worcester is a very dark blue, whilst that of Caughley has a violet tint.

The commonest Caughley mark is a capital C, often drawn like a Worcester crescent, and the word Salopian sometimes appears as an impressed mark.

CHELSEA

The factory was started about 1743 by Nicholas Sprimont and Charles Gouyn, both of Huguenot ancestry.

The earliest products are the 'Goat and Bee' jugs, some of which have the date, 1745, incised into the base.

It is generally accepted that Chelsea was the first manufactory of porcelain in England, although there is some evidence to indicate

167

that the Bow works could claim the honour. The early products of both works were similar but the quality of Chelsea was finer, and noted for its beautiful clear white glaze.

DERBY

The Derby manufactory under the direction of William Duesbury first produced porcelain in the year 1753, and ceased to operate in 1848.

During William Duesbury's administration, the Derby works acquired the Chelsea, Bow and Longton Hall factories, a fact that can cause some confusion with certain articles.

In the year 1786, William Duesbury died, having built up a very prosperous business, and on his death, his son William took over the

Fig. 54 Fine Coalport Dessert
Service of 18 pieces. *c.* 1830.

management. Unfortunately, he only lived to carry on the business
for 10 years, but just prior to his death, he entered into partnership
with one Michael Kean.

In 1808 William Duesbury, the third, entered the business and
later went into partnership with William Sheffield, his father-in-law.
But this period in the history of Derby was not a very progressive
one, and in 1811 the business was sold to Robert Bloor.

Bloor was a poor administrator and maybe because he found the
strain too much, or was lacking in some other faculty, the Derby
manufacturing continued in a slow decline, resulting in Bloor
becoming mentally sick in 1828. From then onwards he took no
active part; he left the running of the business to his manager
Thomason. But the writing was on the wall, and the plant closed
down in 1848.

Early Derby figures, made between 1756 and 1760, were generally copies of Meissen figures; they had pale colouring, and were well modelled. The later figures made between 1760 and 1770 had stronger colours.

The gilding of Derby porcelain is rich, smooth and generously applied. Canary yellow, a beautiful apple green, and a mazarin blue applied as a ground, or used in wide bands or panels, are typical decorative colours and styles of design to be found in Derby porcelain. The handles were always well designed and will frequently be found in the form of serpents and masks.

The decoration of Derby porcelain was of the highest quality, and the beautiful bird motifs, by the painter Richard Dobson, were exquisite. Other painters employed by Derby were George Robertson, famous for his landscapes, Cuthbert Lawson, a painter of hunting subjects, Thomas Steel, a painter of fruit, and William Pegg who specialised in still life subjects.

DELFTWARE

Delftware is a name so Dutch in flavour that it is surprising to find that Delftware was not originally a product of the Netherlands. It originated in Moorish Spain and Renaissance Italy, travelling on its way through Majorca, where it collected the general description of Maiolica. (The name first used in Italy for the lustred wares of Valencia, now a 19th century English name used to describe lead glazed pottery.)

Delftware was produced in England and in Flanders a considerable time prior to the establishment of the Delft potteries. Guido Andries, a maiolica potter, worked in Antwerp about 1508 and this date is generally accepted as the beginning of maiolica pottery in the southern Netherlands. About 1550 the Antwerp potters moved further north and in 1567 Jasper Andries, either a son or grandson of Guido Andreis, moved to England. This dispersion of maiolica potters resulted in the two schools of pottery known as 'Dutch Delft' and 'English Delftware'. The rise of Delft as a pottery centre dates approximately from 1650, and from this period until the middle of the 18th century, Delft attained its greatest growth, and was in its most prosperous period.

The material of Delftware is not stoneware, porcelain, or china, it is a soft earthenware with a lead glaze that has been made opaque with the addition of oxide of tin, or ashes. Painting the designs on this white, absorbent glaze required deftness and a very confident hand. Once the colour had been applied it sank into the surface with a degree of permanence that made corrections difficult, if not impossible.

The Netherlands improved the basic techniques by covering the painted design with an additional lead glaze which added richness. The whole piece was subsequently fired at a high temperature, to 'set' both glazes simultaneously. Further decoration may then have been added in more delicate colours, and then the piece fired again, but now at a lower temperature. This is, in fact, an enamelling process, and compares with similar techniques used on china, porcelain and opaque glass. Early Netherlands dishes and plates were often tin enamelled on the front face only, the under surface being glazed with a transparent lead glaze, through which could be seen the greeny-yellow clay.

The influx of Chinese porcelain, brought by merchant ships around the Cape into Italy, inspired the Italian potters with their Oriental designs of the Ming dynasty, and the influences of the Near and Middle East. Although obviously affected by these influences they developed their own styles whilst making similar wares.

The marks on Delftware are numerous, though the early marks, which were fewer, have proved to be unreliable. From about 1680 onwards, when the industry began to form larger groups, marking became more predominant and it is believed that these marks are indicative of pottery owners, or lessees of potteries.

Delft pottery was mainly produced in the familiar blue and white throughout the 18th century, the Oriental influence being modified by the drapery of Baroque motives, followed by the profuse ornamentation in Rococo style. Earlier wares copy the cobalt blue decoration used by the Ming potters, because of its suitability for high temperature firing, an important factor in porcelain manufacture.

Delftware was not only produced in blue and white; from the late 17th century it was also produced using copper-green, iron-red and yellow, the latter two colours being somewhat rare, the red being a new colour in European ceramics. These colours required high temperature firing, and were fired in the kiln simultaneously with the tin glaze. From about 1720, the process of enamelling by firing additional colours over the glaze at a low temperature, increased the range of colours by adding greys, opaque blues, pinks and lilac.

English Delftware, as previously stated, started in 1567 with Jasper Andries. He is reputed to have settled in Norwich with a fellow compatriot named Jacob Janson, but not being able to find suitable materials in the vicinity for making his apothecaries' mortars and equipment, tiles and so on, petitioned Elizabeth I for a permit to move his operation to London. This was granted, and in the year

171

1571 the partners were settled in Aldgate. It was not long before Flemish, Dutch and English potters joined the community, to start the centre of English Delftware making.

The earliest tin-glazed earthenware produced at Lambeth is estimated to be about 1665, when John Ariens van Hamme, a Delft potter, established his works there.

Bristol, famous for its glass, was also the home of many kinds of pottery, not excluding Delft, which it is estimated was first produced in the village of Brislington in 1650 by John Bissick and Robert Fleming.

Delftware was made at Liverpool from about 1716 by Alderman Thomas Shaw. Other early Liverpool potters were Zacharial Barnes, Richard Chaffers, the Pennington brothers, and Philip Christian. A well known product of Liverpool was their charpots.

Dutch potters were at one time more concerned with making articles that could be used, rather than exclusively ornamental pieces, such as salt cellars, pepper castors, butter dishes, plates, soup tureens and general tableware.

Ornamental figures and animal pieces of horses, frogs, cocks, hens, parrots and cats have been modelled in Delftware, but generally they lack in quality, probably due to the deficiency of modelling skill of most of the potters.

Tiles constitute one of the main items suitable for collectors. These were used in the Netherlands for walls of kitchens, dairies, fireplaces, wainscotings, and cellars, designed as individual tiles, or with patterns that could be used in continuation. Early tiles were decorated with pomegranates and clusters of grapes, flowers and animals, followed later with vases of flowers.

Tiles were coloured with the typical blue, also green, yellow and orange. Occasionally manganese purple was added. The body colour of early tiles was reddish, but later they became buff and were made much thinner.

Tiles produced during the latter part of the 17th century make ideal collectors' items with their attractively designed sea monsters, ships, views, and figures of fishermen, farmers, tumblers and other groups of figures.

Flower vases, candlesticks, goblets, money boxes, wall pockets, teapots, drug and apothecaries' jars, plates, food-warmers, mugs, puzzle jars, bowls and jugs, and wine-bin lables, have all been made in Delftware.

DOULTON

Doulton ware was made from about 1820 to 1854 under the trade name of 'Doulton and Watts'. Then John Watts retired, and Henry

172

Fig. 55 Doulton salt-glazed stoneware. The biscuit barrel 1879, covered jar *c.* 1892–1899, and the jug 1879 were by Hannah B. Barlow. The vase, 1883, with bird decorations was by Florence E. Barlow (*Doulton & Co. Ltd.*).

Fig. 56 Doulton salt-glazed jugs. (From left to right (1) Designed by George Tinworth, *c.* 1874; (2) Arthur B. Barlow 1873; and George Tinworth., *c.* 1874. The colours of the jugs are browns, cobalt blues and cream (*Doulton & Co. Ltd.*).

Doulton continued under the name of 'Doulton & Co.'. The products under the Watts partnership were mainly industrial and utilitarian, but some stoneware jugs and ornamental bottles were also manufactured.

In 1862, Henry Doulton turned his attention to decorated pottery, but his early attempts were not very successful, however. He employed students from the Lambeth School of Art to decorate his pottery, and exhibited at the South Kensington Exhibition of 1871. From this time onwards, Doulton's new Art Pottery was established.

The Doulton stoneware made at Lambeth was a fine quality, salt-glazed stoneware, and most examples carry the personal mark of the decorator, factory mark, and in many instances, the date of manufacture.

Henry Doulton was one of the first potters to employ female labour on a large scale, recruiting the majority of these artists from students who were studying in the Government design schools. They were permitted to express themselves by practising their own individual styles. This was a very successful venture, and some of the students eventually gained a national reputation.

In addition to salt-glazed stoneware, the Lambeth factory produced tiles and architectural terra-cotta work; these were used for decorative features on buildings and for mantlepieces and hearths. Another interesting feature was used in making 'Chine' ware, the body being patterned whilst still soft by impressing it with a fabric material, which gave the effect of a woven pattern. Other bodies used were named 'Impasto', 'Silicon', 'Carrara', 'Marqueterie' and 'Doulton Faience'.

Faience was introduced about 1873 and was decorated by painting, unlike the stoneware, which was mainly incised or modelled. The production of stoneware at Lambeth was discontinued in March 1956.

Collecting Lambeth-made Doulton provides a relatively inexpensive field for a new collector, and the number of examples available is still sufficiently large to allow some discrimination.

An excellent collection can be formed from examples decorated by one of the many known artists, or by collecting only early pieces.

George Tinworth for example, modelled beautiful figures and the like. Other artists worthy of mention are Hannah E. Barlow, Frank A. Butler, Edith D. Lupton, Frances E. Lee, Louisa E. Edwards, Florence E. Barlow and many others.

GOSS CHINA

Goss china is not strictly an antique, since by general definition an antique is required to be over 100 years old. Goss china is only

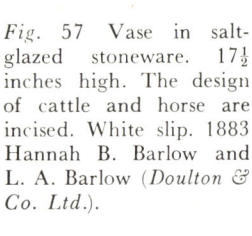

Fig. 57 Vase in salt-glazed stoneware. 17½ inches high. The design of cattle and horse are incised. White slip. 1883 Hannah B. Barlow and L. A. Barlow (*Doulton & Co. Ltd.*).

half this age, but it is fast becoming established as a collectors' item, and no excuse is offered for its inclusion here as a 'young antique'.

This fine quality white porcelain ware was made by William Henry Goss from Stoke-on-Trent, Staffordshire, and decorated with beautiful coloured coats of arms of every English town of importance. Pieces were also produced featuring a few Scottish and Irish towns. These were sold cheaply as souvenirs around the turn of the last century, and were brought back from holidays, or a day at the coast,

Above left. Jug in opaque white glass. Probably mid-Victorian.

Above. Ivory statuette of Fisherman & Son.

Left. A pair of particularly fine Toby Jugs, one with lid. Victorian. (L. Danvers, Isleworth)

Below left. Goss China. Lid of a practical Trinket Box about 4ins. diameter decorated with flags of Great Britain, France, Belgium and Russia.
(David Morley Antiques, Twickenham)

Below. Butter pats and prints.

Above. Chinese mat size 5ft. 2ins. × 2ft. 6ins. with flowers, clouds, bats and show. Bats are good luck symbols the 'show' is the sign for long life. C. 1900.
(Jack Franses of Franses of Piccadilly)

Kashen (Persia) size 5ft. 2ins. × 3ft. 6ins. Traditional floral pattern with medallion. Late, approx. 1950.
(Jack Franses of Franses of Piccadilly)

Persian Tekke 'Bokhara' size 4ft. 0ins. × 5ft. 7ins. Late, approx. 1950
(Jack Franses of Franses of Piccadilly)

Fig. 58 Vase in salt-glazed stoneware. 15½ inches high. The design of cows, horses, and child are incised. White slip. 1881, by Hannah B. Barlow. (*Doulton & Co. Ltd.*).

as presents for friends and family. They ornamented articles such as tiny jugs, spill holders, small vases, ash trays, stud boxes, models of houses, small flat plates, mugs and a host of other smallish items.

Falcon Potteries were started by W. H. Goss in 1858 to manufacture parian holloware, which is a fine grained, waxy feldspathic resembling white marble, mainly for use in the boudoir. These pieces were delicately decorated with floral patterns.

In 1890, Goss developed a variety of porcelain which was ivory in colour, had a waxy sheen and was ideally suited as a base for presenting the coats of arms which were enamelled over the glaze. The credit for the enamelling process goes to Goss's son Adolphus. W. H. Goss made crested china in his early days as a potter, but these were not accepted by the buying public. Probably the crests, originally restricted to public schools and universities, could only be identified personally by a minority.

Genuine Goss porcelain has a quality of its own. Many imitations may be seen in junk shops, market stalls, and even antique shops, but will be found to be of inferior quality. All Goss china bears his mark—a rising falcon; look for this mark before parting with your money.

As a guide to age, from 1891 the trade mark of the falcon had the word 'England' superimposed under it and either 'W. H. Goss' or 'W. H. G.'.

The more valuable pieces of Goss are the larger items, or those depicting two or more coats of arms. It is very reasonable in price, but it will not be long before this relatively new field has claimed the attention of a considerable number of new collectors, and the present 'easy market' will dry up.

MARTIN WARE

Martin ware was produced over a relatively limited period, from 1873 to about 1914, by the four Martin brothers, and although their wares may not rank with some of the more universally known potters for quality, their style and character were so individual that they have now become very collectable items.

The four brothers worked as a team, dividing their labours to suit their individual skills. Their workshop was a studio, and they are considered to be among the earliest of the studio potters.

The team leader was Robert Wallace Martin (1843–1923). Some of his better known works included a series of ornaments in bird forms; these were grotesque caricatures of birds, invariably with large beaks, some of which had removable heads. He also produced other animal forms.

Walter Martin (1859–1912) concentrated on making the large vases, and the production processes of firing and mixing the clay. Edwin Martin (1860–1915) was the artist-decorator, working in relief and incised designs, with floral, fish and seaweed motifs.

Charles Martin (d. 1910) was in charge of their retail shop in Brownlow Street, Holborn, but he also assumed the role of general administrator.

The Martin brothers worked initially in Fulham, then London, and finally in Southall. Their wares were marked by incising the soft clay before firing, with their name, place of manufacture and numbers to denote month and year made.

Martin ware is a salt-glazed stoneware, and the majority is a darkish brown colour. Varied and interesting examples of this unique ware can be seen at Southall Central Library.

MINTON

Minton is a world famous name that immediately suggests fine, elegant, porcelain. It is highly regarded, and the name alone is sufficient to 'hall-mark' it for quality.

Thomas Minton (1765–1836) was an apprentice of Thomas Turner at the Caughley porcelain works, where he trained as an engraver. In 1793 he founded the firm, at Stoke-on-Trent, that was later to become known all over the world. The pottery, however, did not start producing until 1796. Its early examples were of earthenware, usually unmarked, and decorated with blue printed designs in underglazes.

Porcelain production followed after about two years, but the majority of these wares were unmarked, and it was not until about 1805 that the first articles were marked. It is interesting to note that porcelain was not made between about 1817 and 1823.

The early porcelains produced from about 1805 to 1816 were marked with a painted letter 'L', sometimes with a number underneath to indicate the pattern number.

Tea and dessert services, and other fine pieces made at this time, were beautifully decorated with floral patterns by artists Joseph Bancroft, George Hancock, and Thomas Steel.

Identification of Minton porcelain produced during the 1820's and 1830's is extremely difficult for the layman as it was normally unmarked. Factory pattern and design books show the examples produced during this period. They are not normally easily accessible, though a few sample pages have been reproduced in text books.

Between 1820 and 1850, both ornamental and useful wares were produced in literally hundreds of different forms, and decorated in numerous styles. A decorative feature very popular then, and avidly collected now, were floral encrusted pieces. This was a form of embellishment using applied modelled flowers in great profusion, exquisitely coloured. Jugs, vases, and ornamental bottles were popular subjects.

Minton also produced fine quality figures, busts and groups. These were made in glazed and enamel porcelain, and in bisque— unglazed or 'biscuit' porcelain.

179

Collecting antique Minton is expensive, and requires a little expert knowledge, but do not be put off, it is still possible to find later examples at a reasonable price although you may have to search very hard.

PARIAN

Parian ware first appeared in England about 1840, and its development was intended to provide a substitute for Derby 'biscuit' porcelain which was then very expensive, and still is so today. Parian ware was made from a liquid clay, and formed by pouring into moulds. The resultant product was a fine grained, waxy feldspathic porcelain, resembling white parian marble.

Parian was developed in England by Copeland and Minton, and it gained considerable popularity when exhibited at the Crystal Palace during the 1851 Exhibition. It soon became a firm favourite in America for the production of parlour ornaments and busts. Bennington, who first introduced it to America, advertised it in 1852 as 'figures in Parian Marble', but the Americans varied the formula so much, that the examples produced may well be better described as 'biscuit' porcelain, than parian. In Victorian England the new material was an instant success. It provided means of giving miniature 'sculptures' of classical style to a section of the community that otherwise would not have been able to afford such luxuries. Many early examples of statuettes were in fact small reproductions of famous sculptures, but busts of famous people, nymphs, horses, small figures, plaques, vases, ornaments of great variety, and 'useful' ware, in a type of waterproof parian, quickly followed. Although the majority of pieces are snowy white, parian will often be found tinted.

PLYMOUTH

William Cookworthy (1705–1780), a Plymouth chemist, experimented for a number of years to produce a true hard porcelain, and he was finally successful when he discovered the necessary raw materials in Cornwall. He patented his process in 1768, and started a factory at Coxside, Plymouth, Devon.

The early wares were often slightly deformed and decorated in underglaze blue, with Chinese style and floral patterns. The enamelled wares were often decorated with flowers, and bird motifs. Figures, groups of figures, and animal and bird models were included among the early examples.

Plymouth plates, saucers, and even cups, seem to have given this manufactory problems during their early days, because they are indeed rare. Their cup handles are invariably slightly askew, indicating that the cup 'unwound' as it twisted axially during the firing.

Figures are not plentiful, and those that do exist appear to be copies of Bow and Longton. The bases are usually rococo scrolls.

The Plymouth factory only lasted two years. In 1770 Cookworthy removed to Bristol, and established a factory at Castle Green. This new factory was managed by a past associate, Richard Champion, who in 1773 purchased the business.

Under the control of Champion, the quality of the products further improved. Figures of original design, and tablewares, were skilfully made and decorated, but Plymouth porcelain was never really developed to a successful stage. Competition from the many well-established factories did not permit the necessary breathing space, and in 1782 Champion sold the business.

ROCKINGHAM

The pottery at Swinton in Yorkshire was started about 1745 for the manufacture of earthenware, but much of the early examples were unmarked and cannot be identified with any real degree of certainty. Between 1778 and 1806 the pottery went through a phase of changing partnerships, but settled down in 1806 when two of the earlier partners, John and William Brameld, took over the business and operated under the title of 'Brameld and Co.', using an impressed mark 'Brameld'. William died in 1813 and his brother, Thomas, succeeded him.

By 1820 the pottery was a prosperous business with a considerable export trade. But in 1825 they were in serious financial trouble, which resulted in the firm becoming insolvent. The Marquess of Rockingham came to their aid by sponsoring a large sum of money. From this period the Marquess's crest, a griffin, and the name Rockingham were used as marks for 'Rockingham' wares. It was about this time, the early 1820's, that examples in porcelain ware were first made.

The paste from which Rockingham porcelain was produced consisted of bone ash, Cornish stone and china clay from St. Austell and it was in reality a soft paste, but of superb quality and in almost every respect superior to the bone china of the day. It was translucent, hard, and the glaze often shows minute crazing.

Rockingham porcelain was invariably extravagant in design with its pattern of flowers, foliage and so on, and the liberal application of gilding. Ground colours were always beautifully applied and the predominating colours were blue, red and green. If Rockingham is to be recognised for any particular achievement, it must surely be the manufacture of the Royal dessert service for William IV. This service was extremely elaborate in design and a single plate was sold at Sotheby in May 1969 for £340.

Other articles produced were the useful wares, animal models, figures, baskets, ornate vases and beautifully decorated dishes. Figures, groups and busts were also produced in unglazed porcelain.

A guide that may assist the collector, in the absence of a factory mark, is the pattern number. Research has indicated that tea wares are likely to carry a number between 430 and 1565, and where there is a prefix of 2, the probable limit is 100. Dessert services are likely to have a pattern number range from about 430 to about 875.

However, once again, in 1842, the firm found itself in trouble and unable to compete with the more prosperous and commercially-minded Staffordshire and Worcester Potteries, and was finally forced to close.

SEVRES

Sévres, the magic name in porcelain, has almost become a standard reference for elegance, fine workmanship and original design. This French factory was established initially in an abandoned royal palace at Vincennes in 1738.

It was in a favoured position commercially, by virtue of having a monopoly protecting it from competition and giving it exclusive rights to manufacture porcelain. In 1753 it became a Royal factory; a factory mark incorporating the royal cypher was introduced, and the title of the factory became 'La Manufacture Royale de Porcelaine de France'.

In 1756 the factory was re-established at Sévres. Three years later, in 1759, the King acquired a total interest in the company.

The early examples produced at Vincennes were unmarked. They included ice pails, trays and simple forms. Very few figures were made since the paté tendre, or soft paste, did not lend itself readily to moulding in the round or rococo style.

It was not until about 1769, when the necessary clay was found at Limoges, that hard paste porcelain was manufactured. Both hard and soft paste were used concurrently, but the hard paste products were marked with a crown and two crossed 'L's and named 'Porcelaine Royale'.

The decorations of early Sévres products were of an extremely high quality, including the many famous ground colours of turquoise (*bleu celest*), yellow (*jaune jonquille*), pea green, pink (*rose pompadour*), and brilliant blue (*bleu de roi*).

These beautiful coloured grounds were applied leaving panels in which were painted figures, birds and landscapes, framed in rich burnished gold.

Sévres was famous also for its elaborately modelled flowers in porcelain, which were used to form decorative pieces on clocks, candelabra, and many other objects; sometimes they were included on porcelain figures.

Biscuit porcelain, as a material for figures, was used from about 1753. The work of E. M. Falconet, a sculptor who spent nine years at Sévres, is among the best ever produced in the history of the factory.

In 1770 the Sévres factory lost its monopoly, but it is still a flourishing company to this day.

SPODE

Josiah Spode (1733–1797) was once employed by Thomas Whieldon, an early partner of Wedgwood. In 1770 he started the Spode Works at Stoke-on-Trent, making earthenware, often decorated with blue printed patterns underglazed in common with other manufacturers of the times. Excellent basalt ware was also produced which exhibited the fine quality and workmanship associated with Spode.

The majority of the examples of earthenware made from about 1790 had the mark impressed into the body or printed in blue. Josiah's son (1754–1827) who eventually carried on the pottery, added porcelain ware in about 1800 and he is considered to be the inventor of bone china, being the first to use bone ash in his porcelain. Spode's products were always well potted and of a high standard, well decorated and finished with skilful gilding. Up to 1822 Henry Daniel executed most of the enamel painting of Spode porcelain. Daniel later started his own works at Stoke and traded under the name of 'Daniel & Son'.

In 1805 'Stone China' or 'New Stone' was introduced as a cheap substitute for porcelain. Fine tableware was produced in this new material, decorated in patterns of Chinese origin, which were first outlined by means of transfer printing and subsequently coloured by hand. Josiah Spode, the second, died in 1827 and the firm was eventually taken over by the Copelands.

STAFFORDSHIRE POTTERY

Rare examples of Staffordshire pottery figures are now collectors' pieces commanding high prices, but if we turn our attention to the less expensive 'Staffordshire Figures', we enter a field of relatively inexpensive pottery. These figures were intended for the chimney pieces of cottages, not for the china-cabinets of the wealthy. But despite their lowly standing, they represent the sentiment of Victorian folk art, and as such can be fully appreciated.

Whilst the factories of Bow and Chelsea were looking to Europe for their inspiration for their figures, and concentrating on the well-to-do purchaser, the potters engaged on the coarse 'image toys', as these small figures were named by Wedgwood, were in a much less lucrative market and, therefore, could not afford to copy the European styles. Instead they looked at life around them.

Many Staffordshire figures had 'flat backs', meaning that the moulding was not continued at the backs of the figures, where it would not normally be seen. This was an obvious economy to save work on mould making and provided a shape suitable for resting on the chimney corners and mantles. The completely modelled figures such as Jenny Lind, Mrs. Bloomer and similar examples are among the more expensive items.

Many firms were engaged in producing these figures and as the majority were situated in Staffordshire, it has become a general term to describe such wares. They were also made in Liverpool, Leeds, Sunderland, Swansea and Scotland.

The names of such firms are relatively unimportant, and their work was rarely marked; however, Sampson Smith, James Dudson and William Kent, were three of the better known makers who were engaged in making French Poodles, Welsh Sheep Dogs, Spaniels, Greyhounds, and many other items.

Early figures, which were modelled completely (no flat back) were better identified by markings. Ralph Wood Sewer (1715–1772) and Junior (1748–1795) made early Staffordshire figures in pottery to compete with the elegant porcelain of Chelsea, Derby and other factories; these were extremely fine examples, soft coloured, in yellow and green and blue, but unfortunately they are now very rare and expensive.

Thomas Whieldon (1719–1795) who once had Josiah Wedgwood as a junior partner, was another early master potter of note.

The most common Staffordshire item must surely be the Dogs, but figures of Robin Hood, Lord Byron, Soldier Boy, Flute Player, Richard the Third, Shakespeare, Will Watch, Emperor Napoleon, the Lion Slayer, Bag-Pipe Player, Wellington, and Equestrian Dick Turpin, Tom King, General MacDonald, General Kitchener and General Buller are just a few of the varied examples available in sizes from three to about nineteen inches high.

Miniature cottages, churches, summer houses, castles and animals were produced at the same time as the figures and for much the same market.

The miniature buildings were often designed for pastille burning,

Fig. 59 Jug made for the Staffordshire Volunteer Regt., hand painted in multicolours. 1786 (*Josiah Wedgwood & Sons Ltd.*).

which was an aromatic substance burned for cleansing or scenting a room. The smoke issued from the tiny chimney in a most realistic manner, or through detachable perforated lids. There are also cottage money boxes.

There is obviously a great opportunity to specialise if you can afford it—collect early figures and groups; if not, you can make a collection with a theme from any of the following: animals, equestrian figures, military figures, theatrical figures, Royal figures, or even invent a category of your own choice.

Modern reproductions of some of the most desirable pieces were

185

Fig. 60 Tureen, stand and cover, in cream coloured Queen's Ware. Shape No. 2 from Josiah Wedgwood's catalogue of 1774. (*Josiah Wedgwood & Sons Ltd.*).

inevitable, and certain well known figures, such as Shakespearian characters, have been reproduced, often from original moulds. Recognition of such pieces is not difficult if you have handled sufficient 'right' ones; look for glaze, colour, and the 'feel' of the piece. Weight is not an important factor, as some manufacturers seemed to have produced light-weight figures, while others preferred to make them heavier.

WEDGWOOD

Josiah Wedgwood, England's most famous master potter, was born in 1730. He was christened at Burslem on the 12th July, 1730, the youngest son of Thomas and Mary Wedgwood of the Churchyard Pottery. Josiah was the twelfth child of this marriage.

Thomas Wedgwood, the father of Josiah, died in 1739, leaving the

186

Fig. 61 Right: Teapot and cover. Queen's Ware. Hand painted in enamel colours. Painted at Chelsea. *c.* 1773. Height 5⅜ inches. Left: Teapot and cover, Queen's Ware. Hand painted in enamel colours. Painted at Chelsea *c.* 1773. Height 5 inches. Both lent by Mr. G. Duff-Dunbar (*Josiah Wedgwood & Sons Ltd.*).

Churchyard Pottery to his eldest son Thomas. Josiah was then put to work in the family business under the control of his brother, and was apprenticed to him for a period of five years from 11th November, 1744. (The indentures of his apprenticeship can be seen in the Hanley Museum).

On completion of his apprenticeship, Josiah left the family business and went into partnership with a potter named Harrison, who had a works at Cliff Bank.

This partnership only lasted a few years, and in 1754 he entered into a partnership with Thomas Whieldon, of Fenton, the most famous Staffordshire potter of the time, who was noted for his technical skill and knowledge of the trade. At this time Whieldon was making pottery of outstanding quality, including the mottled, agate and marbled stonewares, and the black and coloured glaze earthenware.

Josiah Wedgwood's independent career can be said to have started from the early part of 1759, when at the age of 29, he left Whieldon and leased a part of his cousin's works, known as the Ivy House Pottery. Wedgwood was a ceaseless experimenter, and one of his many early inventions—the famous green glaze—was developed soon after his arrival at the Ivy House Potteries. This green glaze was used on many wares including covered sugar basins and tea-pots, often with gilded mottled springs.

About 1763, Wedgwood was producing a great variety of table-ware and pottery known as ordinary 'Dry Bodies'; that is, pottery with its outer surfaces left unglazed. A speciality of Wedgwood's Dry Bodies was the red terra-cotta or Rosso Antico. Teapots were produced in terra-cotta with white stoneware reliefs, and punch kettles with louped and mottled designs to imitate basket work. Terra-cotta pottery was not a new innovation of Wedgwood's, but in his hands it took on a new freshness, elegance, and precision.

From the early 18th century, Staffordshire potters had been experimenting to obtain a white or light coloured earthenware, to compete with the tin enamelled faience produced in Europe and in oriental porcelains, so highly esteemed by the well-to-do. By about 1765 Wedgwood had perfected a cream ware for plates, dishes, tureens, sauce-boats, cups and saucers, jugs, teapots and general tableware. This very practical 'useful ware' gained Wedgwood royal patronage, and from then on this cream ware was known as 'Queen's Ware'.

The black basalt, or black Egyptian, was used by Wedgwood for vases, candlesticks, busts, and many other ornamental objects. The material was a dense fine grain stoneware, coloured by the addition of clay ironstone and magnesium ore. This mixture, when fired, pro-

188

Fig. 62 Teapot in Black basalt, thrown and engine turned, the knop is in the form of a lion. Height 4½ inches. 1780. The cup and saucer is also in Black basalt decorated in red and white encaustic colours. Height 2½ inches. 1778. *(Josiah Wedgwood & Sons Ltd.)*.

duced a hard, dense stone capable of taking a high polish or engraving as would an agate or blood stone.

Vases and similar articles were often decorated by Wedgwood in encaustic colours. This was a process by which gold was attached to the surface of the black basalt or other dry bodies using japanner's size as an adhesive.

Examples of this type of decoration are now rare, the gold most probably having been worn away with the passage of time.

In 1768 Wedgwood was introduced to a merchant named Thomas Bently. Bently was a well educated man, much travelled, and very much interested in the revival of classic styles. The interest in these styles no doubt largely resulted from the works of art found in the diggings of Pompeii and Herculaneum. Wedgwood and Bently

189

Fig. 63 Early bone china pieces. The teapot has a hand painted landscape. The cup and saucer are the Chinese Tigers pattern, printed and enamelled. The right-hand cup and saucer are designed 'China embossed, gold edge', No. 694. All made between 1812 and 1822. (*Josiah Wedgwood & Sons Ltd.*).

became firm friends, and business partners. They built a new pottery just outside Burslem, a house for the master, and an entire village for the workers. This village was named Etruria. The pottery operated until about 1950, when it was removed to Barlaston, just outside Stoke.

About this time, Wedgwood was producing cane coloured pie dishes in several sizes and generally ornamented with modelled leaves and berries. Other examples were made without ornamentation, except those with crimped edges resembling the rim of a pie.

Josiah Wedgwood required a white stone ware of infinite fineness, capable of being tinted, and hard enough to be polished, so that he could manufacture the reproductions of the 'Greco-Roman' gems of polished stone or coloured glass. He experimented with every kind of likely white material that he could obtain. About 1773 and 1774 he tried hundreds of different combinations using different clays and earths in an endeavour to perfect the whiteness, and reliability during firing, of the glossy white stone ware, or white porcelain bisket.

Wedgwood's tenacity was eventually rewarded, and the answer lay in a sulphate of beryllium associated with lead ore mined in Derbyshire. By 1775 he was producing a fine white terra-cotta. This was a material with a smooth waxy surface, on which cameos were made in relief and closely resembled ivory carvings. The ground was often coloured by hand. It was not, however, the Jasper ware that we know today; this was to come a little later with a mixture of sulphate of beryllium 59 parts, clay 29 parts, flint 10 parts, and carbonate of beryllium 2 parts. Wedgwood found that this porcelain-like material could be uniformly stained by using the ordinary mineral oxides which were generally used in colouring pottery to the various tones of lilac, blue, green and yellow as well as to an intense black. Wedgwood's Jasper was now an accomplished fact.

Although Wedgwood blue ground colour may be the most common, it was produced in a number of other distinct tints, each of which may occur in several different shades. Ground colours vary from a dark, almost indigo, blue through several distinct shades to a pale lavender blue. There are several shades of sage green, and an olive green which ranges from a dark to a lighter shade, this latter colouration being more rare. One other green tending towards blue was also used. The black of Jasper ware was a deep, rich, full black and was used extensively for the reproduction of decorated vases; these beautiful examples had the black body decorated with a relief in white Jasper.

Bently died in November 1780, and was buried at Chiswick on 2nd December, 1780. With the loss of Bently, Josiah Wedgwood carried on the business on his own account for a year and then, on

191

Fig. 64   The Portland Vase. This vase, now in the British Museum, was probably made about A.D. 50, possibly in Alexandria by Greek glassmakers. The reproduction by Wedgwood shown here was made in Jasper and it is one of the ceramic achievements of all time. Since 1878 the Portland Vase has been the registered trade mark of Josiah Wedgwood & Sons Ltd. (*Josiah Wedgwood & Sons Ltd.*).

Beluche prayer rug size 4ft. 9ins. × 2ft. 9ins.
c. 1900.
(Jack Franses of Franses of Piccadilly)

Below. Kurdish Rug. Size 6ft. 4 ins. × 4ft. 1in. Tribal Rug, mainly
undyed natural wools. Geometric pattern including rather delightful
characters (maybe the Weaver's family) of little men and women, dogs,
two birds with legs in the air, and combs of cleanliness. c. 1900.
(Jack Franses of Franses of Piccadilly)

...rbent (Caucasus) size 6ft. oins.
...4ft. 3ins. Typical geometric
...ucasian design. Late, approx. 1950.
...ack Franses of Franses of Piccadilly)

Above. An interesting group of eight figures Nymhenburg c. 1840.
(L. Danvers, Isleworth)

Below. Two fine plates with original willow pattern. Marked 'Booth's Real Old Walow' c. 1850. (L. Danvers, Isleworth)

Above. Three figures, Satzendorf, c. 1930. These are too late to be classified 'antique' but they have been included as antique of the future.
(L. Danvers, Isleworth)

Right. Three Victoria figures, unmarked but of excellent quality. (L. Danvers, Isleworth)

Below. Miniature of a Georgian gentleman. Size of painting 1½ ins. diameter. Signed A. G. dated 1797. Circular frame black japanned. (David Morley Antiques)

18th January, 1790, Wedgwood's three sons John, Josiah and Thomas and his nephew Thomas Byreley were taken into partnership. The title of the company now became 'Josiah Wedgwood, Sons and Byreley'.

Wedgwood's most famous antique reproduction is undoubtedly the Portland Vase. The original of this vase was a Greco-Roman work in glass found in a sepulchre mound a few miles outside of Rome. The vase was enshrined in a marble sarcophagus. The Duke of Portland bought the vase after his wife's death in 1785, and loaned it to Wedgwood so that he could copy it. Examples of the Wedgwood reproduction of the Portland Vase can be seen in the Victoria and Albert Museum.

One of the most eventful and exciting chapters in the history of Wedgwood came to a close on 3rd January, 1795, when Josiah Wedgwood died. It was, however, only the end of a chapter and not the end of the story. The descendants of Wedgwood are maintaining their high standard synonymous with Wedgwood in their new factory at Barlaston.

JASPER WARE

The Jasper ware so beloved by the collector owes its appeal mainly to the relief decoration. These decorations are still made today in much the same way that Wedgwood made them nearly 200 years ago. The beautiful little reliefs, irrespective of their design, were first produced in oak moulds. These moulds had the designs in intaglio, that is, the design was sunken below the surface. Clay of the same composition as the piece to which the decoration was to be added, was then formed by pressing into the mould. The clay moulding was then carefully removed from the mould and applied to the surface of the article by moistening with water. Both the clay of the moulding and the article were at this stage a slaty grey; it was only during the firing process that the colouring oxides became effective, the stained ground taking on one of the famous colours, and the relief becoming outstandingly white.

The high quality of Wedgwood's early reliefs was obtained by further handwork after they left the mould. The moulds had to be designed in such a way that the clay pressed into them could be removed easily; therefore, it was not possible to have any undercutting. Where this was required, skilled workmen were employed to hand finish the little mouldings by accentuating certain lines, and rounding off projections.

The quality of undercutting and finishing is one of the tests for early pieces.

Fig. 65 Vases with covers. L.H. 'Sacrifice to Ceres' in Jasper, white on black. Height 10½ inches. 1790. R.H. 'Chariot of Venus', also in Jasper, white on black. Thrown and turned with scroll handles. Height 12 inches. 1790. Both have applied acanthus leaves and carry the marking 'Wedgwood'. (*Josiah Wedgwood & Sons Ltd.*).

Fig. 66 Early morning teaset, comprising teapot with cover, sugar box with cover, cream jug, cup and saucer and tray. The scenes depict 'Domestic Employment', designed by Lady Templeton and modelled by William Hackwood in 1783. White on blue Jasper. Height 4 inches. 1784 (*Josiah Wedgwood & Sons Ltd.*).

TABLEWARE

Jasper ware tea and coffee sets were produced by Wedgwood with the same degree of attention that was lavished on all his work. It is unlikely that a new collector will be able to buy a complete, early tea or coffee set even if he had the money, such is the demand today for early Wedgwood. Tea and coffee pots could form the basis of the original collection, and then other pieces added as the opportunities arise. Even an odd cup in Jasper ware is an object of beauty, and will not look out of place among your other items of Wedgwood because the saucer is missing. There are many types of Jasper jugs ranging from fairly squat, rotund vessels to the severely upright, with

195

or without covered tops. Your tableware collection can be extended with tea caddies, preserve jars, butter luggers, and sugar bowls, not forgetting the biscuit barrel. All these items of tableware have been made in the typical blue and green Jasper colours, decorated with white Jasper reliefs.

There are also a considerable number of little boxes that were originally designed for the toilet table. Oblong boxes were made completely in Jasper ware, and in other materials such as ivory and wood with inset cameos of Jasper. Dainty and attractive powder boxes were made in tortoise shell and inlaid with Jasper cameos.

Scent or smelling bottles can be obtained in numerous shapes and sizes, and in every colour of Jasper ware. More unusual scent bottles were made in cut glass, with cameos or medallions set into the sides. The more exotic examples of cameos have always been popular in jewellery. They have been made into brooches, clasps, buckles, and lockets hung from a chain around the neck. Other collectable items of jewellery will include cameo rings, scarf and hat pins, and cloak and hair pins.

PLAQUES

Jasper ware plaques are interesting collectors' items. They will often be seen framed and hung on walls, or in collectors' cabinets. These plaques were not intended as an end product in themselves, but were in fact ornamental pieces designed as furniture fittings. These plaques, either round, oval or rectangular, were used either singly or in combination for fireplace surrounds, window shutter decorations, and were inset into chests of drawers, cabinets, book cases, tables, clocks and ink stands. This is by no means an extensive list of the uses found for this most versatile and attractive form of applied decoration.

Vases, urns, and bowls were Wedgwood's pride and joy and are probably sought after by collectors more than any other item of Jasper ware. Very early vases and urns will be well out of the reach of a new collector; they will already be in the possession of a Museum, or a wealthy collector. However, it still may be possible to obtain relatively late examples.

WORCESTER

Although the Worcester factory was founded in 1751, it is unlikely that anything was produced until 1752, when the Bristol factory was acquired. Dr. John Wall, a well known physician, became an important partner, and the period 1751 to 1783 became known as the 'Dr.

Fig. 67   Worcester Jug. 'May Day'. Design printed and tinted over the glaze. (*Worcester Royal Porcelain Co. Ltd.*).

Fig. 68 Worcester Vase and cover painted with onglaze 'dry blue' colours. Worcester First Period *c.* 1765 (*Worcester Royal Porcelain Co. Ltd.*).

Wall Period'. The administration of the actual pottery was under the control of William Davis, another partner. The manufacture of Worcester porcelain incorporated soapstone in the formula, and during the Dr. Wall Period, the porcelain was a greyish colour, but had a greenish tint when viewed by transmitted light.

The glaze was a hard thin coating that had a tendency to shrink away from the foot rim of cups, plates and similar articles, which left a dry, unglazed ring where it had shrunk away.

Early pieces of Worcester were almost indistinguishable from the Bristol examples, including the decoration in underglaze blue, and the more elaborate examples painted in polychrome enamels, depicting Chinese figures with flower and animal backgrounds.

By about 1760, the pottery was producing examples decorated with European figure and landscape subjects executed in a fine, black line. Transfer printing over the glaze was a technique much used from about 1756, incorporating black, lilac and a brick red colouring. By 1770 the decoration of Worcester porcelain became more elaborate, and more like Sévres in style. No doubt, this work was probably executed by Chelsea artists, who moved to Worcester at that time.

Vases, bowls, and other suitable wares, were decorated with beautifully coloured backgrounds, surrounding inset panels, with figures and exotic birds. The most common background colour was an underglaze blue, a popular variation of which was known as 'Scale Blue'. The effect was obtained by painting or 'wiping out' the coloured areas to simulate the scales on a fish. The scale designs were used with overglazed colours in yellow, pink, red and purple, but these are very rare.

Plain, rich coloured grounds painted in sky blue, pink, purple and apple green are also rare. A peculiarity of the apple green was its rejection of gilding, so gilt decorations were always added in close proximity to the ground colour and not over it.

Only a few figure and animal pieces were made, and these also are extremely rare.

In 1783, the Dr. Wall Period ended, and the firm was sold to Thomas Flight. New designs in neo-classic styles were introduced, with fluted forms and Grecian motifs. The central medallion with inset pictures of classical figures and landscapes was much featured.

Flight had purchased the company for his two sons, and when one died in 1791 the surviving brother went into partnership with Martin Barr. Various other changes in partnerships and combines finally resulted in the forming of the Royal Worcester Porcelain Company, in 1862, which is still operating today.

199

Fig. 69 Worcester Plate, part of the Lady Mary Worthley Montague service with blue scale ground (*Worcester Royal Porcelain Co. Ltd.*).

TESTING

Should you wish to test any piece of porcelain for the presence of phosphates, say Bow, for example which should have a positive reaction irrespective of the period, this can be done by subjecting the example to a phosphate test.

First select an area that is free from glaze, usually part of the base,

200

or remove a little of the glaze with a carborundum stone from a part that will not show. Apply a drop of hydrofluoric acid with a wax taper to the cleaned spot, and leave for five minutes. Then wash the spot with clean water and collect the water. A small syringe, similar to those used by doctors for ears, or the small plastic industrial syringe, are ideal for the job. The collected water should then be put into a test tube already containing a small quantity of warmed ammonium molybdate in nitric acid. The presence of phosphates are indicated by a yellow precipitate.

Hydrofluoric acid does give off fumes, and it will also attack glass, so it must be supplied and stored in non-vitreous containers and kept in a safe place away from children.

Once the test has been carried out, thoroughly wash the specimen porcelain in running water to remove all traces of the acid.

POT LIDS

The idea of product marketing by using attractive packaging is not a new one. The 19th century had its share of 'marketing managers', and these have provided an item for modern collectors, namely the pot lid.

The jars for which the pot lids were designed were made to contain a variety of substances, such as meat pastes, pickles, pomades, creams, bear grease, and a host of other such products.

Between 1830 and 1840 a considerable number of different types of pots were being made, and decorated by hand painting, or single colour printed patterns. Earthenware lids were produced a little later, by using a multi-colour print, which was applied by a mechanical process under the glaze.

The printed pattern was applied by transferring each colour from separately engraved plates by the use of transfer paper. This was a very skilful operation, requiring each transfer to be accurately superimposed on the impression previously printed. As an aid to this operation, registration dots, or small circles, were printed on each side of the decoration. Most pot lids carry these marks.

Pot lids are generally known as 'Pratt' after the Staffordshire pottery firm of F. & R. Pratt, and it was this firm that produced the majority of these items. In 1847 Felix Pratt took out a patent which 'productionised' his pot manufacture. This invention took the form of a double gauge to be used in conjunction with the throwing wheel, and it is presumed that the gauges were used to form both the inner and outer surfaces of the pot.

Many pot lids owe their attractiveness to the skill of Jessie Austin, artist and engraver, and a one-time employee of Pratt. His signature

201

Fig. 70 Pot Lid. 5¼ inches in diameter, showing 'The Grand International Building of 1851 (*Loco Antiques*).

will appear on many of the best examples of multi-coloured printed patterns.

There are a great number of different types of pot lids, and it is suggested that the collector should initially concentrate his efforts on items contained in a specific category. Suggested categories are figures, portraits, landscapes, animals and birds, flower subjects, historical pictures, or lids carrying the name of the vendor, or even naming the contents.

Collectors are not usually recommended to accept damaged or faulty examples, irrespective of the price at which these are offered.

Potential pot lid collectors should refer to H. G. Clark's *The Pictorial Pot Lid Book*. An edition was published in 1960, which describes many types.

GLOSSARY

Agate Ware: Wares made to imitate the agate. The effect was obtained by mixing different coloured clays, in which case the colours go right through the body. Another means of achieving the same result was to apply clays coloured on the surface of otherwise plain pottery.

Bamboo-Ware: A type of stoneware similar to the caneware invented by Josiah Wedgwood, but slightly darker in tint.

Basalts: Fine quality black stoneware made famous by Josiah Wedgwood.

Bellarmine: Large stoneware bottle named after Cardinal Bellarmine. Decorated with a bearded mask in relief.

Bisket: Unglazed porcelain.

Black Egyptian: An unglazed black stoneware, Wedgwood's basalts.

Bocage: A flower and foliage background, usually associated with figures and groups.

Body: The potter's clay, the material from which pottery or stoneware is made.

Bone China: So named because white ashes of bone were used in this type of porcelain.

Cane-Ware: Fine unglazed buff stoneware.

Cauliflower-Ware: Glazed earthenware often in the form of cauliflowers and pineapples, etc., coloured green and yellow. One of Wedgwood's products.

Celadon Wares: Wares with feldspathic glaze of a pale grey or blue-green tone.

China-Clay: Fine porcelain clay chiefly produced from feldspar, also known as kaolin.

China-Stones: A crystallised mineral comprising silicates of aluminium with varying proportions of potash, lime or soda, decomposed granite, used with china clay to produce porcelain.

Chinoiserie: Exotic and elaborate decoration depicting Chinese figures, encompassed by flowers, birds and animals, often highly coloured, including gold and silver.

Cloisonné Ware: Enamel metal on which the design is made by thin metal strips. The enamelled colours are contained within.

Combed Slip: Marbled or feathered effect obtained by brushing together two or more different coloured wet slips.

Crazing: Reticulation of the glaze causing minute cracks to appear on the surface. Caused by differential shrinkage of body and glaze.

Creamware: A lead glaze earthenware made of pale coloured clay, usually containing calcined flint.

Enamel: A means of decorating porcelain in vitreous colours, which fuse upon the glazed surface. On soft paste porcelain the enamels are absorbed into the fusible lead glaze, but on hard paste porcelain this does not occur.

Encaustic Painting: An ancient style of decorative art consisting of painting on heated wax. Wedgwood was granted a patent in 1769 for a very similar process involving the decoration of porcelain with encaustic gold bands. It was used by him to decorate some of his early wares in imitation of ancient Greek ware.

Faience: A loosely applied term for all kinds of white pottery.

Famille Rose: A class of enamelled wares characteristic of the reigns of Yung Cheng and Ch'ien Lung; named after the rose colour introduced from Europe.

Glaze: There are many types of glazes, but they are all designed to impart a shiny coating to porcelain which makes them proof against liquids. Glazes can be made opaque, coloured or translucent, depending upon their purpose.

Feldspathic Glaze: Glazes containing feldspar.

Hard Paste: The component materials of porcelain are china clay and china stone, presenting a very hard porcelain when glazed.

Imari: Japanese porcelain decorated in underglaze iron red, blue and gold. The name is derived from a port in Japan of the same name.

Impasto: A thick application of colour which makes the design stand out away from the ground.

Jasper-Ware: A fine grain unglazed stoneware perfected by Wedgwood (see text).

Maiolica: A 19th century English name used to describe lead-glazed pottery of 16th century French style (see Delftware).

Marble Ware: See Agate ware.

Moucha Ware: Made from about 1775 until 1914, the name was derived from Moucha Quartz. A form of decoration with coloured bands into which fern-like motifs have been superimposed.

Parian: A marble-like feldspathic porcelain (see text).

Porcelain: The finest kind of earthenware—white glazed and semi-translucent.

Pottery: Usually refers to earthenware fired at low temperatures. Stoneware and porcelain require very high temperatures by comparison.

Red Ware: Made of red clay pottery.

Registry Mark: See tables at end of book.

Salt-glazed Stoneware: A method of glazing stoneware by throwing common salt into the kiln when it reaches its highest temperature.

Slip: Clay reduced by water to a creamy consistency. Normally used to form decorations or to completely coat with another colour (see Combed Slip).

Soft-Paste: A porcelain made from white clay and soap stone, bone ash or some other material. Not a true porcelain.

Tin Glaze: Basically a lead glaze that has been made opaque by adding tin ashes.

Underglaze Decorations: As the name implies, the decoration was applied before glazing.

19. Antique Prints

Experience gained by actual handling, and critical, visual examination is the only way to familiarise the beginner with antique prints. Obviously, print-sellers will not take kindly to customers who handle every print in the shop and then walk out, but they usually do not mind you looking. If you do handle the odd print, please do so carefully, and never wear gloves. It is surprising how easy it is to transfer dirt and grime from gloves; that is why some print-sellers cover their smaller prints in a clear plastic cover.

Do not overlook the museums, as they often have a large collection. The Curators are usually only too pleased to show a specific print, but do not expect them to let you browse.

Now to the purpose of the collection. It is pointless to collect haphazardly; the scope for print collecting is limitless and the new collector is sure to find a subject that is of particular interest and one in which he would like to specialise. Here are a few suggestions to indicate the possibilities: a particular school or period; a method of engraving; a class of print such as portraiture of fashion; original work only where the print is by and after the same artist or the painter-etcher; or simply take a subject such as topographical views, military, marine, decorative, religious, coaching, racing, games, animals, general sporting and general transport.

Now we come to the matter of buying prints. Ultimately, experience will guide the collector, and of course, there is really no other way, but a few fundamental checks can be made. Examine the impression for signs of wear on the plate, manifest by the lightening or complete disappearance of the more delicate lines; check that the margins are reasonable to ensure that the picture area is complete. If an old print has a particularly good wide margin, it is possible that this may be false. A false margin is nothing more than a paper frame into which the print has been carefully inlaid. To ensure an immaculate fit, the print and frame aperture were cut simultaneously. Obviously it would be nice to insist that every print added to a collection had the full and original margins, but to do this would exclude many otherwise desirable prints. Check the paper, handle it, feel it, hold it up to the light for signs of a watermark, and endeavour to determine if the paper is as old as it pretends. Even if you are unable to do this, the examination will give you experience, which if continually practised, will eventually lead to you 'knowing old paper'.

Today, many fine prints offered for sale have been repaired in some way, such as patches of paper pasted behind tears, and in some instances, the actual print is so badly torn that it is only a backing paper or board that holds the print together. Holes in the paper may well have been repaired by inlaying patches of paper and the lost parts of the engraving added by clever pen work.

Colouring is an important consideration. Ideally, prints with original colour are far more desirable than those coloured by modern colourists. However, the majority of coloured prints available will, in fact, have been coloured comparatively recently. Providing the work has been competently and sympathetically executed, there is no reason why they should be rejected, but many of the smaller book plates offered in gift shops, book-shops etc., for the popular trade, are more often than not coloured by amateurs for the general public and not for discerning collectors. Whilst examining the print for colour, turn it over and examine the back for traces of colour penetration; if this is evident it means the print was inadequately sized before the colour was applied, and is a sure sign of amateurism.

It must not be assumed from the foregoing that only prints in their perfect, original state are worth collecting; if we did implement such a limitation, our collection would be a very small one indeed. Very old prints may well only have a $\frac{1}{8}$ inch margin—the result of earlier trimmings, but providing the picture, title, and any other information is still intact, the beauty of the print is in no way lost. Even minor tears, providing they have been repaired well, need not eliminate an otherwise desirable print, and who knows, you may be able to replace such a print with a better copy in the course of time. The standard of any collection must be set by the collector's personal taste and the financial resources at his disposal.

Now, how much should be spent on a print? How can a beginner know the value of a print? Sorry, there is no specific rule; current demand, rarity, fashion, and condition all influence the final price. Some prints that commanded a few hundred pounds 50 years ago can now be bought for a few pounds, and similarly, the reverse applies. For example, the book containing the small book-plates of Shepherds Views of London (2 vols) could be bought for as little as £6 only 10 years ago, but today you will be lucky to buy a copy for £85.

Do not spend a lot of money until you are reasonably sure of yourself. A lot of interest and knowledge can be gained from prints costing only pence, and if you make a mistake, it will not put you in the hands of the Receiver. Prints of low value can also be used for practice should you wish to try your hand at restoration. A final word concerning prices: sale room catalogues are a good indicator of the prices being paid for good quality prints, but remember that the trade also visits sale rooms, and the retail value could be well in excess of the prices paid at auctions. A better barometer can be obtained from catalogues issued by the various print-sellers and some antiquarian book dealers.

Prints purchased solely for investment will have to be chosen most carefully, for although it is true that selected prints or maps will undoubtedly increase in value, if financial gain is the only motive for collecting, then their real value, in terms of pleasure and appreciation, will be lost. There are many other better ways to invest capital for profit, although there is no reason why one should not collect prudently with an eye to the future.

Good quality prints with reasonable margins, a good clear impression, and no repairs will always command a better price than prints of a lower quality. Early state Speed's maps are a sound investment and so are the maps of Saxton, Jansson, Ortelius etc. Good quality ship portraits, T. S. Boys London Views, original Goulds Birds, etc., are all sound investments providing they are purchased in the first instance at a reasonable price.

METHODS OF ENGRAVING

Prints and maps, as stated earlier, provide one of the most rewarding fields for collectors who have an interest in art and craftsmanship, together with a taste for antiquity. Apart from their obvious craftsmanship and artistic merit, prints also provide historical records of a vast and varied range of subjects. Unlike collections of more bulky antiques, they can be stored very satisfactorily in portfolios which require very little space, and a few selected and well-loved examples can be framed and used to enhance the walls of any room, irrespective of the general decor.

Prints, like most of man's achievements, have passed through many stages of development, resulting in a variety of styles and methods of reproduction. Early prints were made from wood blocks, followed by copper, and later steel. The quality of engraving naturally was totally dependent upon the skill of the engraver, and to a lesser extent, the artistic merit of the picture being reproduced. The fact that a print is old makes it interesting, but not necessarily an item worthy of being included in a collection.

More often than not, prints were produced by an engraver from paintings or drawings by well known artists, but this was not an invariable rule. There are many beautiful examples of prints where the painting and engraving were both executed by the artist.

The majority of prints available to the collector will be those of the seventeenth and eighteenth century, and it will greatly assist and increase our appreciation of prints if first we learn how to recognise the various styles and at the same time learn something about the techniques employed in print making.

WOOD BLOCK

The wood engraver first prepared a suitable block of wood of the appropriate size, by smoothing both faces flat. The design was then drawn on the block with ink or brush, and with the aid of a knife or graver, the engraver proceeded to remove all the wood not marked in ink to a depth of about $\frac{1}{16}$ inch or more, leaving the drawn design standing in relief.

To produce the print, an ink-coated roller was rubbed over the block, so that only the raised design accepted a coat of ink. The paper was then laid on the block and manually rubbed on the back, thus transferring the impression in reverse.

Later woodcuts were made by actually incising the design into the wood with a graver. After inking, the block face had to be cleaned to leave the ink in the engraved channels only. This method required greater pressure to transfer a good impression onto paper.

Early wood blocks were made from relatively thin wood, pear, apple, lime, and other soft woods being the most commonly used. Later blocks were made of boxwood, and thicker in section.

Because the wood blocks did not wear particularly well, it was not possible to obtain very many high quality impressions, and as the life of the block was very limited, so were the total number of good impressions limited from any single block.

LINE ENGRAVING

The block consisted of a sheet of copper, thick enough to be rigid when taking impressions ($\frac{1}{8}$ inch approximately) and flat. The outline of the subject to be produced was first traced on the copper. Then with a burin or graver, which was a triangular tool with a handle that fits snugly into the palm of the hand, the engraver guided this tool with forefinger and thumb along the traced outline, at the same time varying the pressure to cut a groove of varying depths into the metal, to form either a coarse or fine line on the finished impression.

Until about 1820, copper was invariably the metal used for line engravings, although occasionally brass, zinc, iron and even silver were used. From 1820 onwards, copper slowly lost its popularity in favour of steel. Steel, being a harder metal, yielded a greater number of impressions before deterioration of the image.

ETCHING

The engraver first prepared a copper plate with a thin film of wax ground. Then with a needle or similar pointed tool, he proceeded to draw the subject on the wax with sufficient pressure to expose the bare metal underneath. The next step was to protect the back and edges of the plate with a suitable acid-resistant medium, then the plate was completely immersed in acid, which bit into the areas unprotected by the wax. When the lines requiring light treatment had been 'bitten' to the required depth, the plate was removed, and those areas covered with an acid-resistant varnish to prevent any further action by the acid. The plate was then returned to the acid so that lines required to be darker could be etched deeper. Repetitive treatments of 'stopping off' and re-etching resulted in the graduation of lines from the very delicate to the strong and bold.

When the etching stage was completed, the plate was washed, and both varnish and wax removed, leaving a beautifully clean etched plate ready for the first impression to be taken.

DRY POINT

Dry point etchings were made simply by scratching the drawing into the copper plate with a needle-like tool. This action produced a thin line in the copper to receive the ink, and at the same time, produced a ragged edge or burr each side of the line, which also retained a large proportion of ink. The resultant impressions taken from dry point plates were, therefore, richer and more velvety than impressions from line engraved, or acid etched plates.

It will be obvious that good quality prints in dry point are rare. Due to the delicate nature of the burr, it soon wore down so that the number of prints produced whilst the plate retained its high quality was very limited.

MEZZOTINT ENGRAVING

The engraver first polished the copper sheet on the face to be engraved, then with a piece of chalk he marked a series of parallel lines across this face, about $\frac{3}{4}$ inch apart. The first stage of engraving was executed with a chisel-like tool with a curved edge, one side of which was grooved, shaped, and sharpened to form a series of cutting points, or dots. Placing this tool between the first two chalk lines, he rocked it back and forth, and at the same time moved it slowly across the plate, forming a band of dotted indentations in the metal. He then proceeded to treat the next chalk-marked band in the same way, and so on down the plate until the whole plate had been covered. The same operation was then repeated vertically over the plate, and then diagonally at varying angles until the whole surface of the plate was roughened evenly. This was known as 'laying the ground', and if an impression was taken from it at this stage, the result would be a perfectly black surface. The next operation required the outline of the design to be drawn on the roughened surface, then with a very sharp scraping knife, the engraver proceeded to develop the design by carefully scraping away more or less of the roughened surface to produce the variety of graduated tones from very light to black.

STIPPLE ENGRAVING

The copper plate was first given a wax ground and treated in much the same way as for etchings, but instead of drawing lines into the wax, the design was first outlined by pricking dots into the wax. The darker passages were filled in either by larger, or more closely grouped dots. The plate was then immersed in acid to bite the dots into the plate. After this treatment, the wax ground was cleaned off and the engraver proceeded to re-enter most of the dots with a 'stipple graver', to emphasise and develop the final design. Stipple engravings, therefore, are really a combination of the etching, dry point and graver work.

AQUATINT ENGRAVINGS

There were two basic grounds used to produce plates for aquatints; the dust ground and spirit ground. But whichever ground is used the technique is the same.

The cleaned copper plate was evenly coated with a film of finely powdered resin. The various methods used to scatter the resin were to place the plate in a rotating box, by a revolving fan inside the box, or by blowing with a pair of bellows. The plate was then heated to just melt the resin. Spirit grounds were applied on a carefully cleaned plate by covering the plate with a solution comprising resin and spirits of wine. With the evaporation of the spirit, the resin dried, and in so doing, contracted, leaving the resin adhering to the

211

plate in fine particles, which exposed the raw metal around the particles.

When the etching was applied over the resin ground, it bit into the minute exposed areas, but its action was inhibited where covered by the tiny particles of resin. The graduation of tone necessary to express form was obtained by successive applications of acid and by stopping off areas with acid resistant varnish. When a definite or well defined line was required it was added by the etching needle which removed the resin.

LITHOGRAPHS

Lithographs were not produced by any method associated with engraving, but they rank among the best of some of the antique prints. Lithographic prints were produced from a special kind of limestone to which a granulated surface had been added by rubbing the printing surface with a similar piece of stone. This action flattened the surface also. The design was then drawn on the stone, in reverse, with a greasy pencil and the stone treated with a weak acid. Before applying the ink with a roller the stone was first wetted, and because oil and water do not readily mix, only the ink adhered to the greasy drawn design. It was only necessary to lay a piece of damp paper on the stone and press to obtain the final impression.

An alternative method was sometimes practised by first drawing the design with a greasy pencil on a special transfer paper; this was subsequently pressed onto the prepared surface of the stone and the paper removed, leaving the drawn image. Impressions obtained by this method were generally not quite as crisp as those obtained by direct drawing.

SOFT GROUND ETCHING

The plates for soft ground etchings were prepared by coating the polished surface of the plate with a tallow or wax, much in the same way as it would be for normal etchings. A sheet of paper was then laid on the waxy surface and the design drawn with a pencil. When the paper was removed, the wax adhered to the underside of the paper wherever a line had been traced, and in so doing exposed the bare metal in the form of the design. The plate was then immersed in acid and the plate bitten on the exposed areas.

The appearance of a print produced by this method shows the lines to be rough and similar to crayon lines, whilst those produced by a normal etching process are fine and clear.

212

COLOUR PRINTS

The majority of old engravings were hand coloured with water-colours, but these must not be confused with engravings 'printed in colour'. Stipple engravings printed in colour were produced from a stipple engraved plate, with the various coloured inks being rubbed into the required areas by the printer. Excess ink was removed from the plate surface, leaving the tiny pockets of the engraving filled with ink. The subsequent impression resulted in a beautiful coloured print, composed of tiny coloured dots on a white background. Depth of colour tone, or shading, was achieved by the proximity or size of the coloured dots.

Colour prints were produced very early in the history of prints by the Chinese, using various wood blocks to produce the individual colours, but the process used by Jacob Christopher Le Blon very early in the 18th century had a similar basis to present-day technique His process involved making mezzotint plates for each colour, so graduated in texture that they reproduced the required proportions of red, yellow and blue. A fourth plate was used for the addition of black. The plates were inked with their appropriate colour, and printed on the paper, one impression on top of the other, registration of each plate being of considerable importance.

Other colour prints were produced during the eighteenth century from separate colour plates engraved in stipple and aquatint. 1834 saw the beginning of the Baxter oil prints. These were produced from engraved steel plates; the first block engraved became the master, and the subsequent colour plates were prepared by transfers made from this master. The various colours used were mixed by hand to the required tint, plates inked, and print produced by printing one colour impression upon another in accurate register. Later Baxter used a combination of wood blocks and steel plates.

PAPER

It is necessary to know something about paper, and collectors of prints automatically acquire some knowledge by their frequent handling of the material. The paper mark visible when holding a sheet of paper up to a strong light, was impressed into the paper during manufacture, by wire or thin brass formed into the required design and attached to the wires of the mould. The paper in close proximity to the design was therefore thinner, and is more translucent.

It is well known that education during the middle-ages, and even later, was not for the masses. Consequently, not many people could either read or write, so signs had to do the intelligence work, hence

213

the shop signs, barber's poles, public house signs and so on, into paper making, where the manufacturer used a device or trade mark impressed in his paper.

The lines seen on some old paper can give a rough indication of period—from about 1480 they were about $2\frac{1}{2}$ inches apart, or narrower, but prior to this date, they were much wider.

The 'Open Hand' paper mark was in use about 1483, 'Post Horn' about 1670, 'Fleur-de-lis' about 1657, and the 'Cardinal's Hat' dates from about 1649.

Most of the old hand-made papers were coarse, and often of uneven thickness. But from 1801 the machine-made papers made their appearance, being much smoother and of a more even thickness.

The advent of machine-made papers did not mean the disappearance of the wire mould lines; these were still produced in imitation of the earlier hand-made papers, and from about 1815, bleached papers had arrived.

This brief introduction to paper is not exhaustive; indeed, paper and its history is sufficiently diverse to form a complete study in its own right, and whilst some knowledge is essential for print collecting, experience is going to be your best guide in the end.

PROOFS AND STATES

It has been mentioned elsewhere in this book that any plate, irrespective of the style of engraving, will wear progressively as impressions are taken from it. It is a statement of the obvious, but the statement is made to illustrate the fact that early impressions are naturally the sharpest, and have the cleanest and best defined lines. As the plate wears the lines become less distinct and some of the finest details will disappear altogether.

When an engraver is working on a plate, he is invariably working to a mirror image of the final design, working 'in reverse' as it were to provide the negative block. As he proceeds the subject is developed by engraved lines visible in form, but flat and uncontrasting. Therefore, to check his work the engraver will take off a single impression on paper, and from this impression he can ascertain any necessary corrections. Technically, these trial impressions are 'proofs' taken with the object of proving the progression of the engraving and they are an integral part of the process of plate making.

A 'state' defines the condition of a finished plate, or its state at any given time. For example, a first state impression may be printed and issued. Some time later it may be re-issued, but prior to printing the engraver may make some small alteration to the details: impressions from the modified plate would be referred as 'Second State' and so on. Although there is a somewhat hazy distinction between state and proof, they are in practice almost interchangeable, as they both denote the 'state' in broad terms.

A 'Remarque proof' is so called because it has a remarque or small sketch etched or engraved on the lower margin, these sketches being invariably appropriate to the subject matter of the print. Remarque proofs also carried the signature of the artist if he was alive, and the engraver, in pencil, on the left and right of the lower margin. The title of the subject was omitted.

'Artist's proofs on India paper' often followed the Remarque proof. These were proofs taken on a very thin paper made from the inner fibres of bamboo. This paper had a soft, fine-grained texture capable of taking the finest detail. Because of its thinness, it is pasted to a stronger paper for support. Artists' proofs may be produced 'before all letters', that is without title, engravers or artist's name etc., but they may well be signed in pencil by the artist, if living, and the engraver. An artist's proof 'before letters' will not have its title, but could carry the name and address of the publisher on the lower margin. The next set of impressions may be simply 'artist's proofs', the only difference being that the impression is taken in plain paper instead of India paper.

Proofs before letters have a completely blank lower margin, except that the names of both the engraver and artist are printed on the left and right of the margin immediately below the picture.

The next stage in the progression is 'open letter proofs'. These are proofs to which the title has been added to the lower margin, but in outline only; such proofs usually have the artist's and engraver's name, together with the name and address of the publisher.

Finally, we have fully lettered impressions, that is the print in its final form, and these can be on India paper or any other paper.

The various proof stages outlined represent the possibilities, but not all prints go through these individual stages. Some stages are skipped entirely, depending on the needs of the engraver and prevailing circumstances, but it will be seen that proofs represent the various progression stages in the production of the plate, and the final proof stage indicates that the plate is ready for the press to produce prints in a 'First State' condition.

First State prints made when the plate was new obviously will give the finest detail, and when the plate has been worn considerably it is easy even for a collector new to the subject to detect these late pulls by the frailty of some lines or their disappearance entirely, but the various states of the majority of collectable prints can only be ascertained by experience and recourse to works of reference.

MOUNTING

Prints are undoubtedly shown to better advantage when they are tastefully mounted. Even if there is no intention of framing, the mount will protect them from one another in the portfolio, and allows them to be handled by friends without being actually touched.

Prints should never be 'laid down', that is pasted down all over and attached to a board support.

One of the best methods of mounting is by using an overlay. This consists of a backboard of strong card, with a hinged front in which a window is cut to suit the actual picture area and title. The print is attached to the backboard by means of two small strips of masking tape across the two top corners, and the front, or overlay, attached to the backboard by a strip of masking tape along the inside of the top edge. This forms a hinge, and permits the front to be lifted, and the print to be examined, both on the front and the **reverse**.

A final touch can be added by adding a line and wash **border** to the mount, but more about this later.

The solid mount consists of a strong backboard of card**, to** which a cardboard frame is pasted, forming a box. The print **is** attached to the backboard by means of pasted paper hinges **in** much the same way as stamp collectors mount their stamps. With this type of mount no part of the print is covered by the frame.

The window mount is particularly useful for mounting maps that have text matter on the reverse side of the map. It consists simply of two sheets of similar size mounting boards, with identical size windows. The map can be attached to one board by means of a small strip of masking tape and the second board hinged along the top edge either with masking tape, or by pasting a strip of strong paper in this position. A final protection can be added by making an envelope of cellulose acetate sheet into which the complete mount is slid.

To cut the windows in the mount use a specially sharp mount cutting knife; these are obtainable quite cheaply with interchangeable blades, and a bevelled straight-edge. Mark out the size faintly on the mount with a pencil, then with the blade held at an angle and flat against the bevel of the straight edge, make long firm cuts. The precision of the window cutting will add considerably to the appearance of the mount.

Now if you wish to add a line and wash border, you can mark the lines around the aperture faintly with a pencil first, or if you are making a number of mounts it will be quicker to make a little jig.

The jig is simply a strip of Perspex with holes drilled along the diagonals of the border where the two lines meet. A needle is then

216

used to prick tiny holes in the mount, through the drilled holes. Then all you do is connect two opposite prick-marks with a ruler and draw your line. Make certain that the needle fits the holes; a sloppy fit will only result in incorrect positioning and the lines being out of parallel. To draw the line, use watercolour or sepia ink suitably thinned and a ruling pen. After drawing the lines, fill in the centre two lines with a flat wash of colour paint using a flat camel-hair brush. Work from one corner, painting down two sides simultaneously so that the edges always remain wet until finally they meet at the corner opposite to the one started. This will prevent a mark on the finished border showing where you commenced.

One final embellishment can be added to large mounts; this is a thin gold line. The cheapest and simplest method of doing this is to obtain a sheet of gold, gummed, tissue thin paper from your mount supplier, and with a sharp razor blade and a straight-edge, cut a thin strip to the required length. Wet the back, and lay in position on the mount. Mitre the corners for the best effect.

RESTORATION

Cleaning

A print that has dirt and dust ground into its surface, but is otherwise intact, can be greatly improved by being given a wash in cold water. It is advisable to first remove any loose dust and dirt with a soft camel-hair brush, covering the complete surface with short flicking strokes. A rectangular rubber sponge, used dry, will then remove any of the more persistent particles. Care must be taken not to rub up the surface of the print; use only very light and delicate strokes, and *never*, under any circumstances, use an eraser on the inked surface. A very soft eraser, like Art Gum, can be used carefully on the margins and the back of the print. An old fashioned but effective means of lifting out dirt is to use a ball of moist bread. Press the ball onto the print surface and lift; any loose dirt will adhere to the tacky bread, and can be kneaded into the ball to present another clean surface for further applications.

Having dry cleaned as far as it is practical to do so without damaging the print in any way, it may well be that the print is now clean enough. If, however, further treatment is required, lay the print on a sheet of glass or plastic covered board, like Formica, and gently flood with tepid water. It is better to pour the water from a cup than to risk the more violent action of a direct stream from a tap. When the paper is really soaked, pour a cupful of warm water over it to which has been added about a teaspoonful of liquid soap, and then with the palm of the hand held flat gently work the hand

217

over the print to form a lather. It is important to remember that the paper is very fragile when wet, and the hand should not, under any circumstances, actually rub the paper; the lather should form a film between hand and paper, allowing the hand to pass over the print about $\frac{1}{16}$ inch above the actual surface.

Treat both back and front of the print in the same way, then flood with clean water to remove all traces of soap. Lay the cleaned print flat on blotting paper or a piece of towelling, and allow it to dry naturally.

Remember that a print soaked in water is very much heavier than when it is dry, so be careful not to handle it carelessly or try to lift it by a single corner. Transfer the wet print from the board by laying a piece of material over the board and print, and turn the board over, holding the material onto the board by a hand held each end. Then, laying it down on a flat surface, remove the board, at the same time gently easing the wet print away from the board.

Bleaching

Prints are bleached to remove large stains, and the overall dirty brown colouration caused by exposure to polluted atmosphere, smoke and stains caused by water. Bleaching should be the final treatment. Always dry clean a print first then remove any stains requiring local attention such as ink, grease, etc. Only when these have been successfully removed and the print thoroughly washed to remove any residual chemicals, should the final bleaching treatment be carried out.

The majority of bleaching agents are more or less harmful to the paper. Therefore, always use the weakest possible solution initially, and only increase the strength enough to give effective results.

It is assumed that the collector is not in the possession of a fume cupboard, therefore techniques requiring this equipment have been omitted.

Sodium hypochlorite, diluted with water, is probably the easiest and most convenient bleach to use. It is made up in a bath and the print completely submerged. Remember prints should always be laid on a support when they are immersed in a bath so that they can be lifted out without being handled. A sheet of glass or plastic is ideal.

Sodium hypochlorite is commercially available marked '10% w/v available chlorine'. It is always sold in a dark coloured bottle, and it should always be kept in the dark and cool. Generally one volume of bleach to twenty volumes of water will be found effective, but if it is necessary to increase the strength, never use a proportion greater than 5 to 20.

When the print has reached the desired stage of cleanliness, lift out, and wash gently with clean water. Then immerse in a 2 per cent strength solution of sodium thiosulphate (photographic hypo.) to remove any residual chlorine. Finally wash again in clean water and leave to dry.

Chloramine-T is a much safer and gentler bleach. It is obtainable in the form of a white powder, and must always be kept well stoppered. Make up the solution immediately prior to use, 2 gm. to every 100 ml. of water. It can be used in the same way as sodium hypochlorite, but because the corrosive properties are soon lost, only a minimum amount of washing is required, and if necessary, omitted entirely. Solutions of Chloramine-T can be applied to local stains by covering them with a pad of blotting paper, held down with a sheet of glass.

If the stains are not completely removed by the first application after about 30 minutes, repeat the applications of bleach as necessary.

Chloramine-T, because of its gentle action, and the fact that subsequent washing is unnecessary, is ideally suited for treating watercolours, and hand coloured prints.

The retention of colour during any bleaching process is difficult, but the problem can be minimised if you lay the print face down, on a sheet of glass, gently soaking the back with a wet sponge, then applying the bleach. The bleach will permeate the paper from the back to perform a mild action on the front. If sodium hypochlorite is used for this method, a final wetting with 2 per cent hypo. should be given whilst the print is still held face down on the support, followed by clean water. During the whole of this process the object is to prevent any bleach touching directly the front of the print; should it do so it is likely to cause unsightly bleach marks. Now reverse the print on the support so that it is face upwards, and gently wash the front for a few moments with clean water, and leave to dry.

Immersion of India-proof prints is likely to result in the India paper becoming loose or completely free from the backing paper. If this happens it is quite a problem getting it back free of creases. A method often used for such prints is to soak a sheet, or sheets, of blotting paper in a strong solution of sodium hypochlorite, say 4 to 10. When the blotting paper is almost dry, sandwich the print between the sheets, and place between two sheets of glass.

Ink Stains

There are various treatments for the removal of ink stains, but the most effective one to use for a particular stain can only be ascertained by trial. The reason for this necessity is the very great difference in the composition of inks.

First try a 2 per cent aqueous solution of chloramine-T. The stain may require a few applications, but if this does not completely remove it, try a 5 per cent solution of oxalic acid, or alternatively, a 10 per cent solution of citric acid. Wash thoroughly after applying these latter two solutions.

If a more drastic method is required try sodium formaldehyde sulphoxylate. The stain should be wetted and the powdered chemical sprinkled over the stain. This treatment will also bleach out many other coloured stains. Always wash very thoroughly after using this chemical.

One other treatment can be tried if all else fails, but this method has the big disadvantage of being harmful to the paper; however, it is worth trying if it saves a print that would be ruined otherwise. Make a 0·5 per cent solution of potassium permanganate and paint this over the stain; it will form a brown patch. Leave for about five minutes then cover the brown patch with a 2 per cent aqueous solution of oxalic acid. Wash thoroughly in clean water.

Tea and Coffee Stains

First damp the paper and then stipple the stain with a 2 per cent aqueous solution of potassium perborate, and expose to strong sunlight for a few hours. The action of the bleach is slow, so do not become impatient. Should the paper appear to soften, stop the action by flooding with water.

If necessary, a final bleaching can be effected using ethereal hydrogen peroxide, but make sure the paper has been dried before applying the solution.

Tears

When a print has been torn along one of its edges, it is a relatively simple operation to effect an excellent repair. First soak the print in water for a few minutes, then remove and wait until the paper is only just damp. Lay the print face down on a sheet of plate glass, and gently tap the joints until they are welded together. A spoon is an ideal tool for this operation, and it can also be used to smooth the joint by rocking the spherical or curved bowl along the joint. Pressure is obtained by placing the forefinger of the hand holding the spoon in the inside of the bowl, and pressing downwards during the rocking motion. Paste may be applied to the two edges to be joined, but use sparingly.

If the joint requires reinforcing, stick a patch of paper behind it, and when dry, sandpaper the patch to remove the edges and to reduce the overall thickness. Make certain you use similar, old paper. Otherwise it is likely to cause wrinkling during the drying process.

When a print has a piece completely torn away, or a hole, and the collector has the complete piece, adopt exactly the same procedure, but you must position the loose piece accurately, making certain that the feathered edges are lapped correctly. You can check this by turning the support glass, and examining through the glass. When it is necessary to insert a piece of paper, it is important to use paper of approximately the same age, thickness, and appearance. Sometimes it is possible to take a small piece from the margins, when they are very wide. If not, old prints beyond repair or valueless should be retained for this purpose.

The print is laid face down on a sheet of glass and the edges of the hole chamfered. Initially, a very sharp knife or razor blade can be used to remove some of the paper, but it will require the use of fine glass paper to obtain the very fine feather edge necessary for a good repair. Do not hurry this operation and use the glass paper with very gentle pressure, otherwise you will tear pieces of paper away.

Now paste the chamfered edges with a fairly dry paste, and stick the patch over the hole. The patch should be about $\frac{1}{4}$ inch larger than the hole all around. Gently tap with a spoon, and lift away from support to ensure that excess paste has not seeped through and stuck your print to the support. Leave to dry.

When dry, carefully tear away the excess paper, holding the patch down onto the glass at the join as you work round it. Finally, glass paper the back so that the inserted piece of paper is the same thickness as the rest of the print.

When using the machine-made paper, the grain of the paper must be maintained in the patch. The grain can be ascertained by wetting two edges at right angles to each other. The paper will swell across the grain and will crinkle a little.

Keep the joints as clean as possible, because dirty paste, or dirt introduced during repair, will only emphasise the join, which after all, we are seeking to make invisible.

Sizing

After prints have been bleached, especially if they have been totally submerged in sodium hypochlorite, the body of the paper will require strengthening. A simple test is to dampen the print with a spot of water and hold it up to the light. If the spot appears light, and the paper is very absorbent, like blotting paper, the print will need sizing to restore the strength and to render it suitable to take the colour when retouching.

One of the best sizes is the old fashioned jelly size. It is not easy to find a supplier, but when you do, you may have to purchase a whole keg. An average strength size is made by dissolving the jelly with water, 1 volume of size to $3\frac{1}{2}$ volumes of water. Boil for about three minutes in a porringer, or double pan, and apply to the print whilst still hot with a wide soft paint brush, always in one direction only.

An alternative, and more readily available, size can be made from sheets of clear gelatine. Dissolve one sheet of gelatine in a quart of water (strength should not exceed 1·5 grams per litre). Always make this size immediately before use, and apply in the same manner as you would jelly size.

Colouring

After cleaning, it is often necessary to replace the colour in a print that has been lost due to the bleach action and its immersion in water. Also, prints are often found in their original uncoloured state and many collectors will prefer to have colour added to them. Now with regard to the latter the question will arise—'Is an antique print or map that has been coloured recently still a genuine antique, and has the addition of modern colouring detracted from its original value?' There is no specific answer to this question, since after all, the value of any antique is mainly determined by its rarity and the price collectors are willing to pay. The print is still, of course, antique, and although it is obviously more desirable to have one that was coloured contemporarily, it must be admitted that almost any uncoloured print can be made considerably more attractive by the addition of colour, applied skilfully and as near as possible to the colour that would have been applied had it been painted during the period when it was printed originally. The current trend indicates that modern colouring does not detract from the print's value, providing the work is executed by knowledgeable colourists. In fact, the prices are usually considerably higher.

It is interesting to note that during the 18th century and into the 19th century many people would buy uncoloured prints and maps for the pleasure of colouring their own. The results of these amateur colourists are somewhat mixed.

It is not suggested that a collector should go to the trouble of making his own paints in the same manner as the early colourists were compelled to do, but he should study the tints and textures of paint applied by old colourists and simulate these as near as possible by colour mixing. Sometimes it is possible to buy old block colours from an antique shop and these are quite useful for comparative purposes, and for the touch of odd colour that is difficult to mix.

One 18th century book gives formulae for making watercolours, one of which is printed here for interest.

This formula was recommended for copper green:—Take some French verdigris and beat it into a fine powder with about $\frac{1}{5}$ of cream of tartar. Mix the powders in about five or six times their weight of water, then boil until only half of the liquor remains. When cold, strain and let stand until the liquor is clear. There is also a warning of fumes, and a suggestion that the nose should be stuffed, and the mouth covered, to prevent poisoning.

Should you wish to pursue the subject of old colour making, there are some 18th and 19th century books that will provide the necessary information.

Now assuming the collector wishes to try his hand at colouring, he should obtain a selection of good quality sable or camel-hair brushes, and an initial supply of the following watercolours, preferably in tubes because these colours are easier to mix in quantity than block colours: Indigo, Prussian Blue, Burnt Sienna, Raw Sienna, Sepia, Raw Umber, Burnt Umber, Olive Green, Light Red, Vermillion, Gamboge, and a tube of Opaque White. You may wish to increase your pallet in time, but the suggested list is adequate. You also will need a small sponge, and some saucers to mix the colours or pots specially supplied by art shops, and *plenty* of blotting paper.

We are now ready to start. The following suggestions and colours are general; accuracy of tints to periods and styles of engraving must be learnt from experience gained by looking at, and closely examining, old coloured prints. Let us assume we are going to colour 'A View of the House of Lords'. It will at least show how you should approach the subject, but the method of applying watercolour can only be gained by practical experience. Practice as much as possible on worthless prints, checking your results continually with genuine old coloured prints.

Dip the sponge in clean water and wet the front and back of the print. At this stage it is wise to check that the size has been evenly absorbed over the total print area by holding the print up to a strong light. It should appear opaque *all over*; any areas or spots that appear light will not have absorbed size. Colour applied over these areas will immediately soak into the surface and discolour the back, a sure sign that the colouring has been recent and executed by an amateur. If the sizing is not satisfactory, do not attempt any colouring, but put the print aside and give it another thin coat of size at your convenience.

Assuming the print has been adequately sized lay it on its back and blot it. Mix a touch of raw sienna with a touch of light red, then add white until a soft warm cream is obtained—paint the cloud edges and horizon with this colour. Now mix prussian blue with white (make enough to cover the total sky area) until a natural sky blue is obtained and paint the sky leaving the areas already coloured cream. Try to finish the sky whilst the print is still damp so that no hard lines result. Next mix a pale wash of raw umber and paint the stonework of the House and the brick building light red.

The ground can be washed in with a wash of burnt sienna flattened with a tint of sepia. Do not paint over the figures. When dry paint the roof grey made from prussian blue and sepia (Paynes Grey can be used as an alternative).

Now paint the shadow areas with a pale wash of prussian blue.

Finally, paint the figures and coach—faces light red, uniforms correct colours, dresses and coats brightly, but not brilliantly, contrasting.

ARTISTS AND ENGRAVERS

The following is a list of European artists and engravers. It is by no means comprehensive, but it is hoped that those selected are a good cross-section, and produced work that could be of interest to modern collectors.

Name	Nationality	Life Span	Styles
Aliamet, (Jean Jacques)	French	1728–1788	Line and Dry Point
Allais, (Jean Alexandre)	French	1792–1850	Mezzotint and Aquatint
Altdorfer, (Albrecht)	German	c. 1480–c. 1538	Wood and Line Engraver
Amstel, (Cornelis Phoos)	Swiss	1726–1798	Line Engraver
Apostool, (Cornelis)	Dutch	1760–1844	Aquatint
Assen, (Johann Walther)	Dutch	c. 1480–c. 1553	Wood Engraver
Audran, (Benoit)	French	1661–1721	Line Engraver
Audran, (Charles)	French	1594–1674	Line Engraver
Audran, (Gerard)	French	1640–1703	Line Engraver and Etcher
Baldini, (Baccio)	Italian	c. 1436–c. 1515	Line Engraver
Balechou, (Jean Joseph)	French	1719–1764	Line Engraver
Baron, (Bernard)	French	c. 1700–1762	Line Engraver and Etcher
Bartoli, (Pietro Santi)	Italian	c. 1635–1700	Etcher

Name	Nationality	Life Span	Styles
Bartolozzi, (Francesco)	Italian	1725–1815	Stipple
Beauvarlet, (Jacques F.)	French	1731–1798	Line Engraver
Beccafumi, (Domenico)	Italian	1486–1551	Wood and Line Engraver
Beham, (Hans Sebald)	German	1500–1550	Wood and Line Engraver, also Etcher
Benedetti, (Michele)	Italian	1745–1810	Stipple
Berger, (Daniel)	German	1744–1824	Stipple and Etcher
Berghem, (Nicholaas)	Dutch	1624–1683	Etcher
Bettelini, (Pietro)	Italian	1763–c. 1828	Line and Stipple
Bischop, (Jan de)	Dutch	1646–1686	Etcher
Bleeck, (Pieter van)	Dutch	1695–1764	Mezzotint
Blooteling, (Abraham)	Dutch	c. 1634–c. 1685	Etcher and Mezzotint
Boissieu, (Jean Jacques)	French	1736–c. 1810	Etcher
Boulanger, (Jean)	French	1607–1680	Line Engraver
Buhot, (Felix)	French	1847–1898	Various
Burgkmair, (Hans)	German	1473–1559	Wood Engraver
Canot, (Pierre Charles)	French	1710–c. 1777	Line Engraver
Carracci, (Agostino)	Italian	1557–1602	Line Engraver
Chevillet, (Juste)	German	1729–1790	Etcher
Chodowiecki, (Daniel. N.)	German	1726–1801	Etcher
Claude (Gellée)	French	1600–1682	Etcher
Cochin, (Charles Nicholas)	French	1688–1754	Line Engraver
Colibert, (Nicholas)	French	1750–1806	Line Engraver and Stipple
Cort, (Cornelis)	Dutch	1536–1578	Line Engraver
Cranach, (Lucas)	German	c. 1472–1553	Wood Engraver

Name	Nationality	Life Span	Styles
De Bailliu, (Pieter)	Flemish	1614–c. 1660	Line Engraver
De Bry, (Theodore)	German	1528–1598	Line Engraver
De Laune, (Etienne)	French	1518–1595	Line Engraver
Demarteau, (Gilles)	French	1722–1776	Stipple
Drevet, (Pierre)	French	1663–1738	Line Engraver
Du Jardin, (Karel)	Dutch	1625–1678	Etcher
Dürer, (Albrecht)	German	1471–1528	Wood and Line Engraver and Etcher
Faber, (John) The Elder	Dutch	c. 1660–1721	Mezzotint
Faber, (John) The Son	Dutch	1684–1756	Mezzotint
Forster, (Francois)	Swiss	1790–1872	Line Engraver
Freudenberger, (Sigmund)	Swiss	1745–1801	Line Engraver and Etcher
Gaillard, (Robert)	French	c. 1722–1785	Line Engraver
Girard, (Alexis François)	French	1789–1870	Mezzotint and Mixed
Gole, (Jacobus)	Dutch	1660–c. 1740	Mezzotint Line Engraver
Haid, (Johann Jakob)	German	1704–1767	Mezzotint
Holbein, (Hans)	German	1497–1543	Wood Engraver
Hollar, (Wenceslaus)	Czech	1607–1677	Etcher
Houbraken, (Jacobus)	Dutch	1698–c. 1780	Line Engraver
Jacobe, (Johann)	German	1733–1797	Mezzotint
Janinet, (Jean Francois)	French	1752–1813	Line Engraver
Jazet, (Eugene)	French	1816–1856	Mezzotint and Aquatint
Jegher, (Cristoffer)	German	c. 1592–c. 1665	Wood Engraver
Lasne, (Michel)	French	1595–1667	Line Engraver

Name	Nationality	Life Span	Styles
Le Bas, (Jacques Phillipe)	French	1707–1783	Etcher and Line Engraver
Longhi, (Giuseppe)	Italian	1766–1831	Line Engraver
Masson, (Antoine)	French	1636–1700	Line Engraver
Matham, (Jacobus)	Dutch	1571–1631	Line Engraver
Mazzuola, (Francesco)	Italian	1503–1540	Etcher
Méryon, (Charles)	French	1821–1868	Etcher
Morghan, (Rafaelle)	Italian	1758–1833	Line Engraver
Nanteuil, (Robert)	French	c. 1623–1678	Various
Ostade, (Adriaen Janusz Van)	Dutch	1610–1685	Etcher
Pass, (Crispin van de)	Dutch	c. 1565–c. 1643	Line Engraver
Pass, (Simon van de)	Dutch	c. 1590–c. 1640	Line Engraver
Penez, (Georg)	German	c. 1500–1550	Line Engraver
Picot, (Victor Marie)	French	1744–1802	Line and Stipple Engraver and Etcher
Poilly, (François de)	French	1623–1693	Line Engraver
Porporati, (Carlo Antonio)	Italian	1740–1816	Stipple, Mezzotint
Raimondi, (Marc Antonio)	Italian	1480–1527?	Line Engraver
Rajon, (Paul Adolphe)	French	1843–1888	Etcher
Rembrandt, (Rembrandt Harmensz Van Rijn)	Dutch	1606–1669	Etcher
Richter, (Adrian Ludwig)	German	1803–1884	Etcher
Saenredam, (Joannes)	Dutch	c. 1565–	Line Engraver
Santi, (Pietro)	Italian	1630–1700	Etcher
Schiavonetti, (Luigi)	Italian	1765–1810	Stipple
Schongauer, (Martin)	German	c. 1440–c. 1488	Line Engraver

Name	Nationality	Life Span	Styles
Simon, (Jean)	French	*c.* 1675–1755	Mezzotint
Solis, (Virgil)	German	1515–1562	Wood and Line Engraver
Stadler, (Joseph C.)	German	fl. 1780–1812	Aquatint
Toschi, (Paolo)	Italian	1788–1854	Line Engraver
Vaart, (Jan van der)	Dutch	1647–1721	Mezzotint
Vaillant, (Wallerant)	French	1623–1677	Mezzotint
Vandyck, (Sir Anthony)	Flemish	1599–1641	Etcher
Vidal, (Gerard)	French	1742–*c.* 1804	Stipple, Line and Aquatint
Visscher, (Claes Janoz)	Dutch	1580–1609	Line and Etcher
Vivares, (François)	French	1709–1780	Line Engraver
Zorn, (Anders)	Swede	1860–1920	Etcher

GLOSSARY

After: This term is used to denote any print which is not the original work of the engraver, but copied from the original design of a painter or engraver whose name is usually stated; for example, a line engraving executed by W. Byrne using a W. Turner painting as a master from which to copy, would be referred to as 'By W. Byrne after W. Turner'.

Aquatint: A method of engraving using acid and a resin ground (see text).

Block: A block of wood on which designs were engraved, material usually boxwood.

Brief-maler: A name used to describe the playing-card makers of Germany. They were considered to be the initial engravers of wood blocks.

Burin: A graver. The engraver's tool made from good quality hardened steel, one end ground at an angle to provide a fine cutting edge. The other end usually had a wooden handle that nestled into the palm of the hand.

Burnisher: Tool used by the engraver to soften a harsh line. In effect burnishing a line is to polish it by friction.

Burr: The rough edge thrown up along the edge of the engraved line by the cutting tool, particularly on soft metal like copper.

Cameo: The opposite of intaglio. The projection of the design or image above the common ground; a design cut in relief.

Chalcography: The art of engraving on metal plates.

Chiaroscure: The treatment of strongly contrasting light and shade in paintings, a method of producing engravings by the super-imposition of two or more blocks or plates to obtain the effect of light and shade independently.

Collector's Mark: A signature, mark, or device stamped on a print by the owner, to show ownership and to identify it as belonging to his collection.

Counter-proof: An impression taken from a proof on paper still wet with ink and pressed onto another sheet of paper; the design is then shown in reverse.

Cradle: This is another name for the rocker used to prepare the ground for mezzotints. It consists of a flat piece of good quality steel, hardened and prepared with small teeth, to which a handle is fitted. By rocking the teeth over a copper plate, burrs are raised on the surface so laying the grounds.

Cross-hatch: An engraving device to produce a particular effect. It consists of engraving one series of lines over lines already engraved, at right angles.

Cut: A woodcut, or an impression taken from a woodblock.

Dry Point: A sharp needle type engraving tool used in copper plate engravings to obtain very fine lines. Also used for making fine dots in stipple, for fine shading and to produce lines with a burr which held the ink and so produced a rich line (see text).

Etching: A means of producing a plate by etching the lines with acid, and masking with wax (see text).

Etching Ground: The coating of wax or varnish applied to the plate to prevent the acid attacking where not required to do so.

Etching Needles: Tool used to scratch through the wax to expose the raw metal to the action of the acid.

Exc: Excudit, literally 'he executed it', on an engraving usually refers to the publisher, often synonymous with the engraver.

Fecit: Literally, 'he made it', follows the name of an engraver to denote authorship.

Foxed: The brown stains, usually spotted, found on old prints; mainly caused by damp, and perhaps traces of minerals in the paper.

Graver: Tool used for engraving the plate (see Burin).

Ground: The prepared surface of a block or plate prior to engraving, i.e. mezzotint surfacing, and the wax ground prior to etching.

Heliograph: Not a print, more a kind of photograph, obtained by means of the sun and a camera obscura.

India Paper: A tissue thin paper, usually tinted, possessing a soft silky texture and capable of absorbing ink to a much greater degree than normal somewhat thicker papers. Usually mounted on a stiffer paper for support.

Intaglio: The reverse of relief. A design cut below the surface like an engraved plate, a depression.

Laying Down: Prints are said to be 'laid down' when they are pasted to a support of canvas, or cardboard. When a paper of similar texture is used to form a lining it is said to be 'backed'. The latter method is often employed to repair prints with large tears.

Line Engraving: A method of making a plate by engraving lines into the plate to hold ink prior to its transfer to paper (see text).

Lithograph: A print produced from a stone on which the design has been drawn with a greasy crayon (see text).

Mezzotint: A process of engraving using a completely burred plate as a basis, the lighter shades being produced by scraping away the burrs (see Styles).

Needles: Pointed tool used in engraving.

Paper-mark: Same as watermark.

Parcels: Job lots of prints sold in bundles.

Pax: A small plate of gold, silver etc., carrying a picture of the Crucifixion.

Pinx: Pinxit; precedes the name of the painter after whom the engraver produced it; usually engraved just below the picture on the bottom margin.

Plate: The sheet of metal carrying the engraved design.

Plate Mark: The impression made in the paper by the outer edges of the plate when squeezed in the press.

Pontuseaux: The parallel lines caused by the wire mesh of the tray onto which the paper was poured during the process of papermaking. These lines are in fact watermarks.

Proof: Initially this term was used to describe impressions taken to check the progress of the engraving, but now often used to describe prints prior to the lettered impression.

Proof (Artist's): A proof usually carrying the written signature of the artist on the lower margin.

Proof (Engraver's): A proof usually carrying the written signature of the engraver on the lower margin.

Proof before Letters: A print untitled. Prints that do not carry any inscription.

Proof with Open Letters: Print with inscription engraved in outline letters only, the main body of the letters not having been inked in.

Relief: Raised designs (see Cameo).

Remarque Proof: A proof from a plate, usually etched, which carries a small engraving appropriate to the design on the lower margin and usually the name of the artist signed in pencil.

Re-Touching: The reworking of a worn plate by deepening the worn cuts and the re-touching of feint areas, with the object of restoring the plate to its original condition.

Roughing: A wood engraving term used to describe the ground prepared for the drawing. A mixture consisting of Bath brick and water was spread on the block, and when dry, smeared with the palm of the hand.

Rule: A tool used in line engraving to produce a series of close parallel lines.

School: This term has no really precise meaning. In its broadest sense it means that a painting can be identified in respect of its country of origin. It is also used to describe the followers or pupils of a particular engraver.

Scraper: A tool used in producing mezzotint plates to scrape away areas of metal.

Sculp: Sculpsit, literally 'he engraved it', on an engraving precedes the name of the engraver just at the bottom edge of the picture when used.

Shake or Seer: A double impression caused by the paper moving whilst under the press.

Soft Ground Etching: A method of engraving using a wax ground on the copper plate. Paper is placed on the ground and the design drawn on paper. When the paper is lifted, wax adheres to the drawn line, exposing the metal to be bitten by acid (see text).

Solander Case: A box made of cardboard opening horizontally for holding prints.

State: A term used to describe the condition of a plate as it exists for a particular period in its life (see Proofs and States).

Stopping Out: A process used to 'stop-out' or mask a particular part of a plate with wax, varnish or other suitable material so that it was protected from the action of acid for a period during the production of the plate.

Vamp: To renovate, to repair, sometimes with intent to fraud.

Watermark: A number of parallel lines and sometimes a device and name visible when the paper is held up to a strong light.

RUGS

20. Oriental Carpets and Rugs

Presumably a carpet and a rug are one and the same thing. Many reference sources use the definition rather loosely, so we will assume that a carpet covers most of the floor, and rugs only partly do so.

Collecting both carpets and rugs is similar to furniture collecting—they are best acquired for use, unless of course you own a mansion and can hang them on the baronial walls.

Throughout this section the word 'rug' will be used to describe either carpet or rug. Experts may disagree but at least we will be consistent.

An Oriental rug consists of a base, i.e. the Warp and Weft, on which the wool, silks, or hair are woven by knotting. The method of weaving may vary from country to country, but the technique will remain basically the same, and the rug composed of these four elements. It is the variation of these elements that will often provide the only clue to the original location of a rug with any degree of accuracy.

The Warp is the term used to describe the strong, longitudinal threads which run from one end of the rug to the other, and appear in the end-webs and fringes. The warp may be so constructed that the threads lie side by side, all in the same plane; or alternative threads may be depressed so that when viewed from the back, the rug will show one row of prominent knots, and a row of less prominent knots lying next to it. A third alternative arrangement allows one thread above the other so that only one half of the knot is visible on the back surface of the rug.

The Weft is the term used to describe the threads that traverse the rug from side to side, locking the warp in a net-like pattern. The weft threads pass over and under the warp, and may consist of up to four strands.

The Knots. The yarn is attached to the threads of the warp by 'knotting' individual lengths, the free ends forming the pile. There are only two types of knots used on Eastern rugs, the Ghiordes or Turkish, and the Sehna or Persian. The illustrations will show the difference between these two knots.

To complete our terminology—the field refers to the square central portion of the rug, and the border the narrow band surrounding it.

Persian rugs, or carpets, are probably the best known, but Oriental carpets also come from China, Central Asia, Caucasia,

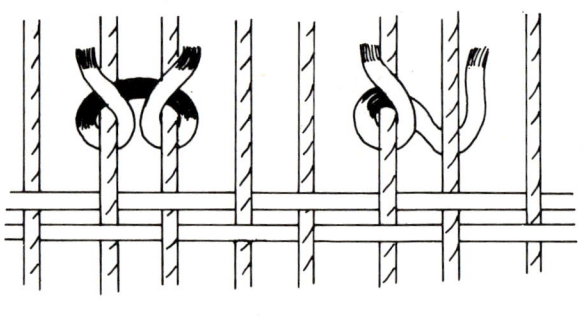

Ghiordes Knot   Sehna Knot

Turkey and India. Together these six groupings represent a kind of classification that is accepted by experts on the subject.

Chinese rugs are obviously Chinese. Their designs are distinctive; Swastikas, Butterflys, Dragons, Bats, The Key, Fret and Emblems, are seen on no other carpets. They date from the late 17th century, but this does not mean that the Chinese were not weaving carpets earlier. It's just that none have survived to provide factual evidence.

Indian rugs are mainly floral, rather more natural than symbolic. During the 16th and early 17th centuries fine carpets were made in Lahore, Agra, and Delhi and some 17 other cities. These early examples resembled the rugs of Persia. By the 18th century, the industry suffered a decline, and although carpets are still being made in large quantities, they are no longer hand woven.

Turkish rugs have a deep, purplish brown colouring and geometric designs, often similar to those seen on Caucasian rugs. The designs, of floral motifs, are conventional and stylised, rather than natural, and this would seem to stem from the Turks' orthodox attitude to religion, and a reluctance to depict living things accurately. A rug with naturalistic designs is unlikely to be of Turkish origin; more likely it will be Persian.

Turkish rugs are invariably tied with the Ghiordes knot. The foundations and pile will be made from wool or goat hair, and the pile longer than that found on Persian examples. Examples likely to be seen will have been made since 1860, although, of course, rugs were made in Turkey well before this date.

Caucasian rugs have been made for thousands of years in the southern part of Russia which lies between the Black Sea and the Caspian Sea. The patterns are invariably of a geometric nature with little or no curves. The 'latch-hook' is a particularly favoured motif.

234

There are three main types—the Daghestan, the Kazak, and the Shirvan. There are other types but they are of less importance.

Daghestan rugs have a short pile of closely woven texture; most Caucasian prayer-rugs are Daghestan. The Kazak rugs are characterised by bold, rich, rather dark colouring and a long pile; Shirvan rugs have a short pile and usually designs of foliage, with flower and leaf forms. All are woven with the Ghiordes knot.

The rugs from Central Asia include the Afghans, Turconans, Beluchis, Bokharas, Youmouds, and Beshirs.

The designs woven into Oriental rugs can be considered in two forms; those used for borders, and those used for the body, i.e. the field.

Borders may consist of a single stripe, or of a varying number of stripes with motifs suitably placed in between (see illustrations).

PERSIAN RUG

Designs

The Herati design is a field design found only in the rugs from Persia, commonly found in the rugs from Herat, Kurdistan, Sehna, and Feraghan.

The Mina Khani is an all-over pattern of Persian origin, but not so common as the Herati design. Found mainly on rugs produced by Kurdish tribesmen.

The Latch-Hook. Almost exclusive to the Caucasus, but sometimes used by the West Asians, and it is rarely seen on Persian rugs.

The Rosette. This is basically, as its name suggests, a flower form, often stylised, common to the rugs of Persia and Turkey.

The Pear is probably the commonest of all Persian designs used repeatedly in the field. It will be found on the rugs from Herat, Khorassan, Sehna, Sarabend, and Shirez.

The Eight Pointed Star may be found on any rugs, with the exception of China. It is a design loved by nomad weavers.

The Elephants Foot is a stylised form represented by a form of Octagon, mainly associated with rugs from Central Asia.

The Octagon. Sometimes found on most rugs with the exception of Persia.

The Cloud Band is like a wavy 'V'. It is a very old device of Mongolian origin found occasionally on 16th and 17th century Persian rugs.

The Comb. The device is not used by Persia but may be found in Caucasian rugs, less often in the rugs of Turkey and Central Asia.

The Swastika is exclusively Chinese.

The Diaper is a term used to describe repetitive designs forming

235

continuous patterns of diamonds, lozenges, octagons, hexagonals, etc. Diaper designs are rarely found in the rugs of Turkey or Central Asia.

The above design motives are by no means exhaustive—pomegranates, scorpions, tarantulas, crows foot, tree of life, and many others will be encountered.

The ability to identify Oriental rugs cannot be gained simply by reading this, or any other book. Obviously it will help to gain knowledge and stimulate interest, but ultimately, a personal acquaintance with the 'real thing' will teach the collector more about colour, texture, patina, and wool than can ever be gleaned from a book. The following is a brief look at some of the better known examples, with pointers to their identification.

Bijars: Strong, coarse weave, with Ghiordes knot, warp doubled under producing a double thickness base. The pile may rarely include part camel hair. Colours mainly reds and blues, with patterns of a simple nature. Borders also usually simple consisting of three stripes.

Feraghans: These come from the plains of Feraghan, between Teheran and Isphahan. The Sehna knot is used in conjunction with a coarse grained weave. Modern examples use the Ghiordes knot. The 'Herati' is a common field pattern; more rarely the 'Diaper', in some form, is used. Animals and birds are not uncommon.

The border stripes may be from three to seven, and usually of elaborate design.

Old-rose pink was a favourite colour for the older examples.

Gorevans: These came from the town situated below Tabriz, adjacent to Lake Urima. The rugs have the Ghiordes knot, the warp has alternate threads slightly depressed, and the rugs are generally coarsely woven.

The colours are shades of terracotta, dark blue and fawn.

The border stripes frequently incorporate the 'Turtle' design, and the field often consist of a single, large geometric medallion.

Hamadans: Hamadan rugs are named after the city of the same name; it is a Persian marketing centre. The Ghiordes knot is used on a warp where all the threads lie side by side.

A large proportion of camel hair is used in the pile, and the outer edging is invariably of plain camel hair.

Natural camel hair, together with green, pink, blue and red are used to form the floral patterns. The field often uses a Diaper design and a central medallion with a projection at each end, known as a pole-medallion. Borders are simple.

Herats: Herat was once the capital of Afghanistan, and until about 1750, the centre of a large rug industry.

These rugs use the Ghiordes knot on a warp which buries one half of the knot, giving a thick foundation.

The field is decorated with the 'Pear' or the Herati design. Medallion

236

centres are uncommon. Borders, comprising of three to seven stripes, have a characteristic main stripe of rosettes and linking vines.

Isphahan: Isphahan was the capital of Persia under Shah Abbas, and in 1600 a royal rug manufactory was producing hunting rugs, but few rugs are made there today. Isphahan rugs are rare, and many so called Isphahans of the 15th to the 17th century, were probably woven in Herat.

The patterns are distinctive forms of foliage and flowers, using the 'Palmette' and 'Cloud Band' motives. The ground colour was usually a deep rose pink, with designs in green, and small additions of yellow, blue and white.

Kashan: Kashan is a city between Teheran and Isphahan, noted for its silk rugs.

The Sehna knot is used to lock the pile to a warp with alternative threads buried, giving a thick foundation.

The field pattern consists of floral designs, with a centre medallion usually diamond shaped with stepped sides. Borders often comprising seven stripes are elaborate.

Kirman: Kirman is a large city in the Southern part of Persia.

The real old Kirmans are truly beautiful rugs with their patterns of red roses in field and borders, often with each petal shaded. The principal border stripe often had a yellow background. The Sehna knot is used on a warp that has alternate threads buried. The modern rugs usually lack the floral scroll work, and invariably contain a central medallion.

Sarouks: Similar to the Kashans, but usually slightly inferior.

Sehnas: This is a relatively easy group to identify because of its distinctive characteristics. The weft of fine cotton crosses the warp once only between each row of knots; all warp threads lie at the same level; and the Sehna knot is used.

The field pattern favours the pear and the Herati designs which are delicately executed. Central medallions are usual, and borders simple and floral. The knotting is particularly close; antique specimens may well have 700 to 800 knots to a square inch.

Shiraz: These rugs were made almost entirely by the nomadic tribes of Kashkais and sold in Shiraz. The Sehna knot is nearly always used but the Ghiordes knot occurs occasionally. The pear chain-medallion, scattered flowers, and birds and animals are quite common design features. The borders are not particularly outstanding; they usually comprise five or more stripes. The pile is soft and fleecy.

CAUCASIAN RUG

Designs

Bakus: These rugs, sometimes called Shirvan, are not too difficult to identify. The field patterns are usually composed of mosaic designs. The rectangular pear and the geometric bird are fairly common motifs.

237

The Ghiordes knot is used. The pile is short, and somewhat dull, but no less attractive for that.

Daghestans: Daghestans are usually Prayer rugs, but they were also woven with a field of diagonals or trellis. They, like the majority of Caucasian rugs, use the Ghiordes knot. The pile is short, and the rugs thin and flexible.

Derbends: These are similar to the Daghestans, but rarely will you find a Derbend Prayer rug. They are dark coloured usually.

Kabistans: These rugs also are similar to the Daghestans—in fact, they can be mistaken easily. Prayer rugs are unlikely to be found, neither will the lattice nor trellis pattern.

Kazaks: The Kazaks have long, moderately lustrous, pile. The patterns are bold, and a favourite motif is the 'Sunburst' design, but the 'Bird' and 'Crab' will also be found.

White is used only rarely, but reds, rose-madder, blue-green, and browns are freely used.

Shirvans: The Shirvan is probably the most numerous of all the Caucasian rugs. Foliage, with flowers and leaf forms, are used in well composed design arrangements. The chain medallion is frequently met, the overall lattice design less frequently so. The principal border stripe is the wine cup, or some variety of it.

Soumaks: The name Soumac is derived from the name of the town of Shemakha. They are easy to identify because of their lack of pile. They are made with a flat stitch that leaves the stitch ends to hang freely on the back. The design is usually centred around three medallions of geometric shape. Colours are usually dark red, blue, green and yellow.

PRAYER RUGS

The Prayer rug is, and was, used by Moslems to cover the unclean ground during prayer. Because of its religious connections, it is not surprising to discover that the basic designs of all Prayer rugs have religious meanings. The Prayer rug consists of a field usually of a single colour and devoid of patterning. The field is capped on the upper end with a Prayer Arch, which symbolises the sacred dome of the temple.

Above the arch there is an area termed the Spandrel, which represents the Heavenly vault. The outer edges of the rug are bounded by straight lines, and some rugs will have the addition of a panel above the Spandrel, or below the field. Occasionally both panels will be present.

Bergamos: Bergamo is a rug-making village near Smyrna. These rugs use the Ghiordes knot, and have a long lustrous pile. The Prayer Arch will be found in diverse shapes, but usually rather plain in design. The field is devoid of patterning, but the Spandrel may be decorated geometrically, or with leaf forms. It may have a panel above the Spandrel or below the field, or it may be totally absent.

Ghiordes: Ghiordes is near Smyrna, and it is the town that gave the Turkish knot its name.

Prayer Arch shaped to simulate a high central spire. Early examples have pillars supporting the Arch. The field is plain, and Spandrel with foliage motives on a blue background. The borders have elaborate patterning and many stripes, and may well eclipse the rest of the rug in elegance.

Kirshehrs: Prayer Arch steep and serrated. Field and Spandrel mainly plain, but both may have floral forms projecting inwards from the sides and base. There are usually two panels.

Koulahs: Prayer Arch fairly flat, either plain or serrated.

The Spandrel extends downwards in two narrow strips, one each side of the Prayer field and it is patterned with an overall flecking design, or with leaf motives. This treatment of the Spandrel together with the unique soft colouring of blues and yellows, picked out in darker shades and white, makes this rug readily identified as a Koulah.

Ladiks: Prayer Arch may be steep and serrated, or may contain three spires. The field is usually a plain red or blue, and the Spandrel is usually very characteristically designed with stemmed leaves. The panel is unusually deep and elaborately patterned.

CENTRAL ASIAN RUG

Designs

Afghans: The Afghan rug is typified by its all-over octagonal pattern, usually of large size, and the fact that the octagons which form medallions, are truly octagonals with really square sides.

They employ the Sehna knot in general, but the Ghiordes knot may also be found in some Afghan rugs. The pile is long and heavy, and may contain camel hair. Afghans are the thickest and heaviest of the Central Asian rugs.

Royal Bokharas: The name 'Bokhara' is given to these rugs because they are sold in the market place of Bokhara in Turkestan. They are really the work of the nomadic Turcoman tribes, and could be better described as 'Turcomans'. The 'Royal' Bokhara has a fine grain and close texture. Favourite colours are deep reds, or brown reds, but white is only used rarely. The patterns delicately woven octagons, often with quartered designs, are arranged all over the field. Alternative rows of diamonds may be interspaced.

The borders are usually simple in design and narrow.

The Sehna knot is used, and the pile short, soft, and luxurious, sometimes with silk and goat hair added.

Princess Bokharas: These Prayer rugs are similar to the Royal Bokhara, but of course, they conform to the usual pattern which includes the Prayer Arch. The field patterns usually consist of the 'Katchli' or 'Christian Cross' design. The field may be divided into four with a band separating each quarter, forming a cross.

Khiva Bokharas: Similar to Royal Bokharas, but slightly coarser, and with a longer pile.

Wine reds more likely than brown or deep reds.

Beshir Bokharas: These are made by tribes near Bokhara. They favour a stylised tree and leaf motif, 'Trees of Life', and lattice designs.

Youmud Bokharas: These are made in a location near the Caspian Sea, and their designs have some affinity with Caucasian patterns. They are brownish red, like most of the Bokharas. 'Octagons' may be replaced by diamond or hexagon patterns, and it is not unusual to find the 'Katchli' pattern used.

Beluchistans: Beluchistan is to the north-west of India, immediately south of Afghanistan. The rugs from this location, termed nomadic, have a long wool pile, to which goats' hair and camels' hair is sometimes added.

Colours predominantly deep reds and browns with natural tan coloured camel-hair. The patterns are hexagons, octagons, and stylised floral motifs. Panels and medallions are also used.

Collectors with little experience of rugs should, in the early stages of acquiring rugs, go to a known expert dealer. His company will be enjoyable and he will be only too pleased to talk 'rugs and carpets', happy to show his stock, pointing out the subtle differences between the various types, colours, weaves, and patterns, and you will have his valuable experience of a lifetime to guarantee that you are getting that for which you pay. The points to note are—is the rug complete? Have any borders been cut-off and professionally finished? Such rugs will have lost a lot of their original value. Are there any obvious repairs? Is the rug in reasonable condition for its age? A worn out rug is a poor acquisition, but a repaired rug, if expertly done, is quite acceptable and does not affect the cost very much. Is it a modern rug that has been treated to make it *look* old? Is the pattern, weave, colour, correct for the type of rug? And so on.

It takes time to acquire practical knowledge and 'book knowledge'; confidence will follow, but meanwhile, do consult your knowledgeable dealer before spending any money.

Below. A selection of silver spoons with marks showing dates between 1798 and 1830. (Mabel Gohm)

Above. Condiment Coaster made from sheet brass with pierced design. Date unknown. (Mabel Gohm)

Goss China. Model of vase dug up near Swindon. One of the larger Goss pieces. (David Morley Antiques, Twickenham)

Goss China. Model of Burton Beer Barrel. approx. 3ins. high. (David Morley Antiques, Twickenham)

Above. (Josiah Wedgwood & Sons Ltd)
'Prior Park, the seat of Ralph Allen Esq.,
near Bath'. Hand coloured line engraving b
Anthony Walker. Published by John Bowl
& Son. 1752.
(Richard van de Gohm)

Left. The Start off Sandy Hook, depicting
the yachts 'Heniretta', 'Vesta', and
'Fleetwing'. Size 14ins. × 24ins. Pub. 18C
(Photo D. C. Gohm)

'A False Alarm on the Road to Gretna'. One
of a pair of coloured aquatints. Size $10\frac{7}{8}$ ins. ×
$15\frac{7}{8}$ ins. By R. G. Reeve, after C. B.
Newhouse. Pub. B. Moss & Co.
(Richard van de Gohm)

(OLD) SHEFFIELD PLATE

21. Old Sheffield Plate

Old Sheffield Plate is a thin but very permanent coating of sterling silver on copper. The coating process was not achieved by any electro-chemical process, but by fusing the two metals together under heat, without any true amalgamation of the metals taking place. This resulted in a material with characteristics that allowed it to be rolled and formed into a thin sheet, and from this the famous Sheffield Plate articles were subsequently manufactured. Unfortunately, the process has now been lost, and superseded by the more modern plating methods.

Until the discovery of 'Sheffield Plate', the medieval practice of plating was carried out by covering a made-up piece in a base material with thin slivers of a precious metal, such as gold and silver. The slivers were beaten down and burnished to give the illusion that the complete article was made solidly of the precious metal.

During the early part of the 17th century, the Sheffield Cutlers had found a means of coating steel and iron with silver. Presumably their method was to solder silver foil, using a tin flux, to an otherwise finished article.

This method or technique is known as close-plating. It was a useful method that was used for a long time afterwards for handles of snuffers, cutting blades, knives and so on. The disadvantages of close-plating were its susceptibility to excessive heat which could melt the solder and cause the silver foil to become detached, or if the article was subjected to moist air or stored in a damp situation, the base material would oxidise, causing a film of rust between the two materials which also had the effect of loosening the foil.

Old Sheffield Plate was invented as a means of providing silverware much cheaper than the solid silver of the day, but as antiques go, its life span was a short one. It flourished from about 1760 to about 1850, until eventually the even cheaper techniques of electroplating ruined the industry.

Good Old Sheffield Plate compares very well with solid silver. The methods employed by the manufacturers were obviously copies from the silversmiths, but even so, the platemakers' difficulties must have been enormous when they first soldered, raised and chased the

241

silver faced copper into representations of solid silver counterparts. They managed to do so, and produced a vast quantity and variety of pieces that lost nothing by comparison with the real silver pieces.

An early problem was the covering up of the cut edges which exposed the copper. Prior to about 1765, it was customary to either apply silver solder to these edges or to roll them over to tuck the raw edge in. A later development was to apply a silver plated copper wire to the exposed edge, which effectively covered the copper and also added strength when required. About 1785 the plated copper wire was superseded by a solid silver wire.

Around 1743, Thomas Bolsover, a Sheffield cutler, made the discovery that silver could be fused to copper; he apparently applied a little too much heat to a knife haft he was repairing made of silver clad copper, with the result that the two metals fused together so strongly that they could not be separated. How Bolsover finally discovered the fact that the two metals, once fused, would react to rolling and forming in the same way as a single metal is not really known, but discover it he did, and in so doing, he made it possible to produce a sheet of copper, covered with a skin of silver, which could be worked as if it were in fact a sheet of silver.

Bolsover's early products made from this 'new' material were mainly limited to small boxes and buttons. However, at that time there was a high demand for such goods, as everyone wore metal buttons, and there was a lucrative market for small boxes as containers for tobacco, patches, snuff and a host of other knick-knacks.

In 1760, Matthew Boulton of Birmingham began to manufacture from this new material and became one of the great names of the day.

Although Bolsover can be credited as the inventor of the process, he made little use of it to produce articles, but it was not very long before others were producing articles in this new technique, and the names Thomas Law, Nathaniel Smith, Jacob and Samuel Roberts, Thomas Bradbury, Winter, Parsons & Co., Matthew Fenton & Co., Joseph Hancock, Charles Dixon, Thomas Leader and Henry Tudor are associated with this period. In the 1760's it was not unusual to silver only one side of the copper, so it is possible to find an early vessel silvered on the exterior and only tinned on the interior. Similarly, a cooking pan could be silvered on the interior surface only. Articles likely to corrode from the chemical actions of their contents were often gilded on the inside as a protection. Such items as salt-cellars, mustard pots and jugs will be found treated in this manner; rarely were the outside surfaces gilded.

Engraving the design on Sheffield Plate presented an obvious problem, as it was all too easy to penetrate the silver skin and expose

242

Fig. 71 Egg cruet, comprising stand and six egg cups. Sheffield Plate (*Adrian Bowyer, Beaconsfield*).

the underlying copper. So other means had to be found. **One** of these was die-stamping, which was achieved by cutting a hard metal block with the required pattern, in reverse of course, and then to stamp the silver clad copper. The impressions from these 'stamps' were clean and resembled the engraving normally associated with silver decoration. From about 1780, a form of engraving known as flat chasing was used to give a very good imitation of the more conventional methods employed by silversmiths. The design was outlined on the article and then the main pattern traced in with a fine steel point; this thin, almost scratched line was then deepened by a series of punches, shading and form being indicated by effective stippling. Conventional engraving was used, however, when the thickness of the silver permitted the use of the graver.

Bright cut engraving, a type of engraving used extensively by silversmiths, came into fashion with plated ware teapots, coffee pots, etc. It is a technique similar to chip carving, in which the line is bevelled in such a way that light is reflected from its facets. With time, and continual handling, the sharp edges become worn and it is difficult to distinguish 'bright cut' from flat chasing.

Pierced decoration was achieved by using various fly punches that did not cut the metal cleanly. The punches pierced the desired shape, but at the same time, dragged the silver cladding down into the aperture and so covered the copper. Unlike silver, Sheffield Plate is not hall-marked. In fact, prior to 1784, it was illegal to do so. From 1784, however, it was permissable for platemakers to put some identification such as their name or identifying mark on their products.

The recognition of genuine old Sheffield Plate cannot be achieved by any precise formula, which of course is not unusual where antiques are concerned. Experience and 'knowing' comes with constant close association with a particular branch, almost to the point of specialisation, and even experts are sometimes misled. However, there are a few guide lines that can be used. When prospecting for Sheffield Plate, inspect carefully, look at the joints and seams with a glass. If you cannot find any seams or joints, they have probably been covered up by electro-plating and you can conclude that it is not a genuine old piece.

When blemishes, such as an area of exposed copper, or a blister, occurred on the plate during the process of manufacture, it would be repaired by first cleaning the affected area, and then by applying thin foils of heated pure silver, under pressure, which were subsequently burnished. Such repairs are almost invisible except when the piece becomes tarnished, when the difference between the two silvers will show.

Although the coating of silver on Sheffield Plate is considerably thicker than that deposited by electro-plating, it will wear with constant cleaning, and if this had been excessive, the base metal will show through in the form of a copper tint. Whether we should add such a piece to our collection is entirely a personal matter.

Worn patches on Sheffield Plate have been renovated by re-plating electrically, a practice which could have taken place during Victorian times or even later. It will be difficult for the new collector to detect such renovations, but as a guide Sheffield Plate has a faint bluish tint, whilst electro-plated silver is whitish. The fused silver of Sheffield Plate is invariably harder than the silver electro-deposited, which is more porous and consequently softer.

Obviously Sheffield Plate cannot in all honesty carry a hall-mark in the same way as silver, but early pieces may appear to be so marked. The workers in plate were trying to copy the silverware of the day and provide a similar article at a reduced price, so why not copy or at least simulate the hall-mark.?

The Assay Offices can of course only certify by marking articles made entirely of silver, and in 1773 the Silversmiths of Sheffield and Birmingham petitioned Parliament to establish assay offices in their towns, with the intentions of putting the platers 'in their place', as it were. They got their assay offices but also a Statute prohibiting the striking of any letters. This was of course unfair to the platers, who now could not even mark their wares with their initials or trade mark. However in 1784 another Statute was passed which allowed the platers to strike their surname, or names of partners, followed by a device (trademark) at the end of the surname, as long as the mark was different from, or could not be, any mark used by the Assay Office.

So any marks you find on Old Sheffield Plate should conform to the above, but there were many irregularities, and many pieces will be found without any marks at all. In fact, it is doubtful if any articles in Sheffield plate were marked before 1784, as there was no compulsion to do so anyway.

Frederick Bradbury's *Guide to Marks of Origin on British and Irish Silver Plate*, of which there are various editions, will provide the best reference source for collectors who wish to study the subject.

Collectors should be aware that the term Sheffield Plate is indicative of the modern commodity produced by electro-plating techniques. The term 'Old Sheffield Plate' refers to the antique. If you are buying the latter, *make certain the vendor describes it correctly* on your receipt.

For the collector interested in Sheffield Plate, the following list gives an indication of the type of articles made and we trust that he will find something to suit his taste and his purse from the extensive range of possibilities:

Toast racks, Candelabrum, Candlesticks, Cheese-toasters, Cake Baskets, Fruit baskets, Tea pots, Coffee pots, Trays, Jugs, Kettles, Wine coolers, Covered dishes, Coasters, Egg stands, Egg servers, Sugar basins, Tankards, Beakers, Snuffers, Inkstands, Spoons and Forks, Fish servers, Saucepans, and so on, the range being almost limitless.

SILVER

22. Silver

Silver and gold are probably the two oldest metals known to mankind their discovery reaching back into the dark ages before recorded history. Old civilisations of the Greeks, Romans, Assyrians, and Egyptians were adorning themselves and their dwellings with beautifully decorated silver. Such is its appeal that even simple, plain surfaces of silver have a lustre and feel that delights the senses of most of us, and especially the silver collector.

Pure silver is very soft, and would not be suitable for utilitarian objects or for working if used in its pure state. Therefore it was alloyed with copper in the proportion of 18 dwts copper to 11 oz. 2 dwts silver, which produced sterling silver, the high quality material from which silverware and plate was made.

Collecting silver can be a very expensive pastime if only the large, fine quality pieces are sought, but if we drop our sights a little, however, and concentrate on the smaller items, we will not find ourselves excluded from the field. Neither will we be forced to accept articles of inferior quality; in fact, it can make the hunt more exciting if our resources are limited. Before we rush out to buy our first piece of silver, it will be as well to learn a little about the subject.

English silver prior to the Restoration is extremely rare. It was a common practice to melt down silver objects to provide the raw material for newer and more up-to-date objects, and sometimes to provide coinage. This practice obviously robbed posterity of a certain amount of silverware, but even more devastation was caused during the Civil War when large quantities of silver plate were melted down to provide coinage to pay the soldiers of both King and Commonwealth.

The designs produced by English silversmiths during the Restoration were greatly influenced by current Continental designs, especially those of the Netherlands, and as the Netherland designers borrowed much from the Italians, it is obvious that English silver of this period was a mixture of influences.

In 1697 the demand for silver to support the trade was so great that the metal became scarce, and it was profitable to obtain the metal by melting coinage. To prevent this happening the Britannia standard of 11 ounces, 10 pennyweights of silver in the pound troy was introduced.

Fig. 72 A Victorian baby's rattle in silver with mother-of-pearl teething ring, bells and whistle. 1851. Probably produced for the Great Exhibition (*Suzanne van de Gohm*).

When the Edict of Nantes, granted in 1598 by Henri IV of France, was revoked in 1685 by Louis XIV, many Huguenots emigrated from France and settled in other countries. Many silversmiths came to England, and brought with them the French provincial influence, which gradually replaced the Dutch styles. The French Huguenots were responsible for the plain silver of the Queen Anne period and the introduction of cut-card work, a method of soldering pierced and chiselled plates to the outside of a vessel for decorative purposes.

During the reign of William III the tea-pot, coffee and chocolate-pot made their first appearance, together with the silver tea kettle and stand. Tea caddies followed in the reign of Queen Anne, usually

247

Fig. 73 Cigarette case in silver. The golfer and the oval frame are embossed, raised from base. 1907 (*Loco Antiques*).

in sets of two or three, so that different types of tea could be blended to taste. Tea was expensive then, and it was usual to provide a lockable case for the tea containers.

Rococo style designs occured in England from about 1740, and embossing, which until now had been little used, became more defined.

A little after 1760, the styles of the neo-classicism period began to have its influence on silver design, and the simpler styles of Adam became much favoured. The tea service was now given a sugar basin and cream jug. Early cream jugs were pear shaped and without feet, but soon afterwards three tiny feet were added. The helmet shape was a typical neo-classic style.

Dinner services in silver were restricted to the wealthy. They did not, however, become widely used until the 18th century, and even then they were soon superseded by porcelain for everyday use.

The Regency period produced much heavy silver, but little domestic silver of any real note.

Victorian silver lacks much of the quality of earlier periods; the styles were mixed and artistically poor.

SILVER IN AMERICA

The raw material for the early American silversmiths was usually provided by their customers in the form of silver coins. In the early days of colonisation, silver was a much prized metal, possessed only by the presumably rich minority. It had a particular significance in terms of wealth conservation; as there were no banks, wrought silver objects became a method of providing financial insurance against a rainy day.

Unlike the English, the early American silversmiths did not hallmark their wares. It was customary to simply stamp the piece with the individual maker's mark, either his name or initials. It is surprising to find the craft of silversmithing flourishing so early in America; even before 1650 there were silversmiths working in Massachusetts, designing examples in the relatively simple English styles of the Jacobean period.

From 1660 to 1697, American silversmiths followed the English trends of the late Stuart and William and Mary period. Typical examples of the wares at this time were tankards, beakers, mugs, porringers, candlesticks, and various cups for tea, chocolate and coffee drinking.

New York, originally a Dutch settlement, became interested in the craft of the silversmith a little later than New England. As may be expected, the styles, at first, were greatly influenced by the styles prevailing in the Netherlands at that time. Most of the early New York silversmiths were either Dutch or of Dutch descent, and the wares reflected the heavier proportions and sizes of the Dutch.

By 1700, silversmiths had become established in other parts of America, particularly in centres that had both wealth and culture.

From 1765 to 1800, new motives were introduced in silver, largely brought about by the classical revival; slim columns, masks, medallions, beautiful pendant husks, swags, and the technique of bright cutting. Although Robert Sanderson (1608–1693) is reputed to have been the 'Father of American silversmiths', the best known must surely be Paul Revere (1735–1818), patriot and craftsman, who learnt the silversmiths trade early in life. He was also an engraver of copper-plates, wood-carver, founder, and even supplied nuts and bolts.

HALLMARKS

The introduction of hallmarks was to guarantee the quality, or standard, of the silver used in the manufacture of a particular article. With English silver we can say that the practise started in 1300, during the reign of Edward I, when the first statute of any importance was decreed. This statute stated that all silver had to be assayed and stamped with the head of a leopard before it was offered for sale. A subsequent law of 1363 specified that the maker add his mark. There were various other statutes made during the next 100 years to strengthen the system, and in 1477 yet another statute insisted that the Goldsmiths' Company of London ensured that the standard was maintained. Approximately one year later, the date letter was introduced and from then hence, the system can be considered to have been established.

English, Scottish and Irish silver is usually hall-marked with characters and symbols that greatly aid the collector. As a guide these are important, but remember it is possible to find good pieces without any marks.

There are normally four or five marks. One mark will show the maker's initials, another the standard or quality mark for sterling silver which is the 'Lion Passant'. (In heraldic terms this means lion walking, or leg raised.) Next comes the date letter, which is a letter on a shield; the style of letter and shape of the shield positively identifies the year of hallmarking, which is usually, of course, the year of manufacture.

We can identify the particular assay office where the article was tested and hallmarked from another mark—an anchor for Birmingham, a leopard's head for London, a harp for Dublin, a crown for Sheffield, a castle for Edinburgh and so on.

Between 1697 and 1720 a higher standard of silver known as the 'Britannia standard' became compulsory. The lion passant was replaced by a figure of Britannia and the leopard's head by a lion's head erased (torn off the shoulder). The sterling standard was restored in 1720 but the Britannia standard with its special marks continued as an optional second standard.

An additional mark, the reigning sovereign's head, was used between 1784 and 1890 to show that the duty had been paid. The duty on silver was abolished in 1890.

Now where do we start our collection? Do we start with tableware, and use it in the home in a practical way? Good usable domestic

Fig. 74 A selection of silver spoons with marks showing dates between 1798 and 1930 (*Mabel Gohm*).

silver will not be too expensive, providing we select carefully. It is worth remembering that since the Restoration almost every type of tableware has been produced in silver. Excluding the obvious knives, forks and spoons which are more useful if collected in sets, there are beautiful single pieces of flatware such as cheese-scoops, strainer spoons, apple corers and marrow scoops. Some of the smaller items of holloware such as beakers and tankards will be a little more expensive, but they can be pressed into use.

Ideal pieces for the silver cabinet are snuff boxes, patch-boxes and vinaigrettes. A vinaigrette is a small box, usually beautifully decorated which has a small grill or grid, to contain a sponge in the base of the box. The sponge was soaked in aromatic vinegar. It was used for inhaling the vapour, which overcame any prevailing bad smells. Vinaigrettes are also known as sponge-boxes, and were produced in materials other than silver, as you will see under the various headings in this book.

251

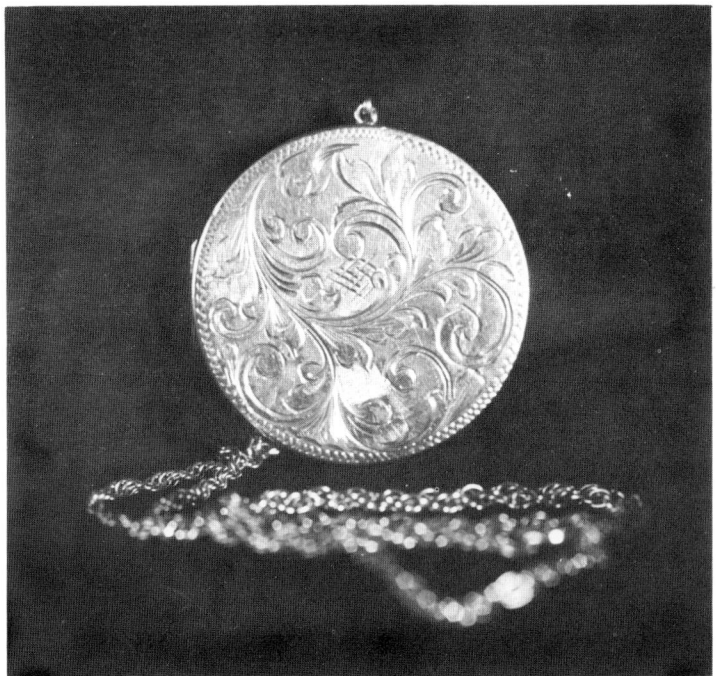

Fig. 75　Silver locket. Interior fitted with two frames to hold photographs (*Suzanne van de Gohm*).

Vinaigrettes date from the times of George III (1760–1820) and were in use up to Victorian times. It is interesting to note that the orange carried by Cardinal Wolsey was, in fact, an orange hollowed out, and a sponge substituted to carry the vinegar, as a protection against the plague and other pestilences.

Collecting vinaigrettes will prove a good introduction to silver; the vast majority are marked, and some experience of the field can be gained with little chance of 'being caught'. They are usually rectangular, but other shapes are not uncommon. The exteriors are usually beautifully hand engraved, and some of the more desirable types have a raised pattern on the lid.

In the same class as vinaigrettes, and an ideal series to combine in a collection, are patch-boxes, used for carrying court plasters, and spice-boxes, for holding nutmeg, which was grated and sprinkled into wine. These small boxes were produced both in England and on the Continent; however, the English type are preferable as they tend to be more robust than the continental variety.

A teapot in Georgian silver makes tea time more pleasurable. The tea tastes better, and one can appreciate the pot whilst drinking. With

Fig. 76 Silver Candlestick, George II. Cast, with Dublin Hall Marks dating the article 1745.

time, perhaps the collector will wish to add a jug for the milk, a basin for sugar and even a tray to put them on. If you advance a collection in this way be certain to obtain the additional pieces in the same style, and near date, so that each piece matches and forms a complete set, rather than add unrelated pieces. A matching set will be more valuable should you wish to re-sell, and remember that such a set is likely to be more valuable than the sum of the prices you paid for each individual item.

Fig. 77 Sugar Caster. George III. Dated 1815. Made by John Crouch.

Whilst on the subject of tableware, salt cellars, mustard pots and the like are relatively cheap. Eighteenth century salt cellars were like a shallow bowl with a moulded base, later ones had three or four feet on which to stand. From about 1765 the shape became oval and the sides pierced, and they contained a glass liner for the salt. Early 19th century salt cellars were sometimes designed as miniature tureens. Mustard, until about the middle of the 18th century, was not premixed in a pot. It was presented at table as a powder, in castors with unpierced lids. The user had to mix his own mustard on the side of his plate.

254

After about 1760, when mustard was premixed, the pots, either cylindrical, or pierced, often contained glass liners and were usually blue in colour. These fairly plain types were followed by oval, and later by the more elegant spherical types.

Candlesticks can be found in great variety. The earliest form, known as a pricket, had a spike on which the candle was impaled. This type, however, is rare in silver. The many-branched table candlestick is also comparatively rare, particularly in matched pairs or sets.

Spoon collecting has many adherents, probably because spoons are not excessively expensive and they offer a wide variety of choice. The spoons of the Commonwealth period had simple rectangular stems without any decorations on the ends. These were followed by spoons with a trifid termination, i.e. the end terminated in three lobes.

Apostle spoons are known to everyone because they are still being produced today. Originally they were made in sets of thirteen, one of which represented Christ, and they were used for christening presents. The Georgian strainer spoon had the bowl pierced or straining tea and a long, slim, pointed stem for clearing the spouts of tea pots. Punch ladles are really special purpose spoons, with a large and deep bowl, and a long slim handle made from wood, whalebone, ivory, silver, etc. In addition to the foregoing, there were spoons in silver for almost every conceivable purpose—marrow spoons, mustard spoons, strainer spoons, caddy spoons.

The field of silver is vast. Any attempt at detailed descriptions of all the possibilities is beyond the scope of any single book.

The following glossary includes short descriptions of generic types of silverware. This, it is hoped, will demonstrate the scope to the novice collector, and aid his armchair thinking on the subject.

AMERICAN SILVERSMITHS

1684–1755	Hendrik Boelen	New York
1654–1729	Jacob Boelen	New York
1693–1745	John Burt	Boston
1656–1722	John Coney	Boston
1645–1718	Jeremiah Dummer	Boston
1675–1757	Cornelius Kierstede	New York
1678–1753	Koenraet Ten Eyck	New York
1624–1683	John Hull	Boston
1723–1795	Myer Myers	New York
1681–1729	Francis Richardson	Philadelphia
1608–1693	Robert Sanderson	Boston
1670–1739	Philip Syng	Philadelphia
1669–1753	Edward Winslow	Boston

GLOSSARY

Acanthus: Foliage design originally used on the capitols of Corinthian columns. The design was used between 16th and 17th centuries for silver, mainly as an embossing.

Almsdish: A circular dish with a flat rim, used for collecting alms.

Annealing: When silver is worked, i.e. formed and hammered, the metal becomes hard and brittle. To restore the metal to a more ductile state, it is carefully heated, or annealed.

Applied: Added to; various parts of silverware are made as separate details, and subsequently joined by the application of solder.

Arabesque: Patterns of flowers and foliage interlaced.

Argyle: A gravy container with a liner for carrying hot water to keep the contents hot. Container usually spouted. First appeared about 1770 and in general use until the early 1800's.

Assay: Test for quality. Metal was removed from the specimen for assay purposes with a scraper.

Bail Handle: A half circle or half looped hinged handle, like a bucket handle.

Baroque: Refers to the late Renaissance period, when decoration became flamboyant with scrolls and natural motives.

Baskets: Baskets were made to contain fruit, bread, cake and sweetmeats. Early baskets are rare. From about 1730 the basket shape was oval, and had swing handles. Wirework baskets with applied decorations made their appearance about 1770. From about 1800 the shape became circular, like the very early baskets.

Bat's Wing Fluting: A pattern used on hollow-ware resembling the outline of a bat's wing, produced by graduated gadrooning—straight or radiating lines with a raised lobe between the lines.

Beading: Like a bead. Ornamental bordering composed of half spheres, resembling a string of beads.

Beakers: Drinking vessels without handles or stems.

Bells: Table bells of silver made their first appearance in the 16th century, but English bells are rare prior to the 18th century.

Bezel: An added inside rim.

Biggin: A type of coffee pot, usually with a short spout, often used with a stand and spirit lamp.

Bleeding Bowl: A bowl used by surgeons to catch the blood when blood-letting.

Bottle Ticket: Small silver plaques hung on bottles, inscribed to indicate contents (see also Wine and Spirit Labels).

Brandy Bowls: Mainly of Scandinavian origin, these bowls were used for serving hot brandy during the 17th century. They were flat, with two handles.

256

THE GAME SECURED.

'*The Game Secured*' *coloured aquatint by J. Harris after W. J. Shayer. (Parker Gallery, London)*

'*The Strand*'. *Coloured lithograph by T. S. Boys. (Parker Gallery, London)*

Brazier: Bowl with pierced base for burning charcoal, used for heating kettles, etc., during late 17th and early 18th century. Superseded by the spirit lamp and stand.

Buckles: Used for shoes, waistbands, and knee straps, now comparatively rare.

Candelabrum: A candlestick to hold more than one candle. English candelabrum before the 18th century are practically non-existent.

Candlestick: There are many styles and designs of candlesticks, either as single pieces, in pairs, or in sets of four, cast, or made from sheet. 17th century domestic candlesticks are usually square, with a square base.

Canister: A box or container for storing tea.

Cann: A type of mug having rounded sides, standing on a moulded base.

Canteen: A portable case for carrying a knife, fork, spoon, beaker, and condiments. Used by travellers during late 17th and 18th century.

Casters: Containers for pepper, sugar and mustard. Mustard casters usually had an unpierced lid. Pepper and sugar lids, or covers, were pierced in decorative designs. During the late 18th century, caster bodies changed to glass, and only the tops were then made in silver. 17th century style was mainly cylindrical, followed by vase and pear shapes during 18th century.

Censer: An incense burner, now quite rare.

Centre Piece: A decorative piece, often very elaborate in design, used in the centre of a table.

Chalice: A cup, used by the Church for consecrating wine.

Chandelier: Hanging branched candle holders.

Charger: A large decorated dish, intended more for exhibition than for utilitarian purposes.

Cheese-Scoop: First introduced in the late 18th century, cheese-scoops had a curved blade with a silver shaft. Handles were made of ivory, silver, or wood.

Chocolate-Pot: Very similar to a coffee pot, but is fitted with a sliding cover finial which exposes a hole to admit a stirring rod.

Coffee-Pot: Early English examples had either straight or tapering bodies, later examples polygonal. Pear-shaped and classical forms appeared from about 1730.

Compostiera: Container for stewed fruits. Usually two silver jars with glass linings, on a salver-like base.

Cow Cream Jug: A jug in the shape of a cow with lid in the back. Milk pours from the mouth. Introduced into England from Holland about 1755.

Cream Jug: Early examples were pitcher-shaped. Pear-shaped bodies supported by three feet were introduced about 1750. Flat-bottomed jugs without feet appeared from about 1800. After 1800 the cream jug tended to be part of a tea set and matched the other vessels.

'C'-Scroll: Describes the shape of a handle which resembles a letter 'C'.

Cupping Bowl: A bleeding bowl.

Cups: Between the 16th and 17th century a vast number of cups for various uses were made, a few examples follow:

Caudle Cup: Two handled cup for serving caudle, and other drinks.

Communion Cup: Equivalent of chalice.

Feeding Cup: Cup with spout for feeding invalids.

Tumbler Cup: Drinking vessel with straight sides and rounded base.

Dram Cup: A shallow bowl, small, with two handles.

Dredger: A kitchen pepper pot with side handle.

Epergne: A table piece containing various dishes for pickles, fruit, etc. usually very elaborate.

Étui: A small case used by ladies to carry bodkin, snuff spoon, etc.

Ewer: Water jugs of elaborate design. Used at meal-times for washing hands in the 16th century.

Finial: Ornamental top to a cover.

Fish-Slice: First introduced about 1750. The slices were made with ivory and wooden handles in addition to silver. Early examples are the most attractive with their pierced and engraved patterns.

Flagon: Container for wine, not unlike large tankards. Not many produced after 1750.

Gadroon: A style of decoration, produced by casting or hammering, used on borders of candlestick bases and the like. The pattern is formed of straight or radiating lines with a raised lobe between the lines.

Goblet: A heavy-based, bulbous drinking vessel.

Inkstand: 18th century inkstands were mainly a tray with inkpot, pounce-box, taper stick and bell, in one form or another. Earlier examples are rare.

Jewel Boxes: Usually rectangular with hinged lids, some decorated by engraving, but majority moulded or chased.

Jewellery: Brooches, bracelets, buttons, pendant lockets, etc., often set with stones.

Ladle: There are various types of ladles, made for specific purposes. Basic shape of a sauce ladle had a deep bowl and a curved handle. Punch ladles had long handles, bowls with double lips date from about 1725. From the 18th century handles were usually horn or whale-bone. Earlier examples had long tapering handles of silver.

Cream ladles were smaller versions of sauce ladles.

Soup ladles were also similar to sauce ladles, but with a long stem.

From the latter part of the 18th century, ladle designs, except perhaps for punch, were made to conform with tea and table sets.

Lemon-Sqeezer: A device for squeezing lemons dating from early 19th century, consisting of hinged levers with depression for holding the lemons.

Matting: A matt surface produced by repeated punching with a burred tool.

258

Mazarine: A flat straining plate used for draining fish dishes.

Meat-Dish: These are found in sizes between about 10 and 30 inches. Usually oval in shape with gadrooned rims after about 1730. From about 1775 beaded rims appear. Early meat dishes have moulded rims.

Moulding: Castings produced from a mould, or border decoration produced by casting or hammering.

Ovolo: A moulding used in the 16th century for border decoration shaped like a small oval. Also used in 18th and early 19th century.

Pannikin: A small drinking cup.

Perfume Burner: These were made in England until about the middle of the 19th century. Late 17th century burners were more elaborate, and they are now rare.

Pin Cushion: Pin cushions with a silver frame may be found from the late 17th century, up to the middle of the 19th century.

Pipkin: A small saucepan-like vessel used to warm brandy. Usually spouted, handle of wood.

Planish: To flatten. Usually executed with an oval faced punch.

Pomander: Box for carrying spices which were used to ward off pestilences, used much the same as vinaigrettes, but often more elaborate in design.

Porringer: A bowl, with or without a lid, having two handles and used for porridge or meats.

Pounce Box: Bottle for holding pounce or sand for sprinkling onto writing.

Pricking: A form of engraving using a needle point to 'prick out' the design.

Punch Bowl: Used from the 17th century, to serve punch. The bowl was circular and often had two drop handles.

Quaich: A drinking cup with two or more handles, originated in Scotland.

Raising: A term used to describe the method of 'raising' silver plate from a flat sheet into a cup shape. This was done by successive hammerings over wooden blocks to stretch and form the sheet. This operation caused the silver to harden (see Annealing).

Reeding: A border moulding of parallel convex convolutions.

Reed and Tie: Similar to reeding, but with cross straps added.

Repoussé Work: A form of relief work obtained by hammering from the under or inner surface, often enhanced by chasing the outline.

Salt-Cellar: 18th century salt-cellars were simply a circular bowl, either with a moulded base or on three or four feet. More elaborate oval shapes with pierced sides and glass liners appeared later in the century from about 1765. A few years later the plain boat-shape was introduced.

Salver: A flat plate or tray for carrying other vessels. Shapes include circular, oval, rectangular and polygonal, with decorative borders and chasing. Often found raised on tiny feet.

Saucepan: Found from early 18th to early 19th century. Basically a cylindrical or bellied body, sometimes lipped, with wooden handles.

Scent Bottle: Those for carrying on one's person were small, and often pear-shaped, and decorated.

Dressing-table scent bottles of the 17th century were larger.

Sconce: A wall light. Consisting of a decorated plaque, from which one or more branched candleholders are mounted.

Silver Gilt: Silver over which has been applied a thin coating of gold.

Skewer: Dates from early 18th century. Meat skewers either had a ring or decorated fan termination to facilitate handling.

Skillet: Saucepan for heating liquids, with legs. Often with covers. Dates from 17th century.

Snuff Box: Found in great varieties from solid silver and with combinations of gem stones, wood, tortoise-shell and many other materials.

Snuffers: An instrument for trimming candlewick, similar to a pair of scissors.

Spinning: A method of producing small hollow-ware from sheet by spinning the material on a lathe and forming with hand-held, polished surfaced tools.

Spoons: These exist in tremendous varieties; the best known is probably the Apostle spoon with its figures of an apostle full length along the finial.

Spoons were also made for many special purposes, including spoons for basting, tea measuring, dessert, egg, marrow, mustard, salt, snuff, straining, table, and so on.

Sucket Fork: An instrument with two-pronged fork at one end and a spoon at the other, used for eating sweetmeats.

Sugar Bowl: Early 18th century bowls were plain circular, or many sided. Later examples were combined to form matching sets.

Sugar Sifter: A ladle-shaped spoon with pierced bowl for sprinkling sugar over food.

Table Services: Complete table services date from the 18th century, where they appeared on the tables of the very wealthy.

Tankard: A beer-drinking vessel, with or without a lid, and a single handle.

Taper Box: Cylindrical box for containing coiled sealing wax taper, dates from about 1700.

Tea Kettle: Designs not unlike teapots; early examples have stands for spirit lamp or charcoal heaters, and late 18th century examples may have a tap replacing the spout. The tea urn made its appearance about 1760.

Tea Pots: English teapots are found with spherical, pear-shaped, oval and semi-rectangular bodies. Squat circular shapes were introduced in the early 19th century, together with sugar basin and cream jug, to form a set.

Teapots can be found from practically the whole of the world.

Toast Rack: These date from about 1770.

Waxjack: Consists of an open frame through which a spindle is fitted to carry a coiled sealing taper. One end of the taper is fed through a ring at the top of the frame. Dates from about the late 17th century.

SNUFF BOXES

23. Snuff Boxes

Sir Walter Raleigh, English military and naval commander, explorer and poet in the time of Elizabeth I, was responsible for introducing tobacco into Britain. Every schoolboy knows this, but the weed was shredded and smoked by native tribes of the Americas well before this period. The habit of sniffing the ground leaf was also practised before the English were aware that snuff existed, but just when this practice began is a matter of conjecture.

The primitive method used for snuff-taking was to insert a forked tube, made of cane, into the nostrils, and to place the other end into a container of powdered tobacco, and then sniff—a somewhat crude procedure which presumably resulted in an ear-splitting sneeze.

Tobacco was once regarded by doctors as a valuable medicine, and during the plague of London, both tobacco smoking and snuff-taking was considered to be a beneficial remedy. Incidentally, the name 'nicotine' was coined after one Jean Nicot, French Ambassador to Portugal, who sent some of the powder to the Queen of France; she was obviously much impressed by its properties and a snuff-taking vogue caught on in the French court.

Strange as it may seem, the Irish were taking snuff long before it became a popular habit in England, and by the middle of the 17th century, they had become really heavy snuff takers.

As may be expected, the Irish had their own descriptive colloquialism to describe snuff-taking—Smutchin was the word they used.

Snuff was carried on the person so that a pinch could be taken whenever required. A convenient method of carrying the powder was obviously to use a small box fitted with a tight lid. Some gentlemen, like Dr. Johnson, had a pocket of their waistcoats lined with soft leather, and they simply tipped the loose snuff into the pocket. Another method was to carry a solid roll of tobacco and a small snuff rasp with which to grate the tobacco into powder when required.

The solid roll of tobacco was known as a Carotte (from the French 'like a carrot') and it followed that a great variety of rasps were made from the middle of the 17th century to suit all needs and tastes. These rasps make excellent and sympathetic items for collectors of snuff boxes.

Snuff mull and tools

Early rasps were somewhat crude, being nothing more than a functional grater mounted as a lid on a simple wooden box. The rasp, or grating element, consisted of a strip of metal, pierced with jagged-edged holes, similar to the present day nutmeg grater.

During the 18th century, when snuff-taking became very fashionable, rasps became more decorative and elaborate. The rasp was provided with a protective cover, often made from wood or ivory, carved with an ornamental design, and decorated with gold and silver piqué work. A pin hinge at one end allowed the cover to be swung away to expose the rasping surface.

Rasps that were used by shops are now relatively rare; these were usually quite plain in design and may measure up to 24 inches in length.

The early Scottish snuff-mill operated on a different principle. It consisted of a small barrel-like container, into which a projecting piece, fitted to the underside of the lid, was forced down onto the leaf tobacco in the barrel. The grinding end of the projecting piece was fitted with a rough surface of metal points, which when rotated acted as a grinding mill.

By the end of the 17th century snuff could be easily obtained already ground either fine or coarse, and plain, flavoured or scented to suit the most fastidious noses, and the snuff rasp virtually fell into disuse.

Fig. 78   Snuff Box in the shape of a shoe. Made of papier mâché with mother-of-pearl inlaid lid, and finely defined imitation stitching. *c.* 1870. (*Loco Antiques*).

Fig. 79   Snuff Box made in papier mâché. The inlay is silver and the interior metal lined. (*Aldgate Ltd.*).

Early snuff boxes were made out of wood, ivory, horn, etc., and suitably carved, but as the habit became more fashionable, the snuff box became more ornate and varied. Collectors will be interested in snuff boxes dating from the early 18th century, because from this date their production became more prolific and artistic, and a much wider variety of materials was used including pewter, gold, silver, papier mâché, and porcelain. Vinaigrettes were made which included a compartment for snuff and even the tops of canes were designed to house a snuff box.

Tortoise-shell, often decorated with piqué work in gold and silver, was a popular material because the tortoise-shell possessed insulating properties that helped to keep the snuff dry, and fresh. Wood, of course, in every conceivable type and combination was used in the manufacture of snuff boxes. The Victorians, always keen on new ideas, incorporated all their inventiveness in trick locks, concealed locks, and secret compartments to protect their snuff; surprisingly so, because it was not a very expensive commodity.

Both simple and elaborate snuff boxes were made from horn; it was an inexpensive material that lent itself to shaping by steaming, and in consequence this led to the production of a great variety of circular boxes, often with impressed designs on the lid.

Probably the simplest and most practical of all the snuff boxes were those made by the Scottish crofters from a piece of natural horn, stoppered with a wooden plug. The more dandified Scot had his piece of horn fitted with a hinged lid, sometimes jewelled and decorated with engraved silver.

Early in the 18th century, the Chinese started to produce containers for snuff. Snuff bottles from the Ch'ien Lung period (1736–1795) are rare; consequently the price will be generally beyond the average collector, but this period in Chinese porcelain is noted for its classical style and some very fine colours in monochrome, notably the flambé copper reds, and the soft enamels that were much used as glazes.

It is interesting to note that many snuff bottles were imported from China in an unfinished state, the silver mounts and stoppers being fitted in Great Britain.

Snuff bottles are obtainable from about two inches to six inches in height; they are narrow necked and have a tight-fitting stopper to which is attached a long-handled spoon for dipping into the bottle and extracting the snuff.

Chinese porcelain is really a subject for the expert; therefore before spending a lot of money on Chinese porcelain snuff bottles, consult a reputable dealer, experienced in this field of collecting.

Porcelain was used extensively as a decorative medium; small

Chinese Snuff Bottle

plaques made in Dresden, Battersea enamel, and in Chelsea were all used to decorate snuff boxes. Whilst lacking the decorative appeal of the Chinese bottles, there are many English and American snuff jars, often carrying the printed name of the vendor, and a description of the contents. Not so very long ago, it was quite common to see rows of these jars in most tobacconists, offering a wide choice of nose-tickling aromatic powders.

Another interesting type of snuff bottle was made from glass and hand-painted on the inside. The painting was executed by inserting a small brush through the neck, and in spite of the apparent difficulty of painting under such limiting conditions, the results were often excellent and composed of fine detail. Such bottles should be judged for quality on the basis of the fineness of the painting.

Snuff boxes in gold and silver are available to collectors with the necessary bank balance, but some very interesting examples in less precious materials are within the scope of collectors with more modest resources; for example, papier mâché. The Victorian snuff box in the form of a shoe was a popular novelty; its detail was fine and even the stitching on the toe cap defined; the lid was quite often tastefully inlaid with mother-of-pearl. The shape made it a little awkward to carry on the person and it can be assumed that such designs were intended for the desk or table top. Other Victorian snuff boxes are more practical, the interior of which will be found metal lined, and with a well fitting lid, often decorated with inlaid metal and ideally suited to a waistcoat pocket.

The shoe was always a popular snuff box shape, and many will be found in other materials, including carved wood with little brass studs to simulate the buttons. The plainer carved wood boxes without the brass studs are of less value and usually of poorer quality.

An interesting oddity comprising a ram's horn, with grooves on the inside for rasping the tobacco plug, and a lid, was known as the 'sneeshing miln'. The small impedimenta required to operate the miln were hung from the lid by small chains—a snuff spoon, a small hammer or mallet, a snuff rake and a hares foot or brush from horse-hair for cleaning up the moustache after partaking of a pinch.

TOYS AND GAMES

24. Toys and Games

Toys and games, in one form or another, have been made and used by men and children from very early times. Dolls made of terracotta, with movable arms and legs, were certainly used by the Greeks, and there is evidence, provided by excavations, of dolls in the days of ancient Babylon. Unfortunately very few examples of very early toys have survived the passage of time.

Toy shops, as we know them today, did not exist generally before the 19th century. Toys were certainly made by adults for their children from early times, but the toys of gold and silver made by craftsmen in the 16th century were a trade side-line to provide amusing objects for adult collectors.

It is interesting to learn that the word 'toy' dates only from the 16th century and did not have the same meaning then as it does today. It referred then to small decorative objects like buttons, shoe-buckles, and other 'gallantries'.

Dolls were being made at Nuremburg at least from the 15th century, mainly by wood carvers, and it is probable that they were being made there even earlier. Nuremburg was still an important toy manufacturing centre during Victoria's reign. Collectors usually concentrate on 19th century examples, when mass-produced toys of great variety were made to supply the increasing demand. Mechanical toys, powered by clockwork of almost entirely German or Swiss origin, were made with great ingenuity, and good quality examples can command high prices.

Like all antiques, good examples are difficult to find at reasonable prices, and toys and games are no exception, but diligent searching will often result in an unexpected find.

ARKS

Model arks, with their numerous animals, were originally intended to amuse children on Sundays. It was a quiet pastime, which had the correct religious associations.

It is difficult to say with any certainty when model arks were first used, but they were certainly a firm, favourite plaything during the 19th century, and they were manufactured in great numbers from about 1840.

Good quality arks must have been expensive, even during those

Fig. 81 Cup and Ball. An excellent example of quality turning (*Victoria and Albert Museum. Crown copyright*).

Fig. 80 Cup and Ball. Victorian child's toy (*Victoria and Albert Museum, Crown copyright*).

Fig. 82   Victorian Miniature Armour for Horse and Man, in the 16th century style.
Height 28½ inches. Not a genuine toy.

Fig. 83 Noah's Ark, made of straw and wood. The animals have been shaped rather crudely but they are all recognisable. This beautiful ark was made by French prisoners-of-war and can be seen at the Bethnal Green Museum (*Victoria and Albert Museum. Crown copyright*).

days; they were generally constructed of wood, with a deep hull that provided storage for the animals and Noah's family, when not in use. The animals were well made, and like the ark, painted in appropriate colours and markings.

Cheaper and simpler arks were made without the deep hull, a single wooden raft serving the same purpose. The animals, mass-produced, were made of wood and plaster, and sometimes quite crudely finished.

As mentioned in the text covering 'Bone Carving', French prisoners-of-war, captured during the Napoleonic wars, applied

270

Fig. 84   'Caroline' cottage showing interior furnishings. 1831 (*Victoria and Albert Museum. Crown copyright*).

271

Fig. 85   A beautiful doll's house made under the direction of Queen Mary. Made in 1887. English (*Victoria and Albert Museum. Crown copyright*).

themselves to many trades, and the making of model arks was one of their activities.

A beautiful example of prisoner-of-war work can be seen at the Bethnal Green Museum; it is made of wood and coloured straw, with a deep hull and inset door, and the 'House' has a porch style door and windows. The animals, although somewhat crude, are recognisable.

Straw-work was an English craft, and to protect the home industry, the authorities would not, at first, permit any good quality straw to be taken into the prisons. However, 'where there's a will there's a way' and when there was a mattress there was straw, so the

Fig. 86 Miniature set of four chairs and two brass folding tables. Presumably made for a doll's house. Victorian. (*Adrian Bowyer, Beaconsfield*).

enterprising Frenchmen found their source of material under their noses. Eventually the authorities gave way and the Frenchmen had their straw.

These early arks were often unpainted, as they were made either of pine with decorative veneer, or were finished with straw-work or marquetry.

DOLLS HOUSES

Dolls houses, known in England from the early 18th century, were originally a German innovation. Initially, they were a toy, designed for adults rather than for children, and were used as demonstration models for teaching girls the intricacies of running a house. As may be expected, these were only to be seen in the houses of the well-to-do, but during the reign of Victoria, they ceased to be the prerogative of the rich, and almost every Victorian child could then boast of a dolls house of their own.

A typical, good quality dolls house of the late Victorian period would resemble a real house of the period, completely furnished with

273

Fig. 87 Mechanical Toy. Made in U.S.A. The figures dance to music from a musical box in the base (*Victoria and Albert Museum. Crown copyright*).

miniature furniture and utensils (see the Miles House at Bethnal Green Museum).

Many of the tiny ornaments, tea-sets, furnishing pieces etc., were made on semi-production lines by skilled craftsmen specifically for dolls houses, and these can form an interesting collection, even if they are not displayed in a dolls house.

MECHANICAL TOYS

These are now in very great demand, especially if they are in good condition and rare. Recent sale prices for such examples exceed £1,000. However, even if the price is above your means it will be interesting to know a little about them.

One such model is an automatous snake charmer, (it is almost too exotic to be labelled 'Toy'), with a beautifully proportioned standing figure of a girl holding a trumpet in one hand, and a snake in the other hand. The figure stands on a plinth which houses the clock-work. When wound up, music plays, her head moves, her breasts rise and fall, the snake wriggles and she raises the trumpet to her lips. What a toy!

Figures of minstrels and musicians which play a tune from a hidden music box, open their mouths, move their heads, and strum on a musical instrument, are more often than not of Austrian origin and can usually be found at a price much lower than that of the snake charmer.

Clockwork rowing boats, clowns that tumble, trees with birds flying around and singing, are just a few of the possibilities the 19th century offered in mechanical toys.

HORSES AND WAGGONS

These were usually a carved horse mounted on a wheeled platform, and propelled by pulling on a length of string attached to the platform. Sometimes two horses were mounted on a single platform.

Carts were attached to the horse, which was between the shafts, by leather thongs or small chains.

The variety of carts, carriages and coaches are numerous and many are finely executed.

DOLLS

Old dolls are collected by a considerable number of people, and they have been doing so for a number of years. Some antique shops even specialise in the subject, so it will not be an easy field to enter.

275

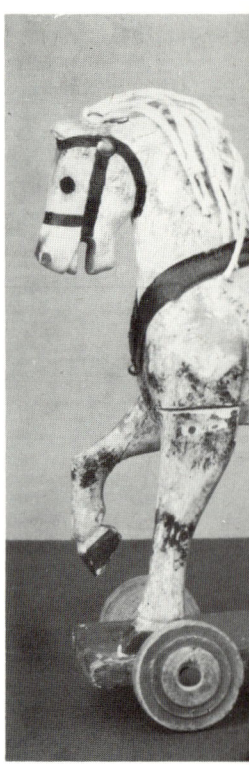

Fig. 89 Child's Toy Horse and Coal cart (*Victoria and Albert Museum. Crown copyright*).

Fig. 88 Doll in costume of 1830. English (*Victoria and Albert Museum. Crown copyright*).

Early European dolls had large heads and faces, and hands made of wood. The eyes were applied in paint. 'Queen Anne Dolls' are similar, but they usually have glass eyes and peg-mounted limbs. Dolls made of wood made originally by peasants of the Thuringian Forest, were known in England as 'Dutch Dolls'; these Dolls had painted hair.

Wax dolls with either wooden, kid or stuffed cloth bodies were made as early as the mid-18th century, but they are generally considered to be a Victorian innovation. Hair was added to some of the wax dolls, strand by strand, using a new technique which employed a hot needle. France gave us the Bisque head and limbs, which were followed by porcelain.

The 'Pedlar' dolls were a firm Victorian favourite, so named because they, in fact, 'peddled their wares' from little baskets or trays.

The latest development was, of course, the 'Sleeping Doll' which closed her eyes when laid flat.

277

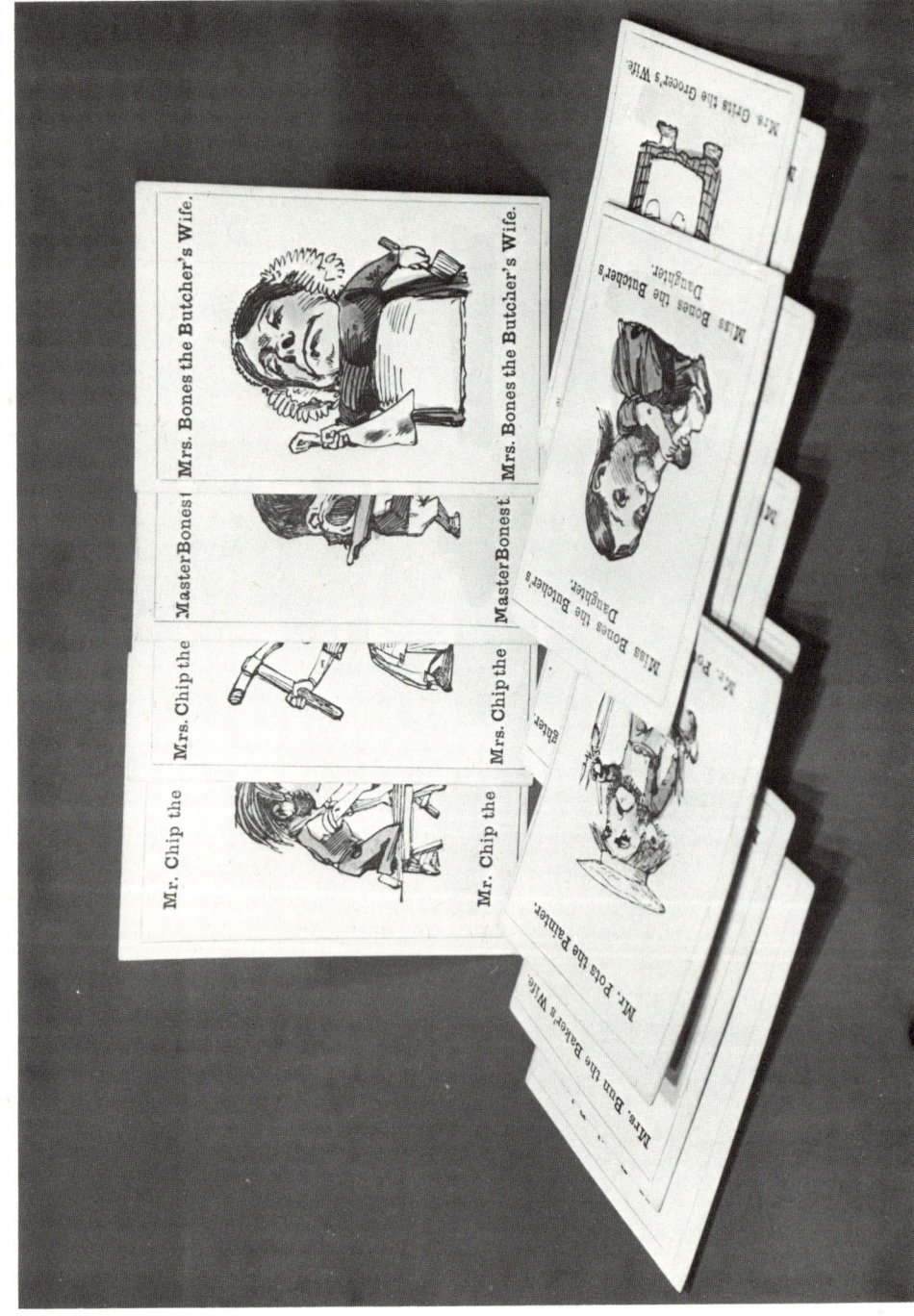

Fig. 90 'Happy Family' playing cards. This pack was produced from hand engraved plates and later hand coloured. Victorian *(R. van de Gohm).*

ROCKING HORSES

Rocking horses of carved wood, mounted on curved rockers, and suitably painted, were a common nursery toy. Many examples of these strong, robust horses have survived from the early 19th century when they were in vogue. In about 1900 the safety rocking horse was made to prevent accidents caused by over-enthusiastic children who 'over rocked', and so came tumbling off. This type of horse was mounted on a strong fixed frame by 'U' shaped links, which permitted a realistic motion although the base was stationary.

CARD GAMES

Card games with an educational bias have always been popular, and they have been produced over the past 100 years or so in considerable numbers. Victorian children were rarely allowed to play games using normal playing cards; these were considered to be the 'devil's cards'.

Specialist collectors are always searching for good quality card games, and they are slowly becoming more difficult to find, except perhaps in museums devoted to toys and with the few antique specialists.

'Happy Families' and 'Snap' have long been in vogue, but here are a few of the lesser known.

'Panki' was a Suffragette game in vogue about 1912.

'Geography of England and Wales', which includes the use of a map, dates about 1799.

'Old Maid', dates about 1900.

'Peter Puzzlewigs Mirthful Game of Alliteration', dates about 1840.

'The Wandering Jew', a German set of cards dated about 1832.

'Historical Lotto', a German set of cards dating about 1890.

The majority of the above card games can be seen in the Derby Museum and Art Gallery at Wardwick in Derby.

TUNBRIDGE WARE

25. Tunbridge Ware

Tunbridge Ware originated in the area of Tunbridge Wells, some 300 years ago. It was a form of veneering used to decorate a wide range of wooden objects, and should not be confused with marquetry or English Mosaic.

The pictures and patterns in Tunbridge Ware were created entirely from wood, using the various natural colours, grains and types. Early Tunbridge craftsmen naturally relied on locally-grown timbers. The beautiful colouring of some of the woods was obtained by quite natural means; for example, 'Tunbridge Green' was obtained from an oak that had been attacked by a fungus which gave the wood a green hue. Sycamore soaked in the mineral waters of the area produced a grey wood. Later the home-grown woods were supplemented by foreign importations which increased the range of colours and added the extra richness of mahogany and red, green, and black ebony. Some 160 different woods were used, some of which were dyed chemically.

The picture or design selected for treatment was first drawn on graph paper and the various woods to be used were indicated by numbering each square. Obviously it was a very skilled operation to plan some of the more intricate pictures, and the designers' knowledge of the technique must have been very comprehensive.

Once the design had been established, the picture was made up from strips of the various woods. Each strip was laid in its appropriate position, and then glued together under pressure. This resulted in a stick with the design running right through, like the place name in sea-side rock. This stick was then cut across to produce wafers about 1/2 mm thick, each bearing an identical design, which were subsequently glued to the article to be decorated. When considering that each strip had to be accurately shaped to form its particular part in the overall design like the pieces in a jig-saw puzzle, one can only admire the skill of the craftsmen whose only tool for this operation was a small circular saw.

Early Tunbridge Ware consisted of patterns made from cubes and diamonds with borders made from thinner strips. The more complicated pictures, usually depicting local views or buildings, date from the 19th century. One of the most ambitious, and probably the finest surviving example of Tunbridge Ware, has 20,000 pieces in an area no larger than 9×7 inches. It depicts the Pantiles, Tunbridge Wells. By this time the craft was no longer confined to Tunbridge; in fact, it was being produced in many other localities.

Tunbridge Ware offers new collectors a wide range of items, and usually they are not too expensive. Because of the method used, no design is really unique, and they may occur on several different pieces. The smaller pieces are much the easier to obtain; the larger pieces are more difficult, but may be studied in the various museums—for example, the Pinto Gallery of the Birmingham Museum and, of course, the Municipal Museum at Tunbridge Wells.

The best period for Tunbridge Ware was the mid-19th century, a period when Berlin wool was very much in vogue, and the Tunbridge craftsmen simulated the wool patterns by using strips of wood no thicker than a darning needle.

The most famous name associated with Tunbridge Ware was that of Thomas Barton, a designer and craftsman who produced work that was of the highest quality, both artistically and practically.

Paper knives, tea caddies, work boxes, jewel cases, ink stands, small pill boxes and even furniture were decorated by the craftsmen of Tunbridge.

WINE AND SPIRIT LABELS

26. Wine and Spirit Labels

Collecting wine and spirit labels is a field where there is reasonable scope and opportunity, and it is one that has not been exhaustively collected in the past; therefore the prices of such labels should be reasonable and it should not be too difficult running them to earth.

Such a collection in itself will not necessarily be sufficiently rewarding for anybody who has the collective instinct, but if associated with another collection such as decanters and sealed bottles they could provide a sympathetic adjunct. The majority of wine labels are made of silver; they may have a curved shape to fit the bottle, be oval, or rectangular and they can be engraved, pierced, or embossed with the name of a wine, which is surrounded with a beaded, or gadrooned border. (Gadrooned means a border ornament hammered, or cast with radiating lobes of curved or straight form.) The labels usually have two pierced holes, one each end, to which a narrow chain or wire is threaded so that the label can hang from the neck of a bottle or decanter to denote the contents.

Although silver wine labels are only minor items of silver, they were produced by some of the great English silversmiths of the 17th century, and will often carry the maker's mark on the back. Some pieces will be found unmarked but this does not mean that they are not genuine. Examples of wine labels before the reign of George III are rare.

Sheffield plate was also used for the manufacture of wine labels, but these are not so easy to find.

Wine labels made of Battersea enamels are probably the most sought after because they were only produced for a very short time between 1753 and 1756. Battersea enamels were made up from thin copper sheet which was covered with a vitreous material to which oxide and tin had been added to make it opaque. After firing, this resembled Delftware. The surface was then painted with metallic pigments and the colours fixed by kilning at a low temperature. The Battersea factory was started by Alderman Steven Theodore Janssen, just prior to 1753. However, he became bankrupt in 1756 and his products were sold off; these included many items that could be considered trinkets—things like sleeve buttons, crosses, toothpick cases and of course bottle tickets 'with chains for all sorts of liquor and of different subjects'.

There were not many painted enamels from Battersea; most of these were transfer printed. The discovery of transfer printing for Battersea has been attributed to Simon-Francois Ravenet, an engraver of note, who incidentally engraved the plates for Hogarth's 'Marriage à la Mode.'

Wine labels are also to be found in porcelain, mother-of-pearl, and a few other materials. The mother-of-pearl labels are quite uncommon. Many of the names on wine labels are self explanatory, but a few will crop up that are not so common; for instance 'Shrub' is a cordial made of fruit juice and spirit. 'Cream of the Valley' was simply another name for Gin. 'Nig' was, in fact, Gin spelt backwards to deceive servants. 'Mountain' was a wine from Malaga. 'Paraketta' denoted an Andalusian wine. 'Montrachet' was a wine from a district of that name. 'Morachee' was probably a corruption of Montrachet.

The best way to collect wine labels and spirit labels would be to generalise. If you confine them to silver they will certainly offer the larger field, but the collection can be made far more interesting if you include the enamels and porcelains; these are, of course, more difficult to find and it is unlikely that you will be able to form a large collection from these choice items only.

REFERENCE DATA

JAPANESE CHRONOLOGY

Jomon Period	1000 B.C.– 200 B.C.
Yayoi Period	200 B.C.–A.D. 500
Tumulus (Great Tomb) Period	A.D. 300–A.D. 700
Asuka Period	A.D. 552–A.D. 645
Early Nara Period	A.D. 645–A.D. 710
Nara Period	A.D. 710–A.D. 794
Early Heian Period	A.D. 794–A.D. 897
Heian or Fujiwara Period	A.D. 897–A.D. 1185
Kamakura Period	A.D. 1185–A.D. 1392
Ashikaga or Muromachi Period	A.D. 1392–A.D. 1573
Momoyama Period	A.D. 1573–A.D. 1615
Tokugawa Period	A.D. 1615–A.D. 1868

KOREAN CHRONOLOGY

Lo Lang	106 B.C.–A.D. 313
Paekche	18 B.C.–A.D. 663
Koguryo	37 B.C.–A.D. 668
Silla	57 B.C.–A.D. 668
Great Silla	A.D. 668–A.D. 936
Koryo	A.D. 918–A.D. 1392
Yi	A.D. 1392–A.D. 1910

CHINESE EMPEROR MING PERIODS
(1368–1643)

Hung Wy	1368–1398
Chien Wen	1399–1402
Yung Lo	1403–1424
Hung Hsi	1425
Hsuan Te	1426–1435
Cheng T'ung	1436–1449
Ching T'ai	1450–1457
T'ien Shun	1457–1464
Ch'eng Hua	1465–1487
Hung-Chih	1488–1505
Cheng Te	1506–1521
Chia Ching	1522–1566
Lung Ch'ing	1567–1572
Wan Li	1573–1619

T'ai Ch'ang	1620
T'ien Ch'i	1621–1627
Ch'ung Cheng	1628–1643

CHINESE EMPEROR CH'ING PERIOD
(1644–1912)

Shung Chih	1644–1661
K'ang Hsi	1662–1722
Yung Cheng	1723–1735
Ch'ieng Lung	1736–1795
Chia Ch'ing	1796–1820
Tao Kuang	1821–1850
Hsien Feng	1851–1861
T'ung Chih	1862–1873
Kuang Hsu	1874–1908
Hsuan T'ung	1909–1912

MAIN PERIODS CHINESE ART

Shang Dynasty (Yin)	c. 1523–1027 B.C.
Chow Dynasty	1027– 221 B.C.
Warring States Period	481– 221 B.C.
Ch'in Dynasty	221– 206 B.C.
Han Dynasty	206 B.C.–A.D. 220
Three Kingdoms	A.D. 220–A.D. 280
Six Dynasties	A.D. 280–A.D. 589
Northern Wei	A.D. 385–A.D. 535
Eastern Wei	A.D. 535–A.D. 550
Western Wei	A.D. 535–A.D. 557
Northern Ch'i	A.D. 550–A.D. 577
Northern Chow	A.D. 557–A.D. 581
Liu Sung (South)	A.D. 420–A.D. 478
Southern Ch'i	A.D. 479–A.D. 501
Liang	A.D. 502–A.D. 557
Ch'en	A.D. 557–A.D. 588
Sui Dynasty	A.D. 589–A.D. 618
T'ang	A.D. 618–A.D. 906
Five Dynasties	A.D. 907–A.D. 959
Sung Dynasties	A.D. 960–A.D. 1280
Yuan Dynasties	A.D. 1280–A.D. 1368
Ming Dynasties	A.D. 1368–A.D. 1643
Ch'ing Dynasties	A.D. 1644–A.D. 1912

MOH'S SCALE OF HARDNESS

The comparative hardness of a mineral (jade, jadeite etc.) is determined and expressed in the terms of the Moh's scale, which

285

uses ten standard minerals for the comparison:

1 Talc
2 Gypsum
3 Calcite
4 Fluorite
5 Apatite
6 Orthoclase
7 Quartz
8 Topaz
9 Corundum
10 Diamond

For example: A mineral with a hardness of 5 will scratch fluorite, but will be scratched by orthoclase.

GENERAL PERIODS

English

Tudor	1485–1558	Reigns of Henry VII
		Henry VIII
		Edward VI
		Mary
Elizabethan	1558–1603	Reign of Elizabeth
Jacobean	1603–1649	Reigns of James I
		Charles I
Commonwealth	1649–1660	Cromwell
Late Stuart	1660–1689	Reigns of Charles II
		James II
William and Mary	1689–1702	Reign of William and Mary
Queen Anne	1702–1727	Reigns of Anne
		George I
Georgian	1727–1820	Reigns of George II
		George III
*Regency	1800–1830	Reigns of George III
		Prince George
Victorian	1830–1901	Reign of Victoria

French

Francois-Premier	1515–1547	Reign of Francis I
Henri-Deux	1547–1559	Reign of Henry II
	1559–1560	Reign of Francis II
	1560–1574	Reign of Charles IX
	1574–1589	Reign of Henry III
Henri-Quatre	1589–1610	Reign of Henry IV

* The Regency period should only cover the period when Prince George acted as Regent between 1811 and 1820, but the periods shown are accepted for period classification of antiques generally.

Louis-Treize	1610–1643	Reign of Louis XIII
Louis-Quatorze	1643–1715	Reign of Louis XIV
Louis-Quinze	1715–1774	Reign of Louis XV
Louis-Seize	1774–1793	Reign of Louis XVI
Empire	1799–1814	Reign of Napoleon

DATES OF REIGNING KINGS AND QUEENS

England

Period	Sovereign
1066–1087	William I
1087–1100	William II
1100–1135	Henry I
1135–1154	Stephen
1154–1189	Henry II
1189–1199	Richard I
1199–1216	John
1216–1272	Henry III
1272–1307	Edward I
1307–1327	Edward II
1327–1377	Edward III
1377–1399	Richard II
1399–1413	Henry IV
1413–1422	Henry V
1422–1461	Henry VI
1461–1470	Edward IV (1st reign)
1470–1471	Henry IV (restored)
1471–1483	Edward IV (2nd reign)
1483	Edward V
1483–1485	Richard III
1485–1509	Henry VII
1509–1547	Henry VIII
1547–1553	Edward VI
1553–1554	Mary
1554–1558	Phillip and Mary
1558–1603	Elizabeth I
1603–1625	James I
1625–1649	Charles I
1649–1660	Commonwealth
1660–1685	Charles II
1685–1688	James II
1688–1694	William and Mary
1694–1702	William III
1702–1714	Anne
1714–1727	George I
1727–1760	George II
1760–1820	George III
1820–1830	George IV
1830–1837	William IV

1837–1901	Victoria
1901–1910	Edward VII
1910–1936	George V
1936–1952	George VI
1952–	Elizabeth II

France

Period	*Sovereign*
1515–1547	Francis I
1547–1559	Henry II
1559–1560	Francis II
1560–1574	Charles IX
1574–1589	Henry III
1589–1610	Henry IV
1610–1643	Louis XIII
1643–1715	Louis XIV
1715–1774	Louis XV
1774–1793	Louis XVI
1799–1814	Napoleon

REGISTRY MARKS

Porcelain, glass, and many other objects can be dated by analysis of the Registry Mark. This mark was introduced by the British Patent Office, and was in use from 1842 to 1883 inclusive.

The mark is a vertical diamond, capped with a near-full sphere, with semi-circles under each point of the diamond (see illustrations).

The hemisphere was reserved for the class of goods, i.e. a Roman IV indicated 'Glass and Ceramics'. The four points of the diamonds indicate year, month and date manufactured, and the parcel number. In the year 1868, the mark was slightly modified with respect to the positions indicating date of manufacture, but the overall shape remained the same.

Index letters from 1842 to 1867:

A = Class
B = Year
C = Month
D = Date
E = Parcel

1842 to 1867   1868 to 1883

Months

Jan.	C	Apr.	H	July	I	Oct.	B
Feb.	G	May	E	Aug.	R	Nov.	K
Mar.	W	June	M	Sept.	D	Dec.	A

288

Years

1842	X	1851	P	1860	Z
1843	H	1852	D	1861	R
1844	C	1853	Y	1862	O
1845	A	1854	J	1863	G
1846	I	1855	E	1864	N
1847	F	1856	L	1865	W
1848	U	1857	K	1866	Q
1849	S	1858	B	1867	T
1850	V	1859	M		

Index Letters from 1868 to 1883 (use in conjunction with changed Registry Mark)

Months

Jan.	C	Apr.	H	July	I	Oct.	B
Feb.	G	May	E	Aug.	R	Nov.	K
Mar.	W	June	M	Sept.	D	Dec.	A

Years

1868	X	1874	U	1880	J
1869	H	1875	S	1881	E
1870	C	1876	V	1882	L
1871	A	1877	P	1883	K
1872	I	1878	D		
1873	F	1879	Y		

Classes

I	Designs in metal.
II	Designs in wood.
III	Designs in glass.
IV	Designs in earthenware, porcelain, ivory, bone.
V	Designs in paperhanging.
VI	Designs in carpets, floor, or oil cloths.
VII	Designs in shawls, printed patterns.
VIII	Designs in shawls, patterns not printed.
IX	Yarn, thread.
X	Woven fabrics, excluding furniture.
XI	Woven fabrics, furniture, printed patterns.
XII	Woven fabrics, patterns not printed.
XIII	Lace and all other articles.

PORCELAIN MARKS

BOW

CHELSEA

Chelfea1745

CAPODIMONTE

CAUGHLEY

SALOPIAN

DRESDEN

DRESDEN

DH

DH/2

DERBY

1750

GOSS

LIMOGES
FRANCE
LIMOGES

MEISSEN

290

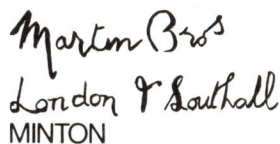 

MINTON

PLYMOUTH   ROCKINGHAM

SEVRES

SPODE

SWANSEA

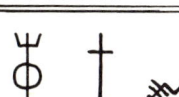  

WORCESTER

291

CANDLESTICK TYPES

1600–1650

1650–1700

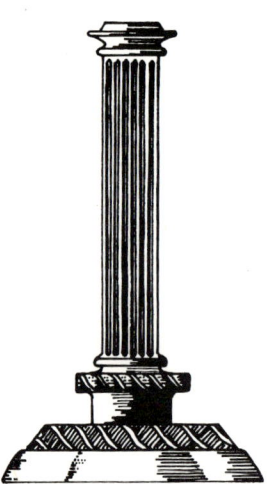

Late 17th Century

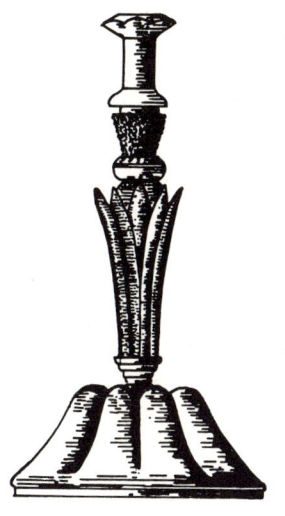

1740–1745

1751

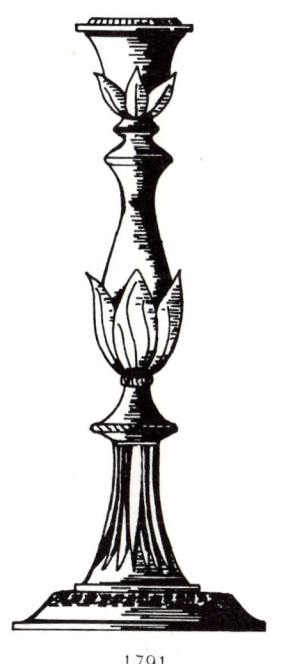

1791

1905

293

RUG SIGNS AND MOTIFS

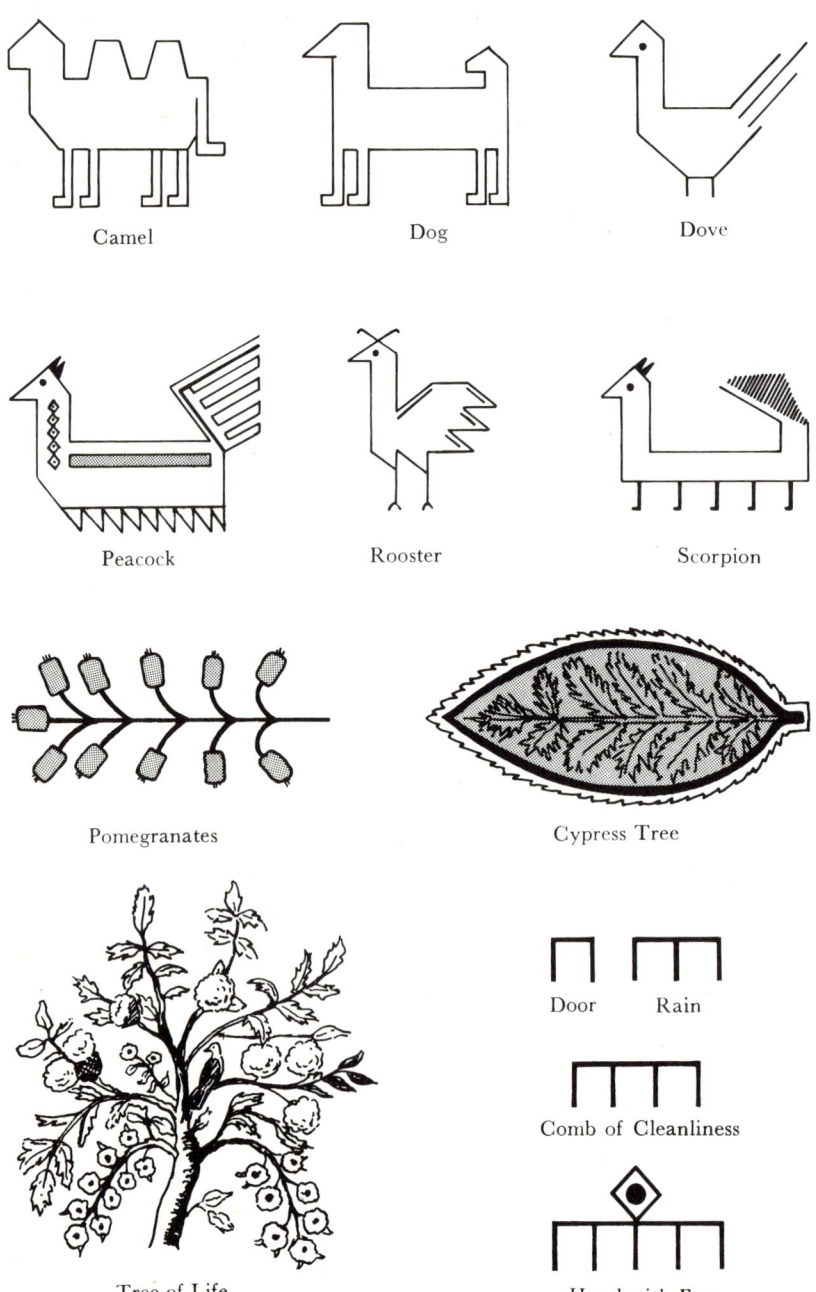

Camel

Dog

Dove

Peacock

Rooster

Scorpion

Pomegranates

Cypress Tree

Tree of Life

Door   Rain

Comb of Cleanliness

Hand with Eye

WINE GLASS BOWL SHAPES

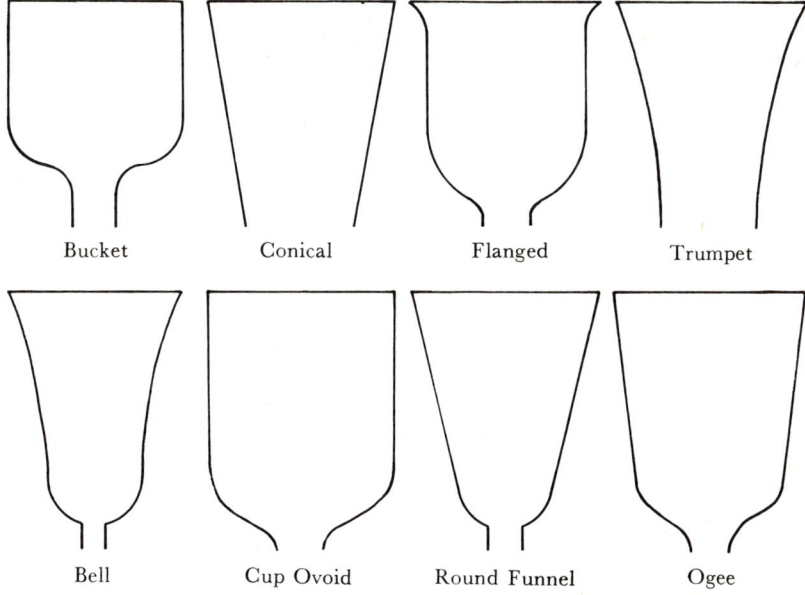

Bucket   Conical   Flanged   Trumpet

Bell   Cup Ovoid   Round Funnel   Ogee

WINE GLASS KNOPS

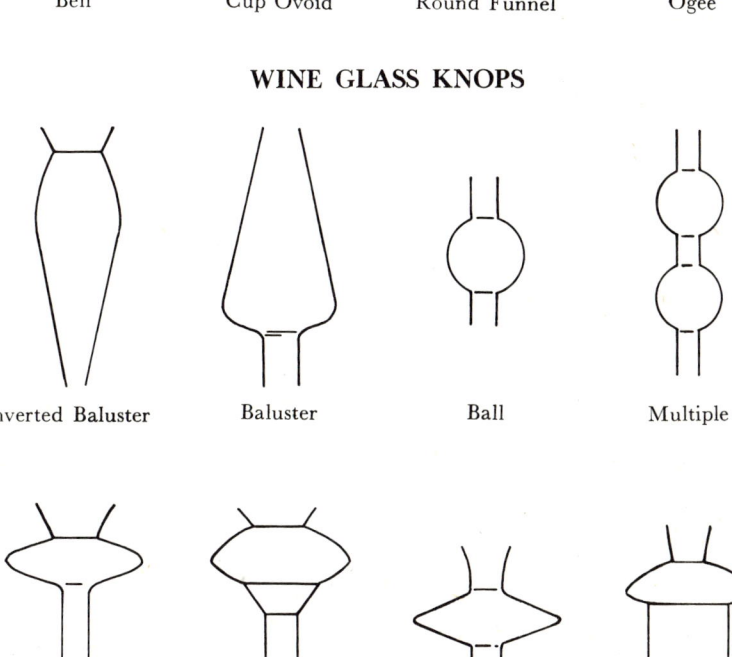

Inverted Baluster   Baluster   Ball   Multiple

Flattened   Mushroom   Bladed   Acorn

| Plain Conical | Folded Conical | Firing | Domed and Folded |

Look for the Hallmark
.. it's your Safeguard

British hallmarks have a long tradition as symbols of integrity. They have appeared on gold and silver articles for over six and a half centuries. Primarily a hallmark certifies that an article has been assayed (accurately tested) at one of the official Assay Offices in the United Kingdom and that the gold or silver content is up to one of the legal standards.

These four examples show that every hallmark consists of several symbols — a maker's mark, standard mark, Assay Office mark and date letter.

This is the information they give:

Maker's Mark, consisting nowadays of the initials of the person or firm submitting the article to the Assay Office, is illustrated by the letters NM in the above examples.

Standard Mark denoting the minimum gold or silver content.

Mark	Standard	Minimum Percentage gold or silver
	Sterling silver Marked in England	92.5
	Sterling silver Marked in Scotland	92.5
	Britannia silver	95.84
	22 carat gold Marked in England	91.66
	22 carat gold Marked in Scotland	
	18 carat gold Marked in England	75.0
	18 carat gold Marked in Scotland	
	14 carat gold	58.5
	9 carat gold	37.5

A carat is one 24th part; thus 18 carat gold means that 18/24ths (i.e. three-quarters) of the alloy is pure gold.

Assay Office Mark showing which Assay Office tested and marked the article.

	London	Sterling silver & gold
	London	Britannia silver
	Birmingham	silver & gold
	Sheffield	silver
	Sheffield	gold
	Edinburgh	silver & gold

The marks illustrated are those used on British wares; different marks are struck on gold or silver articles made abroad.

There were formerly Assay Offices in other towns, each having its own distinctive mark, for example

	Chester		Glasgow
	Newcastle		Exeter

Date Letter indicates the year in which the article was hallmarked. It consists of a letter of the alphabet enclosed in a shield. To determine the date of the marking of an article it is necessary first to identify the particular Assay Office from the Assay Office mark and then to refer to a published list of date letters. This is because each Assay Office uses different alphabetical cycles. The letter is changed in May each year at the London office, in July at Birmingham and Sheffield and October at Edinburgh. Lists of date letters for these offices are given on the following pages. The marks illustrated are for silver articles; on gold the shape of the surrounding shield may be altered but the letter itself is the same.

Hallmarking was instituted in the year 1300 by a statute of Edward I. The designs of the marks have changed from time to time and marks have been introduced for special purposes, for example the sovereign's head between 1784 and 1890 to denote payment of duty. Some of the principal changes are shown in the following lists of date letters. Hallmarking still continues to give the purchaser of a gold or silver article an absolute assurance that the precious metal is up to the standard indicated, as well as providing other interesting and useful information.

London

Year	Letter	Year	Letter	Year	Letter	Year	Letter
		1705		1732	R	1759	D
1678	a	1706	P	1733	S	1760	E
		1707		1734	T	1761	F
1679	b	1708		1735	V	1762	G
1680	c	1709		1736	a	1763	H
1681	d	1710		1737	b	1764	I
1682	e	1711		1738	c	1765	K
1683	f	1712		1739	d	1766	L
1684	g	1713		1739	d	1767	M
1685	h	1714		1740	e	1768	N
1686	i	1715		1741	f	1769	O
1687	k	1716	A	1742	g	1770	P
1688	l	1717	B	1743	h	1771	Q
1689	m	1718	C	1744	i	1772	R
1690	n	1719	D	1745	k	1773	S
1691	o	1720	E	1746	l	1774	T
1692	p	1721	F	1747	m	1775	U
1693	q	1722	G	1748	n	1776	a
1694	r	1723	H	1749	o	1777	b
1695	s	1724	I	1750	p	1778	c
1696	t	1725	K	1751	q	1779	d
1697	a/b	1726	L	1752	r	1780	e
1698		1727	M	1753	s	1781	f
1699		1728	N	1754	t	1782	g
1700	ff	1729	O	1755	U	1783	h
1701		1730	P	1756		1784	i
1702		1731	Q	1756	A	1785	k
1703				1757	B	1786	l
1704				1758	C		

Year		Year		Year		Year		Year		Year		Year		Year	
1787	m	1827	m	1867	m	1907	m	1945	K	1952	R	1959	d	1966	l
1788	n	1828	n	1868	n	1908	n	1946	L	1953	S	1960	e	1967	m
1789	o	1829	o	1869	o	1909	o	1947	M	1954	T	1961	f	1968	n
1790	p	1830	p	1870	p	1910	p	1948	N	1955	U	1962	g	1969	o
1791	q	1831	q	1871	q	1911	q	1949	O	1956	a	1963	h	1970	p
1792	r	1832	r	1872	r	1912	r	1950	P	1957	b	1964	i	1971	q
1793	s	1833	s	1873	s	1913	s	1951	Q	1958	C	1965	k		
1794	t	[lion symbols] 1834	t	1874	t	1914	t								
1795	u	1835	u	1875	u	1915	u								
1796	A	1836	A	1876	A	[symbols] 1916	a								
1797	B	1837	B	1877	B	1917	b								
1798	C	[symbols] 1838	C	1878	C	1918	c								
1799	D	1839	D	1879	D	1919	d								
1800	E	1840	E	1880	E	1920	e								
1801	F	1841	F	1881	F	1921	f								
1802	G	1842	G	1882	G	1922	g								
1803	H	1843	H	1883	H	[symbols] 1923	h								
1804	I	1844	I	1884	I	1924	i								
1805	K	1845	k	1885	K	1925	k								
1806	L	1846	L	1886	L	1926	l								
1807	M	1847	M	1887	M	1927	m								
1808	N	1848	N	1888	N	1928	n								
1809	O	1849	O	1889	O	[lion symbols] 1929	o								
1810	P	1850	P	1890	P	1930	p								
1811	Q	1851	Q	[lion symbols] 1891	Q	1931	q								
1812	R	1852	R	1892	R	1932	r								
1813	S	1853	S	1893	S	1933	s								
1814	T	1854	T	1894	T	1934	t								
1815	U	1855	U	1895	U	1935	u								
1816	a	1856	a	[lion symbols] 1896	a	[symbols] 1936	A								
1817	b	1857	b	1897	b	1937	B								
1818	C	1858	c	1898	c	1938	C								
1819	d	1859	d	1899	d	1939	D								
1820	e	1860	e	1900	e	1940	E								
1821	f	1861	f	1901	f	1941	F								
[symbols] 1822	g	1862	g	1902	g	1942	G								
1823	h	1863	h	1903	h	1943	H								
1824	i	1864	i	1904	i	1944	I								
1825	k	1865	k	1905	k										
1826	l	1866	l	1906	l										

Birmingham

[symbols: anchor]

Year		Year		Year		Year	
		1798	a	1828	E	1854	F
		1799	b	1829	F	1855	G
1773	A	1800	c	1830	G	1856	H
1774	B	1801	d	1831	H	1857	I
1775	C	1802	e	1832	J	1858	J
1776	D	1803	f	1833	K	1859	K
1777	E	1804	h	[symbols]		1860	L
1778	F	1805	g	1834	L	1861	M
1779	G	1806	i	1835	M	1862	N
1780	H	1807	j	1836	N	1863	O
1781	I	1808	k	1837	O	1864	P
1782	K	1809	l	[symbols]		1865	Q
1783	L	1810	m	1838	P	1866	R
[symbols]		1811	n	1839	Q	1867	S
1784	M	1812	o	1840	R	1868	T
1785	N	1813	p	1841	S	1869	U
[symbols]		1814	q	1842	T	1870	V
1786	O	1815	r	1843	U	1871	W
1787	P	1816	s	1844	V	1872	X
1788	Q	1817	t	1845	W	1873	Y
1789	R	1818	u	1846	X	1874	Z
1790	S	1819	v	1847	Y	[symbols]	
1791	T	1820	w	1848	Z	1875	a
1792	U	1821	x	[symbols]		1876	b
1793	V	1822	y	1849	A	1877	c
1794	W	1823	z	1850	B	1878	d
1795	X	1824	a	1851	C	1879	e
1796	Y	1825	b	1852	D	1880	f
1797	Z	1826	C	1853	E	1881	g
		1827	D			1882	h

1883	i	1894	u	1905	f	1917	S	1929	E	1941	R	1951	B	1962	N
1884	k	1895	v	1906	g	1918	t	1930	F	1942	S	1952	C	1963	O
1885	l	1896	w	1907	h	1919	u	1931	G	1943	T	1953	D	1964	P
1886	m	1897	x	1908	i	1920	v	1932	H	1944	U	1954	E	1965	Q
1887	n	1898	p	1909	k	1921	W	1933	J	1945	V	1955	F	1966	R
1888	o	1899	z	1910	l	1922	X	1934	K	1946	W	1956	G	1967	S
1889	p	[anchor] [lion passant]		1911	m	1923	y	1935	L	1947	X	1957	H	1968	T
1890	q	1900	a	1912	n	1924	Z	1936	M	1948	Y	1958	J	1969	U
[lion] [anchor]		1901	b	1913	o	1925	A	1937	N	1949	Z	1959	K	1970	V
1891	r	1902	c	1914	p	1926	B	1938	O	[lion] [anchor]		1960	L	1971	W
1892	s	1903	d	1915	q	1927	C	1939	P	1950	A	1961	M		
1893	t	1904	e	1916	r	1928	D	1940	Q						

Sheffield

Between 1780 and 1853 the crown and date letter are sometimes enclosed in the same shield on small articles.

[lion] [crown]

1773	E	1796	Z	1822	Z	1845	B	1870	C	1895	c	1919	b	1945	C
1774	F	1797	X	1823	U	1846	C	1871	D	1896	d	1920	c	1946	D
1775	H	1798	V	1824	a	1847	D	1872	E	1897	e	1921	d	1947	E
1776	R	1799	E	1825	b	1848	E	1873	F	1898	f	1922	e	1948	F
1777	h	1800	N	1826	C	1849	F	1874	G	1899	g	1923	f	1949	G
1778	S	1801	H	1827	d	1850	G	1875	H	1900	h	1924	g	1950	H
1779	A	1802	M	1828	e	1851	H	1876	J	1901	i	1925	h	1951	I
1780	V	1803	F	1829	f	1852	I	1877	K	1902	k	1926	i	1952	K
1781	D	1804	G	1830	g	1853	K	1878	L	1903	l	1927	k	1953	L
1782	G	1805	B	1831	h	1854	L	1879	M	1904	m	1928	l	1954	M
1783	B	1806	A	1832	k	1855	M	1880	N	1905	n	1929	m	1955	N
[lion] [crown] [head]		1807	S	1833	I	1856	N	1881	O	1906	o	1930	n	1956	O
1784	I	1808	P	[lion] [head] [head]		1857	O	1882	P	1907	p	1931	o	1957	P
1785	V	1809	K	1834	m	1858	P	1883	Q	1908	q	1932	p	1958	Q
[lion] [crown] [head]		1810	L	1835	p	1859	R	1884	R	1909	r	1933	q	1959	R
1786	K	1811	C	1836	q	1860	S	1885	S	1910	s	1934	r	1960	S
1787	T	1812	D	1837	r	1861	T	1886	T	1911	t	1935	s	1961	T
1788	W	1813	R	1838	s	1862	U	1887	U	1912	u	1936	t	1962	U
1789	M	1814	W	1839	t	1863	V	1888	V	1913	v	1937	u	1963	V
1790	L	1815	O	[lion] [head] [head]		1864	W	1889	W	[lion] [head]		1938	v	1964	W
1791	P	1816	T	1840	u	1865	X	1890	X	1914	w	1939	w	1965	X
1792	U	1817	X	1841	v	1866	Y	[crown] [lion]		1915	x	1940	x	1966	Y
1793	O	1818	I	1842	x	1867	Z	1891	Y	1916	y	1941	y	1967	Z
1794	m	1819	V	1843	z	[head] [head] [head]		1892	Z	1917	z	1942	z	1968	A
1795	q	1820	Q	1844	A	1868	A	1893	a	[crown] [lion]		1943	A	1969	B
		1821	Y			1869	B	1894	b	1918	a	1944	B	1970	C
														1971	D

Edinburgh

1705 A · 1706 B · 1707 C · 1708 D · 1709 E · 1710 F · 1711 G · 1712 H · 1713 I · 1714 K · 1715 L · 1716 M · 1717 N · 1718 O · 1719 P · 1720 Q · 1721 R · 1722 S · 1723 T · 1724 U · 1725 V · 1726 W · 1727 X · 1728 Y · 1729 Z · 1730 A · 1731 B · 1732 C · 1733 D · 1734 E · 1735 F · 1736 G

1737 H · 1738 I · 1739 K · 1740 L · 1741 M · 1742 N · 1743 O · 1744 P · 1745 Q · 1746 R · 1747 S · 1748 T · 1749 U · 1750 U · 1751 W · 1752 X · 1753 Y · 1754 Z · 1755 A · 1756 B · 1757 C · 1758 D

1759 E · 1760 F · 1761 G · 1762 H · 1763 I · 1764 K · 1765 L · 1766 M · 1767 N · 1768 L

1769 O · 1770 O · 1771 O · 1772 P · 1773 Q · 1774 R · 1775 S · 1776 T · 1777 U · 1778 Z · 1779 U · 1780 A · 1781 B · 1782 C · 1783 D · 1784 E · 1785 F · 1786 G · 1787 GH · 1788 H · 1789 IJ · 1790 K · 1791 L · 1792 M · 1793 N · 1794 O · 1795 P · 1796 Q · 1797 R · 1798 S · 1799 T

1800 U · 1801 V · 1802 W · 1803 X · 1804 Y · 1805 Z · 1806 a · 1807 b · 1808 c · 1809 d · 1810 e · 1811 f · 1812 g · 1813 h · 1814 i · 1815 j · 1816 k · 1817 l · 1818 m · 1819 n · 1820 O · 1821 P · 1822 q · 1823 r · 1824 s · 1825 t · 1826 u · 1827 v · 1828 w · 1829 x · 1830 y · 1831 z · 1832 A · 1833 B

1834 C · 1835 D · 1836 E · 1837 F · 1838 G · 1839 H · 1840 J · 1841 K · 1842 L · 1843 M · 1844 N · 1845 O · 1846 P · 1847 Q · 1848 R · 1849 S · 1850 T · 1851 U · 1852 V · 1853 W · 1854 X · 1855 Y · 1856 Z · 1857 A · 1858 B · 1859 C · 1860 D · 1861 E · 1862 F · 1863 G · 1864 H · 1865 I · 1866 K · 1867 L

1868 M · 1869 N · 1870 O · 1871 P · 1872 Q · 1873 R · 1874 S · 1875 T · 1876 U · 1877 V · 1878 W · 1879 X · 1880 Y · 1881 Z · 1882 a · 1883 b · 1884 c · 1885 d · 1886 e · 1887 f · 1888 g · 1889 h · 1890 i · 1891 k · 1892 l · 1893 m · 1894 n · 1895 o · 1896 p · 1897 q · 1898 r · 1899 s · 1900 t · 1901 u

1902 w · 1903 x · 1904 y · 1905 z · 1906 A · 1907 B · 1908 C · 1909 D · 1910 E · 1911 F · 1912 G · 1913 H · 1914 I · 1915 K · 1916 L · 1917 M · 1918 N · 1919 O · 1920 P · 1921 Q · 1922 R · 1923 S · 1924 T · 1925 U · 1926 V · 1927 W · 1928 X · 1929 Y · 1930 Z · 1931 A · 1932 B · 1933 C · 1934 D · 1935 E · 1936 F

1937 G · 1938 H · 1939 J · 1940 K · 1941 L · 1942 M · 1943 N · 1944 O · 1945 P · 1946 Q · 1947 R · 1948 S · 1949 T · 1950 U · 1951 V · 1952 W · 1953 X · 1954 Y · 1955 Z · 1956 A · 1957 B · 1958 C · 1959 D · 1960 E · 1961 F · 1962 G · 1963 H · 1964 J · 1965 K · 1966 L · 1967 M · 1968 N · 1969 O · 1970 P

Articles imported from abroad for sale in the United Kingdom are also hallmarked at one of the British Assay Offices. The date letter is the same as for British articles, but the maker's mark becomes the importer's mark and special standard and Assay Office marks are used

Standard Mark denoting the minimum gold or silver content.

 22 carat gold  14 carat gold

 18 carat gold  9 carat gold

·925 Sterling silver   ·9584 Britannia silver

Assay Office Mark showing which Assay Office tested and marked the article.

 London   Birmingham

 Sheffield   Edinburgh

Index

Trade marks

wedgwood

Probably the first mark. Supposed to have been used by Josiah Wedgwood at Burslem 1759–1769.

WEDGWOOD

This is a very rare mark, used at the Bell Works 1764–1769.

WEDGWOOD
Wedgwood

Used in varying sizes from 1759–1769.

WEDGWOOD & BENTLEY

The circular stamp, without the inner and outer rings, and without the word Etruria is doubtless the earliest form of the Wedgwood and Bentley stamp, 1769.

This mark, with the word Etruria, was fixed in the corner, inside the plinth of old basalt vases. It is sometimes found on the pedestal of a bust or large figure. 1769–1780.

This circular stamp, with an inner and outer line, was always placed around the screw of the basalt, granite and Etruscan vases, but is never found on Jasper vases. 1769–1780.

Wedgwood & Bentley

Unique script mark, Wedgwood & Bentley, 1769–1780.

Wedgwood
& Bentley
356

Mark used on Wedgwood & Bentley intaglios, with the catalogue number varying in size, 1769–1780.

W . & B.

Very small intaglios were sometimes marked W&B with the catalogue number, or simply with the number only, 1769–1780.

Wedgwood & Bentley.

Rare mark found only on chocolate and white seal intaglios, usually portraits made of two layers of clay with the edges polished for mounting, 1769–1780.

WEDGWOOD & BENTLEY
Wedgwood
& Bentley

These marks, varying in size are found upon busts, granite and basalt vases, figures, plaques, medallions and cameos, from the largest tablet to the smallest cameo. 1769–1780.

WEDGWOOD
Wedgwood
WEDGWOOD
WEDGWOOD

Varying in size, these marks are attributed to the period after Bentley's death (1780) and probably used for a time after Josiah's death (1795).